Praise for *Carry the Flame*

Carry the Flame tells the tale of a remarkable cadre of men and women who embraced the British vision of Outward Bound, only to transform it into something indelibly Canadian—a way of thinking, practice, and being that could only make sense in a country so vast. We could throw England anywhere to the north, and the English would never find it.

—Wade Davis, author of the Samuel Johnson Prize-winning mountaineering chronicle *Into the Silence*

In this splendid collection of essays and poems, you see campfires and hear the cadence of voices. They come from pioneering wilderness leaders of a life-changing institution talking about going to hard places and doing tough things to find out who they really are. They are practical and poetic, wise and funny. Pull up a spruce bench, lean into the heat of the campfires, and enjoy the conversations.

—Dr. Joe MacInnis, physician, explorer, and author of *Deep Leadership*

Kurt Hahn, Outward Bound's founder, would delight in this compendium! The essays, poems, and photographs within these pages celebrate Outward Bound's core values, evoking Hahn's commitments to experiential learning, adventure, compassion, and, above all, community. This book arrives at a time of increasing alienation, loneliness, and disconnection among the young and old alike. The essays within paint an alternative path, a utopian striving that can help us rebuild the bonds that make us fully human.

—Joel Westheimer, university research chair in democracy and education at the University of Ottawa

I was introduced to Outward Bound's philosophy and programs in 1985. My personal experience was profound. I soon chose to volunteer time by joining the board of directors. The stories and essays in *Carry the Flame* reveal the tenets, passions, and leadership styles that fueled COBWS. This book illuminates the transformative educational experiences that are even more relevant in today's complex world.

—Rose M. Patten, chancellor of the University of Toronto and author of *Intentional Leadership: The Big 8 Capabilities Setting Leaders Apart*

The essays in *Carry the Flame* are written from the heart by early staff, board members, and students of the Canadian Outward Bound Wilderness School. They portray how the development of the school mirrors an Outward Bound course, going beyond any preconceived limitations and working cooperatively to accomplish something beyond any individual's capacity. Using the words of Outward Bound's founder, Kurt Hahn, they did it all with "tenacity of spirit" and "compassion," including compassion for themselves. The school's evolution is a portrayal of love, dedication, and perseverance, delivering an educational experience that should be mandatory for every young person.

—Ted Moores, former executive director and board chair of Voyageur Outward Bound School and former board chair and CEO of Camp Wanapitei

Embark on a remarkable journey through the pages of this book. Reflect on the formative years of Outward Bound in Canada. Fifty-six years later, Outward Bound Canada's commitment to experiential outdoor education endures, enrolling over 4,000 Canadian youth in 2023, in multiple provinces and territories. The stories and insights contained in *Carry the Flame* chronicle the genesis of a school that was, in so many ways, ahead of its time.

—Anne Fitzgerald, chair of the board of directors of Outward Bound Canada

Anyone with interest in the Outward Bound model of education will find the story of the Canadian Outward Bound Wilderness School, affectionately called *cobwebs*, informative and enlightening. Engaging stories, anecdotes, and reflections come together to portray a unique OB community in the most remote location of any of the many OB schools. This is a memoir and a tribute, a reminiscence of a bygone era (not so long ago) when risk and experimentation in educational programming were more possible than today, and a tribute to founder Bob Pieh. A must-have book in the library of anyone interested in outdoor experiential education.

—John Miles, professor emeritus of environmental studies at Western Washington University and author of *Teaching in the Rain*

CARRY THE FLAME

CARRY THE FLAME

THE REMARKABLE STORY OF THE CANADIAN OUTWARD BOUND WILDERNESS SCHOOL

EDITED BY Charles Luckmann

COMPILED BY Charles Luckmann, Alistair McArthur, Wendy Pieh, and Ian Yolles

EARTH AWARE

SAN RAFAEL   LOS ANGELES   LONDON

All you need are these: certainty of judgment in the present moment; action for the common good in the present moment; and an attitude of gratitude in the present moment for anything that comes your way.

—Marcus Aurelius, *Meditations*, 9.6

*The cosmos works
by harmony of tensions,
like the lyre and bow.*

—Heraclitus, Fragment #56

This book is dedicated to staff and board members who were part of the early years at COBWS (1976–1990) but who have since passed away.

COBWS Staff	**COBWS Board Members**	**Council of Patrons**
J. Douglas Bonnell	Bob Couchman	Michel Belanger
Deb Cooke	Ann Hawkins	David Blackwood
Magnus Flood	Karl Harries	David Clark
Steve Fontaine	Jim Hayhurst	George E. Connell
Willie Hauser	Tom Heintzman	Fred Eaton
Tom Heintzman	Tony Long	Betty Kennedy
Guy Lacelle	Samuel Matheson	Donald K. McIvor
Greg Logan	Ed Mercaldo	Joseph A. Peller
Diana Meredith	Ron Patmore	John Rodgers
Mary Morgan	Michael Rosenbush	
Bob Pieh	Omond Solandt	
Viola Pieh	Sandy Treat	
Tom Price	Christopher Trump	
Nancy Suchman		

"Be tough yet gentle, humble yet bold, swayed always by beauty and truth"

CONTENTS

FOREWORD 11
   James Raffan

HISTORICAL PERSPECTIVE 17
   Derek Pritchard

PREFACE 25
   Charles Luckmann, Alistair McArthur, Wendy Pieh, and Ian Yolles

I. CATALYST 29

   Beginnings 33
   Wendy Pieh

   Reflections 36
   Bob Pieh

   Walden V 42
   Andrew Orr

   How to Build a School Out of Nothing 47
   Wendy Talbot

   Something New: Go and Find It 51
   Charlie Orsak

II. VISION 53

   A Perfect Equation 55
   Ken Victor

   People and Place 59
   Philip Blackford

   To Know by Experience 62
   Charles Luckmann

   Sacred Sustenance— Alchemy in Action 87
   Ginger Mason

   Pushing the Envelope of Outward Bound's Four Pillars 94
   (Victoria) Moon Joyce

   Wendell Beckwith 98
   Wendy Pieh

   From Skepticism to Fervent Belief 101
   Ian Yolles

III. HOMEPLACE 107

   The Early Days: Late 1970s to Early 1980s 111
   Alistair McArthur

   Board Member Perspective 115
   Biff Matthews

   The Big Map 117
   Charlie Orsak

   My First Summer at COBWS: Memories, Friends, and Community 118
   Bill Templeman

   Ramblings 122
   Christo Grayling

   Tentfly 126
   Rick Cotter

   Homeplace 127
   Eric MacDonald

   Five Things from My Time Living at Homeplace 131
   Will Pooley

   Black Sturgeon Lake 137
   Ken Victor

   Visits to Homeplace Since 2004 138
   Rob Linscott

IV. COMMUNITY 141

   Community and Creativity 145
   (Victoria) Moon Joyce

   Inclusion and Influence 149
   Philip Blackford

   Reflections 153
   Juliet Westgate (Duff)

   Fire Evacuation 155
   Charles Luckmann

   What Made COBWS Unique 158
   Ian Kilborn

Women of Courage 159
Ruth Goldman

Women of Courage Program
Is the Opposite of Abuse 164
Louise Karch

What Matters 169
Peter Morgan

V. WINTER 175

The Evolution of a
Dogsledding Program 178
Alistair McArthur

The First Winter 181
John Mordhorst

Winter on Black Sturgeon Lake 186
Pamela Ramage-Morin

Winter Reflections 188
David Thomson

Overheard in the Dog Yard and on
the Trail: Imagined Thoughts and
Conversations from Sled Dogs 197
Geoff Murray

Homeplace, Me, and
Baffin Island 200
Paul Landry

Sled Dogs Fly Free: Baffin Island
1987 Reconnaissance Expedition 203
Sara Harrison

VI. STUDENT VOICES 209

A Cold Paddle 211
Patrick Gorry

My Summer 1981 Outward Bound
Course: Memories and Legacy 216
Ilona Hitchcock

So, What Does COBWS
Mean to Me? 218
Amanda Harris

Student Remembrance of the 1980
Fire Evacuation Course in the
Boundary Waters Canoe Area 221
Susie Specter

My Outward Bound Experience
with Apple Canada 223
David Gouthro

If I Live, You Give 227
Bob Ramsay

VII. HARMONY OF TENSIONS 231

The Story of the Bear 233
Charlie Orsak

A Summer Adventure 235
Mary Morgan

On Patterns: Finding
New Leaders 239
Susan Fenton Gibson

The Impact of COBWS
on My Life 243
Rod Taylor

Remembering Bob Pieh,
My Mentor 246
John Huie

Granola Spirit 262
Charles Luckmann

VIII. PREVIOUSLY PUBLISHED 267

Internal and External Rhythms:
The Canadian Wilderness as a
Learning Environment 268
Robert Couchman

The Last Time I Saw Bob 272
Charles Luckmann

Learning to See New Landscapes:
The Canadian Outward Bound
Wilderness School 276
Philip Blackford and Stephen Couchman

CONTRIBUTORS & ACKNOWLEDGMENTS 289

SPECIAL THANKS 293

IN MEMORIAM 295

AUTHOR & ARTIST BIOGRAPHIES 297

APPENDIX: ESTABLISHMENT OF OUTWARD BOUND IN CANADA 313

INDEX 316

FOREWORD

James Raffan

This book is a celebration of a life—a life made up of the many who shaped, and were shaped by, the Canadian Outward Bound Wilderness School (COBWS). Standing at the front of the hall, or perhaps a campfire circle on the metaphoric shores of Black Sturgeon Lake, their faces lit by flickering flames, are Chuck Luckmann, Alistair McArthur, Wendy Pieh, and Ian Yolles, all of whom had leadership roles at COBWS at one time or another, between the school's founding in 1976 and 1990. In their fittingly joint introduction, they say that the impetus for the celebration was the fiftieth anniversary of Outward Bound Canada.

Truth be told, the practical viability of this remote wilderness site, one hundred miles northeast of Thunder Bay, Ontario, was called into question almost from the moment of inception when a rustic forest research facility was repurposed into Canada's second Outward Bound school. COBWS was barely out of its teens when an alternate remote campus north of Huntsville, Ontario, closer to the Toronto marketplace, was considered. And eventually Homeplace on Black Sturgeon Lake was shuttered for good. But while the physical facility may be abandoned, the rich and consequential legacy of what happened there radiates from these pages.

Carry the Flame, like any thoughtfully stage-managed Chautauqua, has a mix of voices: fifty-three essays and poems in all, illustrated with a sprinkling of maps, homespun art, and photographs. The contributions are grouped thematically into eight parts, which allows some contributors to speak more than once without redundancy. The through line is the place, the remarkable boreal oasis in the black spruce forests surrounding Lake Nipigon, and the paddle to Hudson Bay. But apropos of Kurt Hahn and the ideals on which Outward Bound was built, contributions are flavored by the personalities and sensibilities of the individual writers, how they came to Homeplace, what they did there, whom they met, what happened while they were there, and how those experiences have echoed and reverberated in their leaving.

What arises from these pages is a portrait of an educational enclave that was years ahead of its time, made by embracing and embodying Kurt Hahn's broad philosophical notions about what it means to be a complete human being: A person needs to be fit, physically, mentally, emotionally, and spiritually; a whole person needs risk, also known as adventure; a fully contributing person needs craft, making things with their hands and participating in a master-apprentice dialogue; and a person needs compassion—"above all, compassion"—a familiar refrain in these pages.

COBWS aspired to many ideals that are only latterly being realized by the population at large. The school sought to embrace consensus community governance; balance gender roles and power dynamics; practice environmental stewardship and intentional consumption; live simply and lightly on the earth; build human capacity; respect and engage Turtle Island's original inhabitants; and make the world a better place. What a reader learns is that it's one thing to aspire to these lofty goals, and it's another to try to live them in a remote wilderness with a ragtag band of well-intentioned if, in some cases, sparsely skilled idealists.

These tales of foible and misadventure are what give this collection heart and authenticity. What went on at COBWS was serious business, but there's a ring of self-deprecating truth here, including Ken Victor's quip, "Who isn't tempted to say that COBWS was most like a hippie commune for people who wanted to get back to the earth?" And there's telling wisdom and candor in (Victoria) Moon Joyce's observation that, "We [got] good judgment by doing things we shouldn't have done if we'd had good judgment."

Repeated references throughout the book to the tragic death of a fifteen-year-old course participant on a solo expedition in 1979 show clearly that this intentional, if improvisational, community was hell-bent to learn from its mistakes, hard though that was. That COBWS survived as long as it did, in a perfectly improbable location, was testament to the often messy but effective quality of the organization and its people.

For the fifteen thousand participants and staff, onetime executive director Philip Blackford likens COBWS to sourdough bread: "Everyone who experienced COBWS came away with a nub of starter dough.... The initial loaf fed a lot of people. It's feeding people still." With a completely different metaphor, Ian Yolles, another one of COBWS's executive directors, talks about holographic participation: "When a hologram is divided into pieces, each part still contains the entire image within it, although each new image is from a slightly different perspective. The analogy to COBWS holds true." For me, as a person who's never worked for Outward Bound, never been a participant or a leader in an Outward Bound course anywhere in the world, who visited Black Sturgeon Lake precisely once in the 1980s, it's this hologram construct that is most helpful as an interpretive and appreciative device for this collection.

Early on in these pages, as I read them in draft manuscript form, there was a kind of nostalgic wistfulness arising from the stories that brought to mind the image of the multidisc *Woodstock* album, kind of a musical snapshot in time of the guttering idealism of the 1960s. But as I traveled further into this holographic celebration, a surprise emerged: Arising from these pages is a composite image of a man that intensified with each passing reference. That man is COBWS founder Bob Pieh, a teacher, mentor, friend, and colleague of mine at Queen's University, who, thanks to *Carry the Flame*, I see now in a much more consequential light.

In founding COBWS and the Outdoor & Experiential Education program (OEE) at Queen's University's Faculty of Education in Kingston, Ontario (and the Minnesota Outward Bound School, among other creations), Bob did something truly astounding, which was the invocation of experience à la John Dewey and Kurt Hahn as a central tenet of mainstream education. I say *mainstream* because, as an agent of change himself, Bob knew that by creating progressive learning communities within the bigger, more complex, instrumental, and more narrowly focused cultures of commerce and learning, he could make the world a better place by using a diaspora of young, keen, smart, and focused folk who had tasted the transformative power of an alternative approach to life and learning.

I count myself among those who "drank the experiential Kool-Aid" and who, like the contributors to this book, sallied forth unapologetically searching for ways, especially in this increasingly disconnected, virtual world, to connect people to one another and to the natural world through experience. While the whole is completely nourishing, I think my favorite essay is by John Huie. John remembers speaking in 1988 at the third Outward Bound International Conference honoring Bob Pieh. (An interview with Bob during that conference allowed the editor to include Bob as a contributor to *Carry the Flame*.) Later, after the conference, Bob wrote to John, thanking him for his words and saying something to him that crystallized for me Bob Pieh's profound influence on my life: "Thinking about something and being unable to experience the truth of it is like carrying an unlit lantern in a dark room. One can experience the reality of who they are and who they can be by putting themselves to the test. Nothing will light the flame in one's lantern but the wind of one's going. Keep your flame lit, John." Keep your flame lit, [add your name here].

Like Kurt Hahn—and Bob Pieh was like Kurt Hahn in more ways than I'd ever imagined; perhaps even, as Charles Luckmann suggests, an educational prophet in his own right—Bob Pieh wrote very little. He was a quiet thinker, a jackknife philosopher, a man of action. Moved by Hahn, he impelled others into experiences so they might engage the paradoxes of being "tough yet gentle / Humble yet bold / Swayed always by beauty and truth." His work, his way, his wisdom, and his whimsy are written into the practices of people whose lives he touched. Those are the people who animated COBWS. Those are the people who radiate out from the OEE program at Queen's. Those are the people who strung the bow, tuned the lyre, and produced this important and engaging book *Carry the Flame*.

HISTORICAL PERSPECTIVE
Derek Pritchard

Kurt Hahn, the patriarch of Outward Bound, was German born but a lifelong Anglophile. Convinced that the good in everyone could be awakened and developed by the right environment and teaching, he was drawn to the theories of education and drew up plans for a new kind of school, which he first realized in 1920 at Schule Schloss Salem (School of Salem Castle), near Lake Constance, the ancestral home of his benefactor, Prince Max von Baden.

Hahn set up a curriculum borrowing from sources as diverse as Plato, Sparta, Baden-Powell, and the British private school system. Hahn accepted pupils from all economic circumstances, including those with learning and physical disabilities. Hahn and Max von Baden made Salem one of the most famous private boarding schools in Europe.

During the 1920s, following World War I, Germany was in turmoil. The Nazis were ascendant and Hitler came to power in 1933. That same year, after an infamous raid on a Jewish community by Hitler's Brownshirts, Hahn, who was Jewish, led his students at Salem in protest. He was arrested and briefly imprisoned by the Gestapo, only to be released through influential British connections and ensconced on Scotland's Moray Firth. By then he was almost fifty years old, with no home, no job, and little money. What he lacked in these tangibles he more than made up for in dreams and ideas.

This time the result was a second school housed in the castle at Scotland's Gordonstoun. In the first class of thirteen young men, one was Prince Philip, later the Duke of Edinburgh and husband of Queen Elizabeth II. The curriculum required high academic standards and participation in one of Gordonstoun's local services, such as the fire brigade, coast guard, or mountain rescue. Hahn reintroduced the Moray Badge scheme, which also emphasized service, as well as physical fitness, expeditions on land and sea, and a final project. In the United Kingdom, in some format or other, the Moray Badge scheme continued for decades as the Duke of Edinburgh's Award; in North America, without badge or award, it became known as Outward Bound's four pillars.

One of Hahn's ambitions was to use his educational formula in a short-term program nationwide. This became known as Hahn's educational pillars: "an enterprising curiosity; an indefatigable spirit; tenacity in pursuit; readiness for sensible self-denial; and above all, compassion." During this period, a dynamic mix of several singular men led by Hahn resulted in the establishment of the Aberdovey Sailing School in Wales; the founding of The Outward Bound Trust; and Aberdovey's successful transition from a sailing school to an Outward Bound school.

In 1949, I was a participant on a twenty-six-day Outward Bound course at Aberdovey. I was sixteen years old. The structure of the course would be unrecognizable as an Outward Bound course today. It was highly structured and competitive. Prior to the first day of the course, a list of participants was divided into groups of twelve, mixed by race, religion, trade, type of school, and home address. On this course the intake had several apprentices from large companies, and several students from prestigious schools such as Eton and Harrow. The shipping companies and police forces also sent officer cadets. At the end of the first days' activities, an instructor appointed a student watch captain for the remainder of the course.

Every morning at 6:30 we had a morning run and a session of physical training. At 8:00, after breakfast, we stood to attention by our beds for inspection and points were awarded for the watch competition. We wore uniforms and marched or ran in columns between training sites. The majority of the instructors were officers drawn from the merchant marine or armed services. We were required to address them as "Sir." All athletic activities were scored on a merit scale. On completion of a course, one was awarded a badge of merit in different grades. A badge was not awarded if the training conditions were broken, which included a no-smoking pledge for the entire course. The warden considered any transgression as grounds for expulsion.

Each merit badge had a series of standards in five categories. From the outset the badge and award structure was a consistent thread at the majority of Outward Bound schools in the United Kingdom, and in many of the Commonwealth countries. Notable exceptions were in North America.

The Outward Bound courses in the United Kingdom during the 1950s and 1960s, which I experienced as an instructor at Eskdale and warden at Devon, bore little resemblance to the courses and pedagogical values of the Canadian Outward Bound Wilderness School (COBWS). Outward Bound leaders in North America, such as Bob and Wendy Pieh, Joe Nold, Josh Miner, Dan Meyer, and John Huie, among others, added another philosophical level to the Outward Bound I had experienced in the United Kingdom.

My habit when asked to review an essay or book is first to rip through it to get a feel and first impression. This I did with *Carry the Flame: The Remarkable Story of the Canadian Outward Bound Wilderness School.* I concluded that it was not for me!

I then thought of the Outward Bound motto: "To serve, to strive, and not to yield." *Maybe I should have another look*, I said to myself. I read through the book again, and then it was like the sun rising. The authors of seventeen of the essays in this book stood out to me (to use a phrase from this book) as alchemists. These authors are unrecognized, however, mainly because that was not their purpose.

The essays in this book are written with a quiet, gentle, and sincere passion. They are not so much about education as they are about values, community, and principles: engaging with nature; living a simple life; making community decisions through consensus; and searching for equality, regardless of gender or status.

My recollections and experiences with the early Outward Bound schools, however, differ markedly from several of the narratives. Hahn's educational model was very structured. Leaders were appointed; punishments were assigned. Merit was achieved through competition. HRH King Charles III, when asked by a journalist what his experience was like after four years at Gordonstoun, replied that it was "a prison sentence, absolute hell."

None of these differing views about Kurt Hahn and Gordonstoun affect the main themes of this book, however. If anything, they suggest that Outward Bound in North America made a significant contribution in adding the soft skills, or "spiritual elements," to a participant's experience.

In the initial decades following World War II, Outward Bound was almost entirely a physical endeavor with little, if any, reflective or personal growth goals. In North America, on the other hand, the cerebral became an accepted and necessary part of Outward Bound, such as active listening, constructive feedback, improving oneself by reflecting on one's actions, contemplation in solitude, and service to others. The two schools that Bob Pieh created, the Minnesota Outward Bound School and the Canadian Outward Bound Wilderness School, pioneered this transformation.

This astonishing collection of essays and memories illuminates how COBWS took the big ideas of Kurt Hahn, and other writers and philosophers, and reconstructed Outward Bound into a new model. In the jigsaw puzzle of Outward Bound schools worldwide, COBWS is an overlooked piece. If you want to learn more and are curious, then this book is an important tool.

HISTORICAL PERSPECTIVE

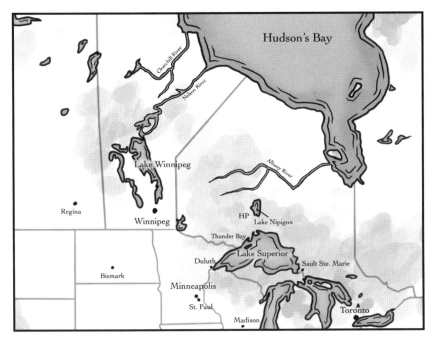

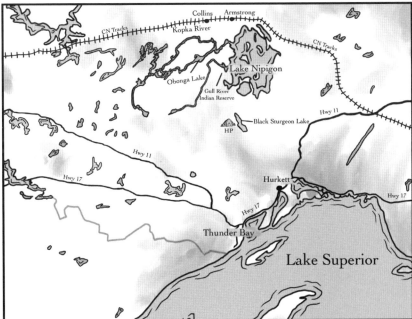

TOP: COBWS's Homeplace location in Northern Ontario. Map (not to scale) by Isabelle Cole.

BOTTOM: COBWS's Homeplace location south of Lake Nipigon and Canadian Northern (CN) railroad tracks. Map (not to scale) by Isabelle Cole.

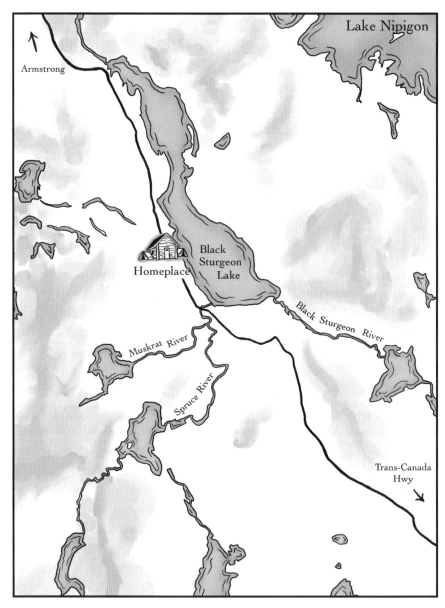

ABOVE: COBWS's Homeplace location on Black Sturgeon Lake. Map (not to scale) by Isabelle Cole.

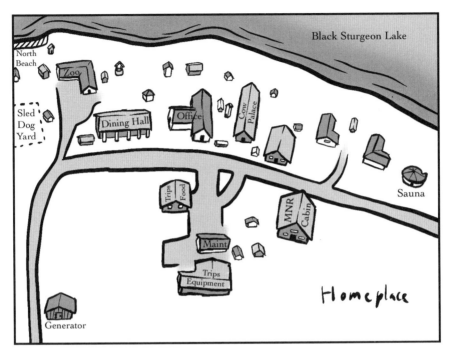

ABOVE: Map of Homeplace site, former Ministry of Natural Resources (MNR) spruce budworm research station. Map (not to scale) by Isabelle Cole.

PREFACE

Charles Luckmann, Alistair McArthur, Wendy Pieh, and Ian Yolles

Outward Bound Canada celebrated its fiftieth anniversary in 2019. During that year, gatherings and conversations commemorated the mountain school in British Columbia, founded in 1969, and the wilderness school in Ontario, founded in 1976. The Canadian Outward Bound Wilderness School was better known by the acronym COBWS, pronounced *cobwebs*. Catalyzed by that milestone, the four of us—Alistair McArthur, Wendy Pieh, Ian Yolles, and Chuck Luckmann—had a Zoom call to discuss Alistair's idea for an article about the early years of COBWS at its base camp on Black Sturgeon Lake, an abandoned Ministry of Natural Resources (MNR) spruce budworm research station, which everyone referred to as Homeplace.

One Zoom conference led to another. Soon we were meeting every month or two; we began recording our meetings and taking notes. The resurrected reminiscences of Homeplace inspired us to keep going. We each had significant memories we wished to explore and frequently talked about Bob Pieh, Wendy's father and the school's founding visionary and first executive director. As the first program director, Wendy, along with her father, set the tone for the early years at COBWS.

Alistair McArthur succeeded Bob Pieh as the school's executive director. Even though his previous experiences at Outward Bound schools in Australia, England, and the United States differed from what he encountered at COBWS, Alistair supported the school's founding principles. COBWS was one of thirty-four Outward Bound schools worldwide. From firsthand experience, Alistair concluded that COBWS was a different type of Outward Bound school. Chuck Luckmann later succeeded Wendy Pieh as program director, followed by Ian Yolles. Ian went on to serve as the school's fourth executive director, following Bob, Alistair, and Peter Turner.

Wendy Pieh reminisced about visitors from several international Outward Bound schools who commented on the special character of COBWS. They felt that COBWS reflected the essence of Kurt Hahn, the founder of Outward Bound, and his beliefs about education.

The more we talked and ruminated between Zoom calls, the more we recognized that each of us strove to articulate what made the COBWS ethos so special. We realized our identities had been shaped by those years. We queried previous staff, administrators, board members, and students, asking them to put words on paper responding to the question, "What made COBWS unique?" Their responses are between the covers of this book.

Carry the Flame: The Remarkable Story of the Canadian Outward Bound Wilderness School is also for the reader unfamiliar with Kurt Hahn, Outward Bound, and Bob Pieh. Hahn was a German Jewish educator, who in the 1930s spoke out publicly against Hitler and the Nazis. Hahn was imprisoned and later expelled from Germany. He moved to the United Kingdom in 1933. During World War II, he started a school for British merchant seamen to improve their survival in the North Atlantic Ocean when the Nazis attacked and sank their ships. After the war, building on insights he had gained during that conflict, Hahn created programs for young men that focused on adventure and experiential learning in the outdoors, risk and confidence building, and service. Thus began Outward Bound, the name derived from British sailors' jargon for leaving the home port.

Bob Pieh was an outdoorsman, athlete, coach, educator, and professor at Antioch College in Ohio for many years. He taught physical education and counseling, which led to taking students on canoe trips. Drawn to philosophy both ancient and modern, Bob agreed with the Stoics that we each create our own reality by the choices we make, and he was influenced by John Dewey's admonition that "We do not learn from experience. . . . We learn from reflecting on experience." Bob was also drawn to Kurt Hahn, who emphasized curiosity, tenacity, self-denial, and compassion.

Bob's love of philosophy, wilderness canoeing, self-discovery, and learning found a natural home in Outward Bound. He owned land outside Ely in northern Minnesota, where he created the Minnesota Outward Bound School in 1963. Bob and his family had spent many summers canoeing in northern Ontario; he saw the possibilities, and in 1976 founded COBWS, which this book is about.

Carry the Flame describes the utopian striving at COBWS during those early years of challenge and uncertainty. Many people contributed to this publication, with essays, art, photographs, donations, and all types of in-kind support. Our collective undertaking to create this book has been worth the effort. We thank the contributors. Moreover, we thank you, the reader, who was ever most in our minds as we assembled these pages.

I. CATALYST

The seed for the Canadian Outward Bound Wilderness School must have been planted during the 1950s and 1960s when Bob Pieh, with his young family in tow, spent summers on an island in Smoothrock Lake, in northern Ontario, which he rented from the Ontario government. Bob wet his chops with Outward Bound when he founded the Minnesota Outward Bound School (MOBS) in 1963 near Ely, Minnesota. Bob had been running a canoe program for teenage boys, called Shining Trails, from the site of a small resort that he had purchased in 1962. Shining Trails featured canoe expeditions into the nearby Boundary Waters Canoe Area (BWCA). Bob began running the first Outward Bound courses from this site in 1964. Jerry Pieh, Bob's son, was the first program director.

A decade later Bob must have decided that Outward Bound needed a true wilderness school. Or maybe he just wanted to return to northern Ontario, a remarkably pristine environment, and fond memories drew him back. He was successful in finding a retired spruce budworm research station on the road to Armstrong, Ontario, the jumping-off place for extended canoe expeditions. The Ontario government was pleased to have the station lived in, watched over, and taken care of, so the government rented it to him for $1 a year. Initially the name was Outward Bound Ontario, but Bob soon changed it to the Canadian Outward Bound Wilderness School (COBWS), pronounced *cobwebs*.

OPPOSITE: *Canoeists* by Lorne Tippett.

A professor at the McArthur College of Education, located at Queen's University in Kingston, Ontario, Bob brought an excited and willing group of his graduate students to the research station on Black Sturgeon Lake in 1976. They all worked together to bring the facility back to life, fixing the diesel generator, repairing the various buildings, and living Outward Bound: morning runs, followed by a dip in the lake; sharing the cooking and cleaning; and making decisions by consensus, whenever possible. Bob's students found themselves participating in all aspects of starting a school in a remote location, a living and learning experiment that they never forgot. This was also the seed for *Carry the Flame*.

Bob ordered canoes on credit, other needed equipment arrived, and soon Outward Bound courses began to be run out of this site, christened Homeplace. Each Outward Bound school has its own program, whether in the mountains, on the ocean, or even in cities. COBWS was in an isolated wilderness setting, surrounded by lakes and rivers that would provide the landscape for its courses.

No mountains to climb, no oceans to sail or row on, just thousands of lakes and rivers, waterways traveled by canoe—you had to learn how to steer a canoe, use a map and compass, and endure portages, which could be swampy, connecting the lakes and rivers. In the summer, there were blackflies and mosquitoes, and in the winter, minus forty degrees and northern lights. This magnificent wilderness lured each group of students, mostly from the urban areas of southern Ontario, on a voyage that would burn in their memories, and maybe alter the arc of their lives.

Consensus decision-making, sharing the workload, and debriefing their interactions and experiences as they went along instilled an ethic of living and working together as equitably as possible. Ideally, students discovered an inner strength, as well as an ethic of kindness and support for one another.

With a Homeplace site that might be habitable year-round, COBWS expanded courses into winter. A dog team arrived from the Northwest Territories. It must have felt like Christmas. Staff built doghouses; administrators purchased winter supplies and equipment; and COBWS established the first Outward Bound program focused on winter travel and camping with sled dogs pulling the load, like a Robert Service poem describing winter in the Yukon.

I. CATALYST

ABOVE: *Solo Paddler* by Lorne Tippett.

In "Beginnings," Wendy Pieh, the first program director, shares her experiences and ideas in creating a community that has minimal hierarchy and embodies the essence of living Outward Bound.

In "Reflections," Bob Pieh reflects on his life, his strong commitment to experiential learning, the educational value of reflection, and debriefing interpersonal relationships. He was a visionary who built a foundation under his dreams.

Andrew Orr joined COBWS as a part of the initial group of Queen's University students who came to Homeplace in 1976 to prepare the site for Outward Bound courses. In "Walden V," he finds inspiration in the vibrant community and its mission. Andrew spent his professional life in education and in various roles within Outward Bound Canada.

Wendy Talbot also joined the initial group of Queen's University students in 1976. In "How to Build a School Out of Nothing," she stresses that working together, being an outdoor community, and maintaining a sense of humor capture the essence of COBWS.

Bob Pieh lit a flame for others to follow. His genius was in helping others discover their beauty, something new within themselves, as Charlie Orsak's poem at the end of this section fittingly captures. Two years after opening COBWS, Bob handed the administrative reins to Alistair McArthur and left the program in the capable hands of his daughter, Wendy Pieh. —Ed.

ABOVE: Bob Pieh in 1977. Photograph by Andrew Orr.

ABOVE: The north beach. Photograph by Rob Linscott.

BOTTOM: An outhouse, 1982. Photograph by Peter Morgan.

OPPOSITE TOP: Homeplace from above, 1980s. Photograph by Peter Morgan.

OPPOSITE BOTTOM: The dining hall. Photograph by Rob Linscott.

TOP: The office, as seen from the driveway. Photograph by Rob Linscott.

BOTTOM: Women's whitewater staff training with (Victoria) Moon Joyce, Ruth Goldman, Nathalie Belanger, Martha Badger, and Bertha Bumchuckles. Photograph by (Victoria) Moon Joyce.

TOP LEFT: Students on the Funger Lake portage, 1988. Photograph by (Victoria) Moon Joyce.
TOP RIGHT: Educators' course with Kathleen Boylan, 1988. Photograph by (Victoria) Moon Joyce.
BOTTOM LEFT: Women's staff training with Amanda Harris, 1980. Photograph by (Victoria) Moon Joyce.
BOTTOM RIGHT: Daniel Vokey briefing participants on marathon route. Photograph by (Victoria) Moon Joyce.

ABOVE: Women's course, looking down from the top of portage. Photograph by (Victoria) Moon Joyce.

RIGHT: Students comparing portaging bruises from the Kopka River portage, 1978. Photograph by (Victoria) Moon Joyce.

OPPOSITE TOP: Gull River expedition, 1977. Photograph by Andrew Orr.

OPPOSITE BOTTOM: Student marathon, Black Sturgeon Lake, 1986. Photograph by David Thomson.

TOP: Paul Landry and Matty McNair during a fire evacuation from Homeplace, 1980. Photograph by Charles Luckmann.
BOTTOM: Start of staff marathon, Black Sturgeon Lake, 1986. Photograph by David Thomson.

TOP: Staff training, Black Sturgeon River, May 1982. Photograph by David Thomson.

BOTTOM: Ian Thomson demonstrates whitewater maneuvers on a section of the Black Sturgeon River known as "The Washing Machine." Photograph by Mark Zelinski.

TOP: Women's staff training, 1980. Photograph by (Victoria) Moon Joyce.
BOTTOM: End of course staff banquet, 1981. Photographer unknown.

TOP: Staff departure, 1985. Photograph by Daniel Vokey.

BOTTOM: Women of Courage course. Photograph by (Victoria) Moon Joyce.

ABOVE: Don Kafrissen and Diane Gallagher at Claghorn Bluff, 1976. Photograph by Andrew Orr.

RIGHT: The wall challenge, 1977. Photograph by (Victoria) Moon Joyce.

OPPOSITE: Students enjoy the majestic view of Northern Ontario's boreal forest while rappelling the 50-meter surface of Claghorn Bluff. Photograph by Mark Zelinski.

ABOVE LEFT: Winter course, 1980s. Photograph by Peter Morgan.

ABOVE RIGHT: Winter course, 1980s. Photograph by Peter Morgan.

BOTTOM: John Mordhorst on the winter course. Photograph by (Victoria) Moon Joyce.

TOP: Tanner. Photograph by David Thomson.
CENTER LEFT: Chip. Photograph by David Thomson.
CENTER RIGHT: Nancy, circa 1984. Photo by David Thomson.
BOTTOM: Sam. Photograph by David Thomson.

TOP: Dog sledding. Photograph by Mark Zelinski.
BOTTOM: Part of the Baffin Island recon group, 1987. Photograph by Sara Harrison.

Beginnings

Wendy Pieh

Bob Pieh, my father, ran a small pilot Outward Bound program in Canada in 1975. He had founded the Minnesota Outward Bound School (MOBS) in 1963, and he decided that he wanted to establish another Outward Bound school, this time in northern Ontario. He remembered the summers that our family had spent on Smoothrock Lake, where we rented an island from the Ontario government. He went exploring in the north and discovered a spruce budworm research station that was no longer in use on Black Sturgeon Lake, about one hundred miles northeast of Thunder Bay, fifty miles of which were logging roads.

He wandered around the site and thought, *This is perfect*. The area was pristine, with access to a truly wild system of lakes and rivers to the north, an ideal location to have the independence to create an Outward Bound school that would focus on his ideals: service to others, discovering the power in each individual to be more than they ever thought, to share and to learn through direct experience and reflection.

This research station was like a small village. As you entered, you drove past the kitchen and dining hall on the left and up to what had been the office and infirmary, plus some outbuildings. There were several family homes, an antique generator, and electrical service to all the buildings. To Bob, it felt like home.

Being Bob Pieh, he thought, *I'll ask the Ontario government to rent it to us for a dollar a year*. Of course they did, and COBWS was born. So was Homeplace, and we all felt right at home.

I leaped at the opportunity to join him as the program director. Over the years I had been developing my own sense of the power of community and a concept of my ability to contribute. At the age of sixteen, I had read *The Way of*

Life According to Lao Tzu, translated by Witter Bynner and originally published in 1944. In it, Lao Tzu described leadership:

> A leader is best
> When people barely know that he exists . . .
> But of a good leader, who talks little
> When his work is done, his aim fulfilled
> They will all say, "We did this ourselves."

Our second summer, in 1977, my father had to leave early, and he hired Tom Price, an old friend from England, to be our interim director. Tom had been the warden (*director* to us) of the Outward Bound Mountain School in Eskdale. Now of course I am not prejudiced, but somebody from England, where they are all correct and proper, as interim director? *Oh, dear!* To top it all off, he wrote that he would be arriving at ten o'clock. I got up in the morning to a message from him that I wasn't at the airport, so he checked into the Salvation Army for the night, and could I pick him up there? *Yikes!* He'd come in on the evening flight, and I had thought it was for the next morning! There were a few cracks making the rounds that I should bring him a tin cup full of stew, which really helped.

Tom Price was a leader in the Lao Tzu mold and one of the most amazing people I have ever met. First he apologized, assuming he had misinformed me of his arrival time—very un-British. A mountaineer and avid hiker, he was excited to be coming to a place that was on the water. Part of what was so impressive about him was that he was never self-centered and had an unending curiosity and amazing humility. His job at the time was as an inspector of schools, and he traveled around the United Kingdom, visiting what we would call public schools. He said he learned the most by never offering criticism, working hard to meet with and compliment staff on all the positives he could see. When he returned several months later, all the activities and practices that he might have criticized were completely gone.

He acted as a friend and companion to me, not as my boss, and I listened carefully to everything he said. (Well, he was mostly quiet and smiling, yet he would talk about anything and share his thoughts when asked.) I was honored that he came to spend time with us when I was the director of the Outward Bound school in the Kingdom of Lesotho, a small country landlocked by the Republic of South Africa. Tom passed away in 2013 at the age of ninety-four. You can learn more about him from his book *Travail So Gladly Spent*, published in 2000.

Alistair McArthur, who came in as the permanent executive director after my father, made all the difference. He is Australian and had a broad background with Outward Bound, most recently as the program director at the Colorado Outward Bound School. He arrived full of enthusiasm and curiosity about how we did things here in the wilds of northern Ontario, Canada. I immediately felt at home with him and knew he would help us move forward. His enthusiasm to learn and grow together with us set an excellent example in leadership for all of us. He had—and still has!—a great sense of humor.

Alistair must have been somewhat flummoxed as I talked about how important it was that the staff have a break in the summer to play together, which was much more important than having courses going on that would bring in more income. Yet he must have said to himself, *Okay, I'll just have to find more money*, and was completely supportive of how COBWS was evolving. He did everything he could to support and guide us as we moved forward into an amazing community and an outstanding Outward Bound school. To save the school money, he even hitchhiked north from Toronto for a visit!

Alistair showed his strength and compassion during the time around the drowning of Mark Bateman. Mark's mother, Irene, had worked in the Toronto office, typing our staff manual in order to raise the funds for Mark to have a scholarship on a summer course. To our caring and sharing community, Mark's drowning in July 1979 hit us like a ton of bricks. Alistair came to Homeplace to offer his support and to take care of all the things that immediately needed to be done. He gave us permission to be ourselves in sorrow and pain. I think back to (Victoria) Moon Joyce singing on the lawn, the tears, and the fellowship of powerful community that we were at Black Sturgeon Lake.

I have so many memories of when we laughed and learned together. I've taken the COBWS philosophy to every place I have worked, whether a small farm, a group home for juvenile delinquents in Alberta, an Outward Bound school in southern Africa, or as a state representative in Maine for eight years. Anywhere you go, whatever you do, you can make a difference. COBWS taught me that.

Reflections

Bob Pieh

At the third Outward Bound International Conference in New York, in September 1988, Ken Victor, guest editor for *The Journal of COBWS Education* 5, no. 1 (June 1991), interviewed Bob Pieh, who had received the 1988 International Conference Service Award "in recognition of his creative energy and outstanding service as founder of two Outward Bound schools and as a caring servant-leader to youth." The edited responses to the interview follow. —Ed.

When I was a senior at Madison Central High School in Madison, Wisconsin, my father died. It was the height of the Great Depression and pretty much a shakedown for the family—my mother, my sister, and me. What happened was that the kids at school got together, all twenty-eight in the senior class, and asked their fathers if they had any work for me, and various projects came up. The guys at the golf course whom I caddied for called me more often and tipped me more; I got more lawns to cut and snow to shovel. There was quite a concerted effort to help me, which really got to me in terms of what's possible within groups when they're sharing and feeling comfortable doing that, [providing a positive benefit for] not only the recipient but also the others.

There are a lot of things that I think my high school prepared me for. Madison Central High serviced the suburban groups who were the elite and also the town, which was lower class economically. Quite a bit of rivalry expressed itself in amateur sports and so on. I was a good student—in fact, straight A's—and an athlete, which was an unusual combination, and so I knew people in every area of town: I knew the south-side neighborhoods that hated the Italians; I knew the Italians because of my part-time work running the softball and basketball leagues; and the Irish I knew too. This created a lot of acceptance of me by a cross section of ethnicities. What I'm driving at is that one of the things that pleases me is that my roots in community go way back, and when I needed a boost, I got it.

As I look back, I know I was given a lot of help, support, and recognition. That kind of support, and that kind of base, I think, created in me a better understanding of all the segments of a potential community.

When I was at the University of Wisconsin–Madison, I met Art Thomsen, who had a tremendous influence on my life. He was the head of the Physical Education Department, and every noon, he and others got together for gymnastics. I couldn't believe what they were doing, and he invited me to get involved. We built a strong relationship; he became my substitute father. He taught me about the natural environment and how physical activity lent itself to [including] much larger concepts, like those of community and personal growth. Later, at Antioch [College] in Yellow Springs, Ohio, I was able to use these ideas to bring faculty and staff together on the playing field to work out their conflicts through healthy and fun competition.

I got hooked on group dynamics at Antioch. Doug McGregor, the new president, brought along with him Nick Knickerbocker, a colleague from MIT. Nick became a buddy of mine, and we taught group process together. I was able to tap both Doug's and Nick's excellent knowledge of group dynamics, consultation, and taking responsibility for decision-making. Doug revolutionized the efforts of the college to involve students and faculty in government, which was in the college charter. He and Nick were powerful examples for me.

I was on a PT boat in the Philippines during the war. One of my jobs was to arrange housing when our squadron would arrive at an island, and I always took care of the enlisted men first. I also arranged the food, and again, I put the enlisted men first on the list. The officers couldn't understand why suddenly the enlisted men were performing better, seemed happier, and were more contented. I learned a lot from that.

By the time I started the Minnesota Outward Bound School (MOBS), I was sold on the concept of community. It influenced my attitude in terms of administration, stressing the importance of adequate consultation, listening to grievances, and so on. A director can prevent community or enhance it. So one of my roles was to be sure that people understood themselves, that issues were addressed fairly and openly. I had to be open to criticism and to admit my mistakes. We had to look at mistakes so they wouldn't happen again. We did, as you probably know, have that drowning death the first summer, which really shook us badly.

The site for the community was ideal in terms of its natural beauty. Sigurd Olson, a friend of mine and one of the reasons we acquired the property, used to come out to bless the groups in his own way before they went off on the big journeys, the expeditions. That was good. We had Rena Weisinger as our head cook, who was everybody's mother, and ex-trapper John Sansted was the site manager. Art Thomsen, a great swimmer and my mentor and teacher when I was a student at the University of Wisconsin, was our waterfront director. He would go out to the dock in the evening, and the harmonica would come out, so there was that kind of lightness. It didn't mean that there weren't times when I had to make a final decision, but at least the staff would listen to one another, and I'd listen to them.

I was invited to join the new Faculty of Education at Queen's [University] and to write my own ticket. It was almost too good to believe. The two deans agreed that we were going to have community service as a curriculum requirement, and the three of us had almost a year to prepare before the school opened. I didn't have to adroitly explain the things I wanted to do—human relations, group process, using the outdoors for teaching, community service.

All students who enrolled in the Faculty of Education would do a term of volunteer service in the community, and this was attractive to them as a way to explore service before you got too far down the road. My job was to make the contacts in schools, social service programs, and the local prisons. Students were expected to put in a set amount of hours per week, to keep a journal, and to discuss it with their faculty counselor. It was a great success and a real help to the involved organizations.

I started COBWS because it seemed to be needed. I didn't want to call it Outward Bound Ontario, because that was not a big enough name. I had learned things from starting MOBS—I was going to say that I have an addiction to Outward Bound, but I don't feel that's it. But I believe very much in Outward Bound, if effectively organized. It can make a major difference in the short term: People can learn to motivate themselves and to develop a deeper capacity for relationships, which also means they can get reinforcement for their growth.

Plus, it seemed to me that the deserted government site on Black Sturgeon Lake was perfect. Our family used to go on canoe trips in that area; we went past this place that had been, at times, used for forestry research and odds and ends, and it seemed a natural. Plus, I had gained so much from Outward Bound. It's fun, really fun, and I had sufficient contacts at Queen's to make the recruitment of staff fairly easy.

It took some time and red tape to obtain the site. We got some support from people in government, and we guaranteed them a type of development that would enhance the site. I didn't want COBWS to be developed like MOBS, and anything that was developed I felt should be a product of the community, even to the extent of electricity and plumbing. I wanted it to be developed naturally, in harmony with the environment.

As far as staff goes, there was a lot of choice from the Faculty of Ed people. We had a shakedown; I knew the staff, they knew me, and we had that to build on, so it was easier to handle issues and to reinforce one another.

I wanted people with emotional maturity so there wouldn't be any hang-ups that would get in the way of communication. Maturity is first with oneself, accepting the fact that we've all got our problems. I see having patience as an aspect of maturity, not interfering too soon in a situation when there's learning happening, where if you do interfere, you stop the learning. I was also happy to get breadth—someone who was a photographer, someone who liked to paint, someone musical—and it was nice to have someone who knew the difference between a hammer and a chisel. We sure needed that our first year!

In group facilitations, at staff training, and otherwise, you'd be asked, "If you could change something about yourself, what would you change? If it is possible for you to change, would you like our help?" The idea was that we'd like to help, we'd like a community where people help one another and don't resent it, and if you don't hear us, is it okay to go ahead and pin you down rather than getting mad and cussing? We all need help, and we'll go a lot further if we have help, but our help can't be typical. You can't tell people what to do. You can only say,

"Have you thought of trying . . . ?" Which means the option's yours, recognizing the limitation that there are some things about you that I don't understand, but that's not your problem, that's my problem, and I'd like to understand and I'm interested. It's much easier, then, to let it hang out. It means that others aren't going to be as irritated as they might be by that bad habit because they know you want to change. It's possible, it seems to me, to get people to talk about how they'd like to change—some people think I'm too risky here—but if people don't talk, that's a clue, too, that they're not ready. A capacity for growth and a willingness to accept that growth is a community effort: That kind of openness I valued.

The other thing that struck me, and still does, is people hearing one another. People think that they know what you're going to say next, so they don't hear what you do say. They also don't pick up things that you might want to get out but that aren't easy to get out. My feeling is that if someone can't listen, it's hard for them to hear anything! And if someone working with a group can't listen, how are they going to hear the group? They might stereotype a group based on inadequate evidence because they haven't heard the group.

Mutual understanding, acceptance, knowing you well enough to know what you've got to give, and also knowing where you are in terms of areas where you may need help are basic ingredients to becoming a community.

Whether the staff or the administration made a decision depended on the implications of the decision, because I had ultimate responsibility, and it would be me and the trustees who would face the music. This did not mean that the administration was superior but that staff and administration have different responsibilities. If I had questions about a decision being made, I would question the analysis and point out holes, not question the persons involved but the decision-making itself. If the decision in the end made sense, perhaps I would want to implement it gradually in order for it to succeed.

It was very important that no one make dictatorial, bulldozing, or insensitive decisions. In a community, you can play power games, and that needs to be challenged. When groups came to me with a tentative decision, I would ask, several times, if they all agreed. Usually I had a hunch about things we might need to reconsider before making a decision that we would all have to live by.

* * *

Size can affect community because interactions are affected by size, and a lot depends on the nature of the interactions. Some Outward Bound schools in the States strike me as getting very big, and I'm a little worried about that; things can get lost. Even if the director is an advocate of community, it can get so big that there isn't the chance for the kind of communication that adds muscle—jointly imposed—to what the expectations are.

If groups get too big, people don't have time together, especially staff, and they are our primary resource. Nor does the administration have adequate time, and I think that lack of time sets a tone and [establishes] procedures that do not reinforce community, which I would fight for because I think community is essential.

For example, despite the efforts to have a good staff and an effective staff, sometimes a kind of weeding is needed—altering a staff member's role or suggesting that maybe this isn't the place for them. I need to have time with you to sort things out, to be together—not always in the office, but around—to be able to say to you, "I get the feeling your interests are elsewhere," or whatever.

In a community, these things can happen. If you have a record of consistency and caring, then you don't have to beat around the bush when you're raising a problem with someone. I resent it when people beat around the bush with me. I tend to say, "Let it hang out. If it's wrong, I'll let you know; if it isn't, I assume we've both got a problem." In a community, conflicts can be effectively resolved.

Another thing about a community is if you have a mature staff, then there are several people whom less experienced staff feel free to go to. They may be scared or confused or have had a near miss that they are afraid to tell me about. Yet they need advice and can trust a more mature staff member to maintain their confidentiality and to give them support. In an atmosphere of trust, an important aspect of community, these interactions and relationships can be fostered. Someone can say to me, "Bob, did you know so-and-so . . . ," and I can make myself available to that person, take a walk, go for a canoe ride. I myself must be trustworthy and not judgmental, which fosters a kind of exchange and openness that you don't often see.

Walden V

Andrew Orr

It was early March 1976, and I noticed an eight-and-a-half-by-eleven-inch poster titled *Walden V* stuck to a wall. One of the professors of Queen's University's Outdoor & Experiential Education (OEE) program was looking for volunteers to drive up to northern Ontario and open the base camp for a new Outward Bound school.

This was at McArthur College of Education at Queen's, where I was a student. I had never heard of Outward Bound. I wasn't even part of the OEE program. But we had one more student-teaching round coming up in April, and this sounded like a much better way of completing the requirement than standing in front of a class of snotty-nosed kids for another week or so.

McArthur College was relatively innovative for the time. We all had to do student-teaching rounds. We knew the evaluation that we received from each teacher would be important. Obviously, the student-teaching report from our final placement would be the most critical one for our future employment. Thus, normally we would all play it safe and choose a placement where we would be most likely to get the best possible evaluation.

But the college wanted us to try new things, to have the confidence to use our skills in ways that might challenge or inspire us. And to not get fearful about failing just as we were about to launch. So in an inspired move, they made the final student-teaching round unevaluated. If you were a secondary teacher and wanted to try elementary, go for it! No harm done!

Bob Pieh was the professor in charge of OEE. He founded MOBS in 1963 and subsequently moved to Queen's. Unbeknown to us, he had been tasked by

I. CATALYST

Outward Bound Canada to establish a new program in northwestern Ontario. He secured the use of an abandoned Ministry of Natural Resources (MNR) research facility on Black Sturgeon Lake, north of Nipigon. It needed work, and the timeline was tight. He needed free labor and got the project approved as a student-teaching round. I was in!

So in April, I and a bunch of other aspiring student teachers drove from Kingston past Wawa and up Black Sturgeon Road to what would become Homeplace. Don Kafrissen, who was in the technological education program at McArthur College, had arrived about a week earlier to get the old Witte one-engine generator started. At least we had power.

When we rolled in, people were still checking out the buildings. There were two cabins down at the south end that nobody had looked at yet. It was suggested that we go down and see whether they were habitable. We did, finding a comfortable, small, two-bedroom cottage, and moved into what would become Southern Comfort.

The site had been abandoned for a number of years, but the roofs were good and the buildings in reasonable shape. The work involved getting the rest of the infrastructure working, such as the electrical. And digging up all the water pipes that had frozen. It was determined that the water tower was not usable. The interiors of buildings had to be repurposed. There was brush to burn along the shore. And so on.

Work commenced on new major projects. Additions were needed for more staff accommodation. The dining hall had to be expanded.

Housing was gender-specific, and most of the guys were assigned to the large dormitory-style building at the north end. It became known as the Zoo. The cabin south of the office became the Cow Palace. (The story behind this name is not quite as sexist as it seems. There was a small chain of convenience stores in Thunder Bay called Cow Palace. Before the cabin was named, one of the women came back with a shopping bag with the name and logo. It was adopted by the residents.) Bob was in the next cabin south, the Director's. Every afternoon at five was cocktail hour in the lounge in the Zoo, with the bottles lined up on the mantle above the fireplace.

Bob had a very unobtrusive presence, but he was clearly shaping what was happening. We didn't learn anything about Outward Bound programs those first weeks, but we did catch on very quickly that this was about more than just building the physical infrastructure for a school.

Walden V, for example. Many of us were aware of the literature of the time on utopian communities, such B. F. Skinner's *Walden Two*. The name of this project implied to us that a certain kind of community was to be part of this. But why did Bob specifically choose Walden V as the name? And what exactly was the model? We had no idea.

The ways of decision-making were subtly introduced, although I don't recall any kind of formal meeting, let alone a community meeting. Rather, it was in the way Bob dealt with everyone, either one-on-one or during a gathering, such as a meal, that was happening anyway.

I recall going to see him at Director's with a problem that I felt required spending some money. I knew things were very tight, so I needed to get his okay. I knocked. Bob opened the door, naked except for the towel he was holding from his shower.

"I can come back later."

"No, Andrew, come in."

So I explained the problem to the naked Bob. I wanted the go-ahead.

He smiled. "Whatever you think is best."

I left. And, of course, found a way to do it without spending any money.

You never just spoke with Bob; you had a conversation. Unhurried. Inquisitive. As the opportunity presented itself. Famous was the knock on the door of the two-holer privy to make sure it was unoccupied before going in, only to hear Bob say, "Come in."

"I can come back later."

"No, come on in."

I'll spare you the metaphors, as I'm sure you can imagine your own. But it was never a short visit.

The crew evolved through the late spring. Most of the student teachers returned home after a couple of weeks. Intrigued by what was happening, some of us stayed on. Other people started arriving to finish the preparations, senior people such as Wendy Pieh, who would make the program actually happen. The nature of the community was in flux. How much direction and how much process? I recall finding a document in the office that was titled "Welcome to Portage." It listed lots of rules, such as curfew times and other such things. Quite different from what we ended up doing. To the best of my knowledge, that document was never implemented. But there was certainly a period of conflicts as the nature of the community developed.

One memorable moment occurred one morning after breakfast. Some of the guys who were doing the heavy construction work felt they were not getting enough food from the vegetarians who had recently been volunteering to do breakfasts. So the guys made a run to town and then signed up to make breakfast, which turned out to be steak and eggs. Bob spoke for half an hour afterward on moderation without ever mentioning steak or eggs.

The first students arrived in July, the morning after the tables were assembled in the newly expanded dining hall. The first course was Wilderness School Standard Course 3 (WSS-3). Why not 1? Apparently there had been two courses the year before in Quebec. That was news to us. But the school was launched.

So what did I take away from this?

I subsequently visited Outward Bound schools in many parts of the world and came to understand that although there is a common inspiration and purpose, there is no one model. It became clear to me that Bob was intent on creating a certain kind of community, not just because it would be nice for the staff but also because it would inform the kind of program this Outward Bound school would be. That community would include shared purpose, values, skills, and connections. The skills and attitudes that would make this community work would help us be better instructors. Working through and resolving our own conflicts, as well as helping one another expand and evolving our visions, would help us become better leaders.

I drove back from Homeplace in early August that summer with fellow McArthur student Doug Bonnell. The initial season wasn't over yet, but we both had commitments for our first full-time jobs—Doug in southern Ontario, me in the Caribbean. We had no idea where this project would end up, nor did we understand what it was really all about, but we felt that something significant had happened. So as we drove, we scratched down some words and phrases from the time, just over fifty of them, to capture the moment. They ranged from the concrete (*the Zoo, Ainer's, four-holer, mystery meat*), to language ("*In terms of...*," "*And so forth...*"), to process (*sharing*), and things that would only mean something to those who were there (*BS time, moose turd pie*).

Interestingly, the word *community* was not one of them. There had not yet been a community meeting. We weren't there yet. Bob was still helping us form. However, we were on the way, learning how to navigate, even if Doug and I weren't aware of it at the time. But looking back, the idea and the trajectory were clear. And we were seeing, again in hindsight, how to lead with a light touch.

How to Build a School Out of Nothing

Wendy Talbot

We had no GPS, no phones, no radios, no vehicles (except for staff vehicles), and no money. But we were young and keen and didn't know any better. It was an adventure that became life-changing and challenging. Many of us grew up at Homeplace, in a manner of speaking. Some of us still have not figured out what grown-up is.

Homeplace was first an MNR research station studying the effects of spruce budworms on the boreal forest. Walking into the camp was like going back in time: dishes left on tables, lab equipment everywhere, petri dishes and Bunsen burners scattered about, thousands of little bugs in trays stuck with pins, and buildings in need of repair.

Staff learned how to build everything from bunk beds to window dormers. For example, the kitchen addition was built by those not on the trail with students. It was a great way to spend your days off. There were special groups of staff who lent whatever skills they had to build Homeplace. One of my favorites was the bare-chested women roofers. Sunscreen was not as prevalent back then, but no delicate body parts were burned.

One fall we got a load of logs donated to build the Snail—a replica of Wendell Beckwith's original design. We peeled each log by hand! We learned quickly to be instructors, climbers, whitewater paddlers, and carpenters. Driving the bus and dropping off students for expeditions was always an adventure; leaving groups at the right location was never guaranteed. But groups always made it home—eventually—and once there, ate some of the best meals one could ask for. We had exceptional kitchen staff; they fed us and provided lots of fun!

With secondhand equipment and canoes and loans from MOBS and the Queen's University OEE, we put together our first courses. We also borrowed instructors from MOBS.

Expedition drops-offs became our first Outward Bound challenge. Changing flat tires was an integral part of staff training. Repairing road washouts became an opportunity in bridge building. And the dust! No one who has lived through a ride in the Dustbin will ever forget riding in the back of that old delivery truck during the dry summer months. Rock climbing staff endured a blanket of dust on each trip to the rock site, the Claghorn bluffs, a few miles north of Hurkett, Ontario. As they disembarked from the Dustbin, students looked on with uncertainty and disbelief . . . but for us, it was just another trip down the road.

Portages, if they existed at all, were mere jungle trails. In the early years, axe-toting instructors pioneered routes and cleared trails. Incredible terrain; high, impassable rapids; and magnificent, clean, clear lakes—we drank from them without water purifiers. And then there were the bugs! Words cannot do them justice. Fashion back then was something to be forgotten. If you have ever spent a twenty-eight-day course in wet wool from constant rain, no explanation is needed. The locals thought we were a paramilitary hippie commune, which of course is a contradiction.

Dogs were also a part of Homeplace. My colleagues knew my passion for these incredible animals. Who could fault Ticcanaf, my black Labrador, doing a 5.9 climbing move into the garbage trailer, or Kishline, a German shepherd–Siberian husky mix, chasing a bear that had just absconded with a fifty-pound pail of honey? We never did get the honey back, but Kishline came home.

The sled dogs played a vital role in the winter programs. They were tough, stalwart, and funny, especially when they were peeing on someone else's pack. We had a snowmobile donated one winter—a controversial gift. On its first venture north up the lake, it broke down. We sent the dogs to drag it home . . . which they did.

There were hard times and struggles; it wasn't all paradise. Difficult courses, problem students, challenges with staffing, accidents, and relationships—some good and some not so good. We had our share of problems. The school constantly struggled with money and not being able to pay bills or salaries, as meager as they were. Of course, we didn't do this for money.

COBWS was a lifestyle, a passion, and not for everyone. Tragedies with the sled dogs and the first, and thankfully only, student fatality, Mark Bateman in July 1979, kept it very real.

Overriding it all was a sense of doing something extraordinary, of having purpose and a community that could and would pull together, especially during the difficult times.

Homeplace was not just about staff. Students who experienced the atmosphere, the work ethic, and the overall connection to community left with a greater sense of what Outward Bound could represent as they moved forward.

There are many stories of Homeplace, from the collective experience, to individual struggles, to mistakes that helped us grow and better ourselves. The people who lived there through their mistakes and successes became, if not necessarily adults, creative, talented, and valued members of their future workplace communities. Some of us may never become adults. The wisdom of growing up at Homeplace is difficult to match. For those who came after, those early years were perhaps difficult to comprehend. We grew in experience and wisdom of what could be done if we pulled together and took this with us as we each eventually left Homeplace for our own reasons.

It was a different era. Could Homeplace happen today? Perhaps not in the same way. It was a time when some choices were limited and others more profound. We didn't have cell phones, and for years we only had a radiophone at Homeplace—it worked . . . sometimes! So we learned quickly that getting into trouble meant you had to get out of trouble on your own or, when available, with the help of others nearby. We didn't have as many rules or laws, which made risk-taking possible and demanded that we figure it out.

And the national debate was only just beginning about instructor certification. Did it make us better, safer instructors? Or was it an obstacle to doing what we did best? We had to think it through. We were forced to be unorthodox, creative, and at times a little outrageous. Were technical skills more important than knowing how to work together in an experiential atmosphere in the deep woods of northern Ontario? These arguments were just beginning to surface at community meetings. They might or might not persist today because the choice is not there. Regardless, the environment has changed. What we did back then I do not believe could happen now.

When I look back, the responsibility we had at such young ages was quite remarkable and, in hindsight, profound. It took a lot of people to make Homeplace the community it became. Those of us there at the beginning were truly lucky and fortunate.

Should Homeplace happen again? Perhaps. I think the premise, philosophy, and spirit of Homeplace are even more important today. We need another Homeplace, if only in our minds and attitudes, to teach us how to live, how to support the best of whom we can become.

Something New: Go and Find It

Charlie Orsak

We journey away from people,
Seeking wild adventure—only to find
Together we are the beauty.

The Wall

Lorne Tippett

II. VISION

Kurt Hahn and Bob Pieh were visionaries, Confucian in their beliefs that education is the antidote to human suffering. Each started two schools; each implemented an innovative curriculum based on ancient and modern philosophers, including Plato, Heraclitus, Emerson, and Dewey. Both men were shaped by the events of World War II.

Hahn's second school, the first Outward Bound School established in Aberdovey, in 1941, turned into a worldwide movement of more than thirty schools on four continents. Pieh established the second Outward Bound School in North America in 1963, the Minnesota Outward Bound School (MOBS), on a piece of family property near the town of Ely, Minnesota, bordering the Boundary Waters Canoe Area. MOBS was the first Outward Bound school to offer courses for women in 1965. Pieh's second school, which this book is about, was founded in 1976 on the shores of a large lake in the wilderness of northern Ontario.

Hahn's educational precepts have been articulated as his five pillars: "an enterprising curiosity; an indefatigable spirit; tenacity in pursuit; readiness for sensible self-denial; and above all, compassion." Pieh's maxims are contained in a koan-like poem he wrote: "Be tough yet gentle / Humble yet bold / Swayed always by beauty and truth."

Both men used the wild outdoors as a classroom and risk as the magical ingredient for change. For Hahn it was sailing programs on the North Atlantic.

OPPOSITE: *The Wall Team Challenge, Ropes Course* by Lorne Tippett.

For Pieh, the classroom was a multiweek canoe expedition in the BWCA, Quetico Provincial Park, and farther north in the Canadian bush of northern Ontario. Charles Luckmann describes in his essay a standard canoe expedition in "To Know by Experience." In her essay "Sacred Sustenance—Alchemy in Action," Ginger Mason outlines alchemy in action with food designed for these expeditions. (Victoria) Moon Joyce discusses in her essay "Pushing the Envelope of Outward Bound's Four Pillars" how COBWS pushed the envelop by growing physical fitness; learning through expeditionary challenge and adventure; meeting obstacles with self-reliance and discipline; and developing compassion for others through service.

As Ken Victor ruminates in "A Perfect Equation," Pieh sought a remote site for his school on Black Sturgeon Lake to hone his philosophy using a focus on community and grassroots leadership, which Wendy Pieh defines as "lead from behind." Both Bob and Wendy Pieh were attracted to the hermitage of Wendell Beckwith, inventor and philosopher, who lived on Whitewater Lake and practiced a Thoreau-like contemplation of the natural world, as a model for their own beliefs that personal growth is best achieved through reflection, as Wendy describes in her essay "Wendell Beckwith." Bob Pieh often used the expression "Dunk 'em and dry 'em," interpreted as give students a challenging experience and then have them reflect on their actions. Philosophers call this "doing the work."

Surrounded by religious believers in Outward Bound, Ian Yolles lays out a skeptic's path to conversion in his essay "From Skepticism to Fervent Belief." And Philip Blackford, in his essay "People and Place," paints the vision he found at Homeplace on Black Sturgeon Lake in four words: community, consensus, compassion, metaphor.

In the history of Outward Bound, recorders have often labeled the key ingredients of its pedagogical vision as *pillars*. Community, consensus, compassion, and metaphor are a good start in labeling the pillars of COBWS. —Ed.

A Perfect Equation

Ken Victor

COBWS was the second school founded by Bob Pieh. And I'm quite sure the uniqueness of it can be partially traced to what was learned from his first school, MOBS. When I showed up at MOBS in 1972 to take a course, the school was a mere nine years old. When I returned in 1979 to instruct, the school was—for better or for worse—in what I would call production mode, focused on rolling out its wilderness product to customers. Wonderful people were doing great work, slotted into a system focused on efficiency. What lessons Bob took from the evolution of MOBS I can't say, but there's no doubt that at COBWS he created a very different culture and school than those of his earlier effort.

My first experience with COBWS was in the spring of 1981. Chuck Luckmann, the program director at the time, picked me up in Thunder Bay for the long drive to Homeplace. Chuck used the drive to help me debrief my time at MOBS, where I'd been perceived as a bit of a rabble-rouser—I'd thought the staff ought to unionize—and he gently asked me penetrating questions and offered wise counsel. He also recited poetry and let me know, as we turned onto the COBWS road, that we were on the "driveway to Homeplace." By the time I got there—*Oh my God, where the hell are we?*—I knew I was someplace different. How different and in what ways, I had yet to experience.

The formation of community at COBWS can't be separated from its geographical isolation. The school was self-contained and, other than those road trips to get the essentials, self-reliant. It was as if this community, this isolated outpost, was the world. I remember how surreal it felt the first time I joined one of those road trips into Thunder Bay to pick up supplies. I'd been at Homeplace for so long that I could see civilization with new eyes—cars, traffic lights, a mall with a Canadian Tire. Wow.

Without it being said, that isolation put a kind of pressure to bond on those who showed up at Black Sturgeon Lake. We are the world, as the song says, so let's build it right.

Yes, building it right meant creating community, but it's perhaps more accurate to say that COBWS was, at its heart, communal. More accurately still, who isn't tempted to say that COBWS was most like a hippie commune for people who wanted to get back to the earth? That sounds about right except for one distinguishing feature: This particular commune intersected with, and was shaped by, the purpose that brought everyone together—to serve as an Outward Bound school.

The community had a meaningful mission that it took to heart. It had people who were passionately committed to the educational ideals of Kurt Hahn and who were able to articulate them and question them and revel in them. We were on the shores of Black Sturgeon Lake to bring people with us into an experience of Hahn's pillars of Outward Bound: "an enterprising curiosity; an indefatigable spirit; tenacity in pursuit; readiness for sensible self-denial; and above all, compassion." To live these meant focusing our curiosity on how to become excellent instructors, on understanding one another, on understanding ourselves. They meant that we were tireless in our learning and in our community building, that we gladly let go of the excesses of civilization, and that we remembered how each of us has our flaws and our failings and our shortcomings and are magnificent nonetheless. In other words, "Above all, compassion."

Along with Hahn's pillars, we valued democratic practices and radical equality. And the two were intertwined. Community meetings were practice fields for democracy, for citizen engagement, for the voiceless claiming their voices, and for having the powerful surrender their privilege because, well, there really wasn't any other choice. If you thought your position guaranteed you a platform, think again. I remember when some new board members came up for the first time and attended a community meeting; what puzzled them was that no matter how intently they observed the proceedings, they couldn't figure out who was in what role, and they had no idea who held a position of power. After all, whose voice is most important in a meeting where every voice is equally respected? The answer: the voice that offers the most useful and compelling point of view. That could be anyone's. And often it was.

I suppose there's one aspect of Homeplace's radical equality that needs to be mentioned even though it seemed to be such a given to me that I didn't notice it; it just was. I'm referring to the equality of men and women. Maybe because Outward Bound contains physical challenges, people assume testosterone ought to naturally be in the ascendancy. That thinking was, and remains, nonsense, and COBWS would have none of it. If some men were bewildered at certain times by it, they would surely have a chance the next time to demonstrate that they had evolved.

Power wasn't the only thing that mystified visitors. Some visiting board members wanted to see job descriptions, as they were sure we needed them, but we didn't have any, or none that would pass their official HR inspection. What we all shared was a sense of what needed to be done. Some people, of course, were charged with being mainly responsible for certain things—trips for food, the site, equipment—but that didn't take the place of an ethic of participation. Things got done because they needed doing. And oftentimes they got done joyfully. Weren't the dishes meant to be washed to a chorus of "Barrett's Privateers"? When things fell between the cracks because we weren't sure who was supposed to deal with them, it wasn't long before someone would reach in and pull the things out and do what needed to be done.

And then it would be time for another song, eh, or perhaps a round: "Wearing my long wing feathers as I fly . . ."

If the work of the community was held together by participation and contribution, the off-hours were about creation. I have an idealized vision, I suppose, of our earliest ancestors who gathered around fires. Once their needs for food and clothing and shelter were met, what then? I like to think they nurtured community. They became storytellers and ritual-makers, artists and dancers, singers and pranksters. COBWS had all that. When the work was done, we were spontaneous and playful and irreverent. We would've made our ancestors proud.

There's one last thing to mention, and it is likely the hardest to describe. There was something spiritual about COBWS. I hesitate to use the word *worship*, but the shoreline of Black Sturgeon Lake was a good spot for reflecting on our place in the universe, for experiencing that we are part of something much larger that is mysterious and ineffable. The lake was our daily sermon, reminding us that we are small, that we live in the presence of an immensity and beauty we had best honor with our praise and our care. And in that immensity we realize the only thing we had was one another, and we honored that, too, by our love and our care.

And every summer, and maybe not until August, these awarenesses would take hold. Perhaps it would happen at a circle before dinner outside the kitchen. Someone would give a reading, a gentle breeze would move across the lake, and the beauty and the love and the gratitude would land. And frankly, it didn't need to be named. We felt it, and we knew; all of us knew.

So what made COBWS unique? Here's a perfect equation:

isolation + Hahn's pillars + democracy + equality + sacred beauty =
the unique COBWS community

Of course, that's nonsense. I'd say anybody who thinks there's an equation that can get at the ineffable magic that was COBWS should think again. As Einstein put it, "Not everything that matters can be measured." And COBWS mattered, more than anyplace else in my life, and I'd hazard a guess I'm not alone in that.

People and Place

Philip Blackford

*What do we live for, if it is not to make life
less difficult for each other?*

—George Eliot (Mary Ann Evans), *Middlemarch*

My first experience of COBWS was as a guest at the end of staff training in 1981. I had come to see a friend, who after having been a student herself the previous fall had returned that spring as an intern. My dad was a high school physical education teacher and deeply involved in camping when I was a kid, so I grew up loving both the outdoors and experiential learning. I had read about and been drawn to Outward Bound for years, but I had also come across a fair bit of bad press that portrayed Outward Bound as a macho, quasi-military organization. I was concerned my friend might be getting herself in over her head with a bunch of loonies and wanted to check it out.

I pulled into Homeplace just before lunch and have this vivid memory of gathering in the dining hall with a group of thirty complete strangers, all of whom simply radiated life. It made my head spin! One thing that struck me immediately was a greater sense of balance in terms of gender expression—men who appeared comfortable with their feminine sides and women who were in touch with their masculine selves—than I had ever experienced anywhere before. It was exhilarating. I'm pretty certain that within the first couple of hours of being there I had—unconsciously, at least—determined where and with whom I wanted to spend the next chapter of my life. I applied and was hired as an intern the next year by Ian Yolles, who was program director at the time. Alistair McArthur was executive director.

It's absurdly reductionist, but in my mind, four foundational and enduring elements that contributed to making COBWS unique were (and bear with me here; I'm going for alliteration) community, consensus, compassion, and conscious use of metaphor.

Our reputation within the wider Outward Bound community as "that mystical little school in the north woods" was due in part to Homeplace's being the most remote school in the world (we needed to rely on one another more than other schools). But that wasn't the whole story. Our commitment to community, collaboration, and cooperation was a conscious choice, and by the time I arrived community meetings were legendary. The simple fact that we chose to stagger our course calendar so that everyone could attend the monthly meetings is proof of that commitment. Most organizations would have conveniently forgotten that efficiency is a means to an end, not an end in itself, and squeezed in a couple of extra courses.

Community meetings were also a perfect opportunity to reinforce our predisposition toward consensus decision-making—difficult and time-consuming, perhaps ("Where on the agenda should we put life-jacket policy?"), but entirely worth it. Not only does a preference for consensus contribute to greater clarity, cohesion, and accountability, but it also reduces the tendency to blame others when things don't go well.

Which leads to . . . "and above all, compassion." I remember in the mid-'80s hearing Marilyn Ferguson, author, editor, and influential proponent of what became known as the Human Potential Movement, deliver a keynote address to a group of several hundred educators. (Being a poor, starving Outward Bound instructor at the time, I had snuck into the conference and was standing quietly at the back of the hotel ballroom.) She opened her talk by saying, "Regardless of what subject you teach, the most important thing any of your students will ever learn from you is who you are."

She let that sink in for a moment, then asked, "How many of you here team teach on a regular basis?" Fewer than 10 percent of the audience put up their hands. But of course I immediately thought of us. Then she said, "The most important thing your students will learn from you is how you relate to your partner." What really blew me away wasn't just the provocative nature of her discourse.

It was the realization of how central the qualities of empathy, caring, compassion, and respect *were* to how we tried to live and work together at COBWS.

In his 1980 article "Can the Mountains Speak for Themselves?" Thomas James did an exceptional job of exploring the complexities of what were then (and may still be) two seemingly divergent schools of thought on how best to conduct an Outward Bound course: An Outward Bound experience on its own is enough to result in meaningful learning, and sincere, nonjudgmental facilitation can enhance the learning derived from the experience. In my mind, these two points of view really aren't mutually exclusive. As with most things, it's a question of balance.

I'm grateful that COBWS was fully committed to experiential learning and also encouraged sensitive and appropriate instructor-facilitated reflection. In fact, in support of this, Ian somehow managed to get his hands on enough first-edition copies of Stephen Bacon's *The Conscious Use of Metaphor in Outward Bound* for everyone attending staff training in 1983 to have their own copy.

I remember, as a wet-behind-the-ears intern, dropping by the ropes course one day in time to overhear my more experienced colleague Marian Flammang engage a young, at-risk student. She asked him if it would help to remind himself of how proud he was feeling (having just then mustered up the courage to successfully cross the beam) the next time he felt pressured by his friends to do something wrong. I thought to myself, *Wow, that's going to stick.*

To Know by Experience

Charles Luckmann

> *The key to the improvement of mankind does not lie in understanding society intellectually but in developing active methodologies capable of stimulating the growth of persons.*
>
> —Paulo Freire, *Pedagogy of the Oppressed*

I met Bob and Wendy Pieh in the summer of 1973 at MOBS. They made a significant impression on me. I was twenty-two years old, and this was my first Outward Bound experience. I went on to work at another Outward Bound school for three years, as well as two adaptive programs similar to Outward Bound but with different clientele. At the end of 1978, after a summer of canoeing and archaeology in Labrador, I was surprised to get a call from Wendy asking me to consider working for the new Outward Bound school in Ontario, COBWS.

I didn't have any money. I wanted to return to Canada, so I said, "Sure." In April 1979, I took a bus to Thunder Bay to attend staff training. The COBWS staff training was unique. It wasn't hierarchical, and everyone had an equal voice. It was kind of like a commune, utopian. COBWS was also way off the beaten track, which appealed to me.

Following the COBWS staff training, I taught my first Outward Bound course in Ontario from May 15 to June 8. My co-instructor was Chris "Kit" Bresnahan. Our eleven students were picked up at the airport in Thunder Bay and transported one hundred miles to where Kit and I met them for the immersion phase of our course on the Spruce River, a tributary of Black Sturgeon Lake. My journal for that time began when the students got out of the van, collected their personal gear, and assembled in a circle near where Kit and I had put six canoes, eighteen paddles, twelve life jackets, two Duluth packs (canvas packs designed specifically for canoeing) filled with food and cook gear, and two more Duluth packs filled with three four-person tents. We also had eleven stuff sacks, in which the students would pack their personal clothing, and six empty Duluth packs, two people sharing each pack.

The educator Kurt Hahn founded the first Outward Bound school in 1941 in Wales during World War II. He wanted to better prepare British seamen to survive in lifeboats in the North Atlantic when German submarines torpedoed and sank their ships. Our eleven students were now in their metaphoric lifeboats. I still have their names in my journal—five men and six women, all from cities in eastern Ontario, ages seventeen to twenty-six. Kit and I gave each one a large stuff sack measuring twenty inches long and sixteen inches wide and told them their extra clothes should fit inside.

The students had been sent a clothing list, basically one set of clothes to wear and one set to keep dry, plus a heavy sweater, a wool hat, and a sun hat. Kit and I provided them with rain gear—a green poncho that fit over their head—and a sleeping bag. They could also take with them a swimsuit, a towel, and a few toiletries and personal vitamins and medicines. In their suitcases, they left behind their travel clothes, watches, money, other valuables, and anything they couldn't fit into their stuff sacks, which they would be living out of for the next twenty-four days. They were now in a place away from their usual society.

They arrived around five in the afternoon, hungry and tired from their travels. Before they could eat, they had to pack up, load the canoes, and paddle a mile to our first campsite. Some of them didn't know how to keep a canoe going straight. We zigged and zagged from the mouth of the Spruce River to our campsite on Black Sturgeon Lake, which was only a couple of miles from Homeplace, the base camp for COBWS.

Beginnings can be the hardest part. Our students appeared apprehensive with this unexpected start, dropped off far from any town in the middle of nowhere—the Canadian bush! Luckily, the weather was pleasant and there were few biting bugs. Blackflies wouldn't be out in force for a couple more weeks; mosquitoes got bad later in the summer.

As the students set up their tents and rolled out their sleeping bags, Kit and I started a fire and cooked their first meal. We emphasized keeping the brigade, as we called our group, healthy in the days to come and demonstrated safe outdoor-cooking sterilizing habits: scrape, wash, rinse, sterilize. Later that evening, as we sat around the fire and after introductions, we discussed a few key tenets of the Outward Bound educational philosophy as articulated by its creator, Kurt Hahn. The following is copied from the journal I kept at the time, which I used in presenting Kurt Hahn and his philosophical assumptions to students (my journal didn't record the source):

- persons have more resources and are more capable than they think they are
- a small, diverse group of people have the resources within it to successfully cope with significant physical and mental challenges
- adolescents are capable of adult decision-making and responsibility
- more can be learned by presenting problems rather than solutions
- a period of solitude and contemplation contributes to greater understanding of self in the broad scheme of things
- stress and shared adventure are important catalysts in the discovery process
- the single most important determinant of a person's future is what they think of themselves
- significant, long-lasting learning can be achieved through an intensive, short-term experience
- one reveres life for having experienced it in real, dramatic terms
- from such experiences one learns to respect oneself
- from respect for self flows compassion for others
- compassion for others is best expressed in service to mankind
- the morally responsible [person] is the aim of the training, not to produce an artist, intellectual, or woodsman

Kit and I also reviewed the itinerary with the brigade for this twenty-four-day course. We emphasized we were a self-contained unit, a small community responsible for one another's safety and well-being. Everyone said they were happy they had signed up. Most expressed feelings of boredom with life, being in a rut, seeking a catalyst for a new perspective. They had read the Outward Bound literature; they were hopeful. Most also said they were looking to learn outdoor skills.

The first three days were called *immersion*—an initiation into the Outward Bound curriculum and pedagogy. After breakfast on the first morning we did a swim test and practiced swamped canoe rescue. The water was cold, so we had tents, sleeping bags, and hot drinks ready in case of hypothermia.

At lunch Kit and I introduced them to the first aid kit. One of our Duluth packs, where the first aid kit could be quickly found in an emergency, had a large cross taped on it. After lunch we paddled two miles to the whitewater site at the Split Rapids Dam, where the Black Sturgeon River cascaded from the lake in a series of rapids. Here we met two other instructors who had wet suits for everyone. We spent the afternoon whitewater canoeing—learning different canoe strokes such as the pry, draw, and cross bow draw.

The Class II rapids had some large standing waves and powerful eddy lines but no rocks or logs to maneuver around. It was a great way to get them thinking about how to handle a canoe in moving water. Everyone had fun. A few said it was scary.

After an afternoon of whitewater practice, students stripped off their wet suits and we paddled the short distance back to our campsite. Kit worked with several students to prepare and cook our supper. Morning and evening meals would be prepared over an open fire. We meant to live as wildly and simply as possible. Before supper Kit or I would read a short poem or another piece of literature that celebrated our relationships to the land, food, one another, and our life journeys. We were attempting to create a group identity that was mutually helpful, consensual, interdependent, and inspirational.

> *I wanted to live deep and suck out all the marrow of life . . . and, if it proved to be mean, why then to get the whole and genuine meanness of it . . . or if it were sublime, to know it by experience . . .*
>
> —Henry David Thoreau, *Walden*

* * *

After breakfast on day three, we paddled to Homeplace and spent the morning at the ropes course. The ropes course had a tension traverse stretched between two trees. Students tried to cross a quarter-inch wire using a rope tied to the far tree for balance. The rest of the brigade would carefully spot each person as they moved across the wire in case they fell, which happened often. The course had rope bridges to cross and an assortment of individual climbing activities, with the user protected by a harness and belay (to arrest a fall).

A prominent group activity was the Wall, which was twelve feet high. The brigade had to figure out how to get everyone over the Wall without props of any kind. I've seen many groups struggle for a long time, but eventually they solve the problem, and everyone is moved from one side of the Wall to the other by hanging one person down and the last person on the ground hangs on as both are pulled over the top of the Wall.

Sometimes, if the last person is small, they can climb up the person hanging there. It helps, however, if the person being lowered down the wall is wearing a tightly cinched belt. I've seen people almost have their pants stripped off as the last person hangs on to them or climbs up over them. The Wall was one of my favorite team-building activities.

Kit and I discussed with the brigade their decision-making process and how they figured out how to get everyone over. Ideally, students had already begun to gain confidence in how they worked together as a team. Activities such as the trust fall also increased students' faith in each other that the other members of their brigade would catch them when falling backward from a modest height.

In the afternoon we took the brigade into the Map Room and began to plan their fourteen-day expedition. One wall was covered with topographical maps of the nearby canoeing wilderness, hundreds of square miles of northwestern Ontario where few people lived, now part of Wabakimi Provincial Park. The immersion phase of a COBWS course typically took place on or near Black Sturgeon Lake, not far from Homeplace. There were six other courses happening simultaneously, so we had to schedule and coordinate each brigade's time at the whitewater and rock climbing sites and time at Homeplace for expedition planning. Our time to rock climb wouldn't come until after the expedition, at the end of the course.

The Map Room was a favorite place. Here we surveyed the seemingly infinite possibilities, which seldom failed to inspire. Whereas immersion was close to Homeplace, our expedition departed near Armstrong, an Ojibwe outpost on the Canadian Northern Railway, farther up the gravel road and another fifty miles from Homeplace. COBWS used a few standard places to start and end each expeditionary course, typically at Bukemiga Lake, south of Armstrong, or Little Caribou Lake, north of Armstrong.

Instructors often experimented with different routes, however. Major destinations for expeditions were Smoothrock Lake, Whitewater Lake, Whiteclay Lake, and Cliff Lake. But there were thousands of lakes to traverse. Our group settled on departing from Little Caribou Lake, paddling and portaging three days north to Whitewater Lake, then, after a visit with the inventor and hermit Wendell Beckwith on Best Island, traveling two more days by canoe and portage to Scrag Lake for a three-day solo.

After the solo portion, the brigade would be on its final expedition for four days, traveling south (without Kit and me) along the Ogoki River and eventually to the Kopka River and the pickup on Bukemiga Lake. We had no way to communicate with Homeplace, no satellite phone or the like. We were on our own, completely self-contained. We had to handle any emergency ourselves and arrive at the pickup destination fourteen days later, on time.

At the time I didn't fully appreciate the enormous responsibility Kit and I, the school's directors, and the board of trustees were assuming for the participants. Risk was an essential part of our curriculum. If handled properly, as Kurt Hahn had demonstrated, it would lead to a stronger sense of self. The Kurt Hahn pedagogy taught that taking risks was fundamental to learning and developing a positive self-regard. It was the single most important factor influencing a person's destiny. For an Outward Bound school to exist at all, to fundraise, to charge tuition, to insure the school against accidents, and to implement Kurt Hahn's pedagogy, school trustees had to believe a certain level of risk was critical to shaping individuals and society.

Of course, food planning would be a crucial component too. And the kitchen staff at COBWS was missionary in its zeal to educate staff and students

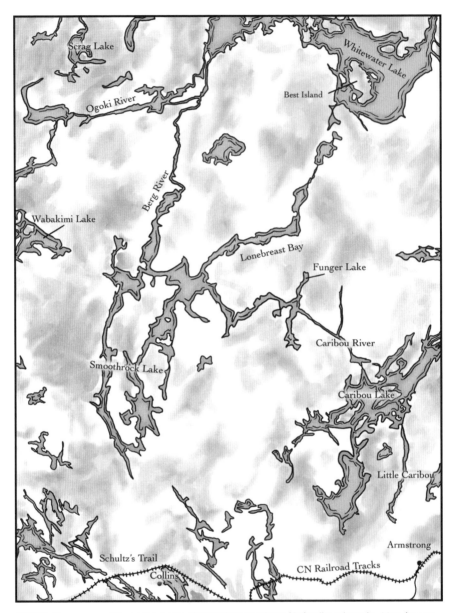

ABOVE: Canoe expedition area north of Canadian Northern (CN) railroad tracks. Map (not to scale) by Isabelle Cole.

II. VISION

about healthy trail food to support a *small planet*, the term used in the 1971 best-selling book *Diet for a Small Planet* written by Frances Moore Lappé, which noted the environmental impact of meat production as a contributor to global food scarcity and climate change.

Ginger Mason, aka Bertha Bumchuckles, supervised the kitchen and the trips food program. She was probably either vegetarian or forced to feed everyone on a budget of a dollar per day per person, or both. Bertha had mimeographed pages of sample recipes with food quantities for groups our size and gave the brigade a tour of the warehouse, which resembled a small food co-op. Sizable quantities of bulk foods were stored in large tin garbage cans (to keep the mice out). All eyes of our brigade were wide open in amazement. They would be eating mostly a vegetarian diet and preparing homemade food from scratch over an open fire. The only meat was canned chicken, tuna, and sardines.

Each person would need approximately four thousand calories per day, comprising carbohydrates (50 percent), proteins (25 percent), and fats (25 percent). Bertha discussed with the brigade the importance of complementary proteins (to get the most value from their food). She gave them sample menu plans and the quantities of grains, noodles, or legumes needed. The students would need to decide how they wanted to pack the food—by each day or pantry style. They chose both, packing the basic meal items for each day and then a pantry of staples for baking (flour, oil, sugar, baking powder, powdered milk) and condiments (salt, pepper, spices, seeds).

The following day the brigade baked granola, Logan bread, and flapjacks to take with them on the trail. The industrial-size Homeplace kitchen could accommodate different items being cooked simultaneously.

We all knew what granola was, but how many in the brigade knew about Logan bread? Our bodies crave fat after a day of exhausting labor, even more so when camping and nights are cold. Logan bread is rich in oil and butter as well as nuts, sugar, raisins, and molasses. It's also the perfect bread when winter camping because it doesn't freeze.

Logan bread is made with many cups of flour. Flapjacks are oatmeal-based. They are kind of like granola bars with peanuts, soy grits, and powdered milk.

The sweetener for flapjacks is usually honey or maple syrup. They tend to crumble, so we packed them in old milk cartons. "One flapjack a day keeps the doctor away," I used to say.

At the end of a busy day, we took a sauna together in the Snail, which was large enough to accommodate all thirteen of us. We poured water on hot rocks; the resulting steam caused our bodies to perspire. After it became too hot to breathe, we walked a few steps down the beach to the lake, where we immersed our steaming bodies.

The combination of hot steam and cold water invigorated body and soul. Our bodies tingled with delight, releasing any vestiges of anxiety or tension anyone may have been feeling. (Since my days at COBWS, I've felt that a sauna once a week for all people would put an end to war.) Summer solstice was arriving soon—there was some daylight left. By the time we left the sauna, stars were beginning to pierce the fabric of sky.

Our last full day at Homeplace was busy cooking and packing for our expedition. It was a Herculean task assembling all the food and equipment thirteen people needed for fourteen days in the northern Canadian wilderness. When we were finished, we had three food packs weighing approximately a hundred pounds each.

Like the challenges at the ropes course the day before, the students were demonstrating the teamwork and confidence to pack everything they would need for their expedition—in twenty-four hours! Our brigade of individuals was solidifying into a team. We cooked and packed and planned late into the night.

Of course, what made it possible was that the staff at Homeplace had already shopped for and organized what the brigade would need. The amazing, wonderful energy of the Homeplace staff assisted in getting the brigade on the trail the next day.

Midmorning on May 20, we left Homeplace in a small school bus, bound for Little Caribou Lake, which lies a few miles north of Armstrong, Ontario—an outpost on the Canadian Northern Railway. North of the CN tracks, water flows through wilderness to Hudson Bay. Thirteen of us piled our Duluth packs filled with food and personal clothing into the back of the bus, which also hauled a trailer carrying our canoes, life jackets, and paddles.

II. VISION

Duluth canvas packs are so named because they are manufactured by the company Duluth Pack in Duluth, Minnesota. In the twenty-first century most canoeists use plastic food barrels and waterproof packs. Duluth food packs are heavy and cumbersome, and care has to be taken to waterproof personal gear and put all food in plastic bags.

Before plastic bags were ubiquitous in wilderness travel, we used to apply paraffin to cloth bags to waterproof them—more labor-intensive but better for the environment. As much as possible, however, we saved our plastic bags (cleaning and reusing them once we returned to Homeplace). We practiced leave-no-trace camping and recycled everything we could.

Recycling was part of the ethos; the staff at COBWS took seriously the threat to the earth from human activity and embodied a deep ecology of place. We didn't want to contribute to the erosion of our local wilderness, which we used as a classroom. But of course we did. Our footsteps deepened portage trails, the vehicles we drove contributed to greenhouse gases, and our fires left scars (unless properly removed). A group of thirteen had to properly dispose of their excrement, too, which we did in individual catholes or group latrines. The beauty of canoe travel is that water is your highway, and aside from a few bubbles left in your wake, canoes leave no trace.

In the first couple of days of an expedition, a typical brigade like ours acclimated to all the chores of a wilderness expedition. Little Caribou Lake is a good place to begin. It's a slender lake, ten miles long and only a quarter mile wide. We moved slowly down the lake, practicing our J-strokes, the stroke the stern paddler uses to keep the canoe going straight. At the end of Little Caribou Lake, the brigade accomplished its first portage—or carry—into the larger Caribou Lake.

Within a few days our students would be able to portage all their gear in one trip. Kit and I taught everyone how to lift and carry a canoe. Our canoes were aluminum, the workhorse of the early days of canoeing before Royalex plastic canoes made by Old Town and Mad River became popular. Two personal packs could be carried by one person, typically one pack atop the other. Tumplines were used to distribute the weight. When used properly, it's amazing how a tumpline placed over the forehead takes the weight off the shoulders and transfers it to the legs.

At the beginning, the food packs were especially heavy. Two people were needed to lift a food pack so a third could slip into the shoulder straps and position the tumpline. In these first days it was strenuous and difficult to carry a food pack. The bigger and stronger young men carried them. A couple of the young women with us were petite, weighing slightly more than a large food pack. Luckily, our little community had a mixture of sizes, and the larger men took their role of carrying the food packs in stride.

That initial night of the expedition we camped at the end of the first portage trail. We divided the brigade into food groups of three to four people. Each night a different group would cook and clean up. Kit and I would take turns helping and advising. After the meal we'd sit around the fire, talking and massaging one another's shoulders.

It was late May, and daylight remained until ten o'clock. The weather was glorious. In fact, my journal indicates it hardly rained at all during our fourteen-day expedition. Rain can be a stressor, as can the blackflies and mosquitoes later in the year.

Kit and I had planned a different stressor for that evening: a first aid simulation. I had purposefully gone down to the water, telling our brigade that I was going to check the canoes. Kit excused himself from the group and walked into the woods. A few minutes later his screams could be heard. He had cut his arm, and fake blood was streaming from it. It looked real. A couple of students took charge, looking to apply pressure to the wound.

Most of the students just stood around, looking scared. Of course they couldn't find the first aid kit. Soon they guessed it was a trick. But our point was to be prepared for an emergency. We were on our own. Autonomous. We had to know where the first aid kit was at all times. (It's easy to lose track of it while portaging.) Kit and I debriefed the simulation. We stressed that accidents could happen at any moment. We ran through possible evacuation scenarios. For the first week of the expedition, Kit and I spent an hour each day teaching first aid and possible responses. We wanted them to be prepared for a life-threatening emergency. They had to realize it could happen.

* * *

I witnessed an emergency with the Cornell University Outing Club during a course I was co-instructing with (Victoria) Moon Joyce in August 1979, while we were camped with our brigade on Butland Lake, along the Pikitigushi River, just north of Cliff Lake. The Pikitigushi River flows south into Cliff Lake and has some rapids that need to be lined or portaged. One afternoon, two tandem canoes, with four occupants pulling frantically, approached our campsite. (One doesn't actually paddle a canoe, but rather pulls it through the water.) They stopped and explained that they had an emergency—could we help?

"What happened?" I asked.

"One of our group fell on rocks portaging a canoe from Cliff Lake into Butland," they explained.

I grabbed the first aid kit, got into one of their canoes, and we quickly returned south to the portage trail separating Butland and Cliff Lakes. They took me across the portage to where Barney Solit was lying. I did a survey of his body; he was conscious but had no feeling below his neck. One of his group mates told me that Barney had tried to walk up the river with the canoe instead of using the portage trail and had slipped on rocks while carrying the canoe.

"What should we do?" they asked.

"There's no nearby help," I said.

As luck would have it, the day before our brigade had run into Vic Pelshea, an archaeologist who was surveying the numerous Indigenous pictographs on Cliff Lake. He and a pilot had flown into the lake site in a small bush plane.

"When you came up Cliff Lake, did you see a plane?" I asked.

"No," they said.

"An archaeologist is camped here," I said, showing them where on the map. I gave them Vic's name and said his plane must have a radio. "Go find him!"

As two people paddled away to look for Vic, we got Barney as comfortable as we could and covered him with a sleeping bag. I kept traction on Barney's neck and asked him a few questions. He was from Columbus, Ohio. He was a sophomore and twenty years old. They had been out for a week. A dozen people comprised the coed group.

In a couple of hours, Vic arrived. He did have a radiophone. He made a phone call to emergency services. By canoe we were easily twenty-four hours from help. But soon there was a helicopter on the way. I had the Cornell group clear an area for the helicopter to land. Shortly before nightfall the helicopter arrived and flew Barney to the hospital in Thunder Bay.

Later I learned he indeed had been paralyzed from the neck down when he fell with the canoe. The Cornell group may have contributed to his paralysis by moving him from where he fell. They were in shock. I told them we would help them again the next day to decide on the next course of action. They agreed to stop by our camp on Butland Lake.

A couple of weeks later, Moon and I visited Barney in the Thunder Bay hospital. He was in traction—screws in the top of his skull, which were attached to a cable, kept his spine aligned. Barney's parents were there. They were concerned, as were we, but Barney was surprisingly ebullient. "A beautiful young man," I recorded in my journal. A few weeks later, when I inquired, I learned Barney had died in the hospital of a stroke.

I relate this story to show how quickly an accident can happen. Over the years I became more and more conservative in my course planning, imagining what-ifs and preparing my students for an emergency at any time.

* * *

On May 21, the brigade prepared to paddle northwest across Caribou Lake, a large lake with numerous islands, to Outlet Bay. After breakfast, Kit and I taught them how to navigate with a map and compass. Caribou Lake was the perfect place to practice these new skills. The day was exceedingly warm, and a couple of students wanted to take off their bulky life jackets. The lake and weather appeared benign, but the lake water was still cold, and an accidental immersion could cause hypothermia. We reinforced our policy to wear life jackets at all times when on water.

Our destination, Outlet Bay, was the headwaters for the Caribou River, which we followed downstream. We camped at the far end of the fourth portage. By now we'd done five portages, and the group was getting the hang of it. Lots of extraneous items slow you down, and the students were learning to keep all items tucked away in the Duluth packs. Each canoe had three paddles. The paddle blades would be wedged under the front seat, the paddle shafts jammed under the shoulder yoke on the canoe's middle thwart. The person carrying the canoe on their shoulders would use the secured paddle shafts to help balance the canoe.

Most of our canoes and packs could be taken across the portage in one carry, which was our goal. In these early days, a few students had to go back for the packs they couldn't carry on the first trip. Most efficiently, when beginning a portage a pack would be lifted from the canoe and placed on a person's back.

One person could lift a pack filled solely with clothes; two people were needed to lift the food packs.

Usually when lifting a canoe, it was easiest with two people; however, only one person carried the canoe using a canoe yoke, which rested on their shoulders. Canoes would be carried across and then placed directly in the water, awaiting the packs. It was easiest to wade into the water to load and unload the canoes; everyone had wet feet all day. Because the canoes and packs were bulky, you wanted to streamline your efforts.

I enjoyed portaging. After using the upper body paddling for a couple of hours, it felt good to exercise the legs. On the Caribou River, however, the distance was short between portages, and the students were soon exhausted from the frequent unloading and loading of the canoes.

The next day, on our way to Whitewater Lake, we elected to do a one-mile portage north from Funger Lake instead of paddling the extra twelve miles across the north end of Smoothrock Lake and into Lonebreast Bay. One could call it a shortcut; normally, it would take four hours to paddle the twelve miles in windless conditions.

It took us four hours to do the portage! Much of it was across boggy land. With a heavy load, such as a food pack or canoe, the carrier would sink to their waist, necessitating crawling out of the pack's shoulder straps or out from under a canoe.

At first the students were frustrated, but soon the comedy of the travail had everyone laughing. It was a wet, mucky mess carrying our canoes and gear from Funger Lake to Lonebreast Bay. Luckily, the day was gorgeous and warm. And one could admire the insectivorous pitcher plants growing atop the spongy bog. At the end of the portage we were all wet and muddy and smiling. The best things in life are not things.

On May 23 we reached Whitewater Lake and headed for the northwest bay on Best Island, where we'd find the inventor and hermit Wendell Beckwith. I had not met Wendell before, but Kit had during the previous summer. Wendell had supposedly invented the ink for the ballpoint pen before removing himself to Best Island. When we arrived, I found him to be short in stature with a long white beard; he resembled a wizard, I thought. Wendell was overjoyed to see

ABOVE: *Wendell Beckwith's Snail Cabin* by Lorne Tippett.

us and told us where to camp. First, however, he gave all of us a tour of his three handmade cabins. Wendell had lived on Whitewater Lake since 1961, when the local, Indigenous Ojibwe still occupied it.

The first cabin Wendell built in summer 1961 was erected quickly so he could survive his first winter. In the following years he built a magnificent second cabin, which he filled with Ojibwe artifacts. Wendell was an accomplished artist and craftsman.

He was an excellent storyteller, too, describing to the students his first years on Whitewater Lake with the Ojibwe. He told us how they would come over and watch him work. Wendell showed us the first chair he made on Best Island.

"One day," he said, "an Ojibwe person asked me why I was building a chair. 'To sit in,' I told him. But the man responded, 'When you want to sit down, *just sit down!*'" Wendell demonstrated by quickly plunking his butt on the ground and simultaneously laughing at the same time, which soon had us all laughing.

Then he turned reflective, as my journal notes indicate, and said he found it profound and symbolic that the Ojibwe left Whitewater Lake in July 1969, the same month and year Americans landed on the moon.

The following day, Wendell told the students he came to Best Island to practice "pure research."

"What's that?" one student asked.

Wendell laughed. "If I knew what I was researching, it wouldn't be pure," he explained.

Later he showed us an invention of his that allowed him to observe the sun and moon at the same time when they both were in the sky. Unfortunately, he said, long periods of observing the sun had ruined his eyesight.

One of the many truths Wendell discovered by close observation of nature was that it was organized around pi, the ratio of a circle's circumference to its diameter, which is approximately 3.14159. One of the paths he took to reach this conclusion was to measure the slopes of thousands of spruce trees. The slope is the ratio from the height of the tree to its greatest width. Wendell measured from the height of the tree to where the outermost branches at the bottom of the tree sprout from the trunk. He discovered that the average slope of a spruce tree is pi.

The Snail, his third livable structure, Wendell said was now his winter living space. (The sauna at Homeplace was modeled on Wendell's Snail.) It was a small one-room cabin built into an earthy berm. Three walls were encased by earth; only the wall with the door was uncovered. The ceiling was thick plastic, also covered by earth and then a top layer of moss. His goal was a structure easy to heat in the winter. Once snow fell, the snow would offer additional insulation. Water doesn't freeze when it has twenty-four inches of insulation, Wendell explained.

Inside the Snail was a small woodstove; the stovepipe extended upward through the layers of plastic, earth, and moss. Like everything Wendell did, it was intentional and artistic. His little cabin was built to resemble the shell of a snail. The roof, which was only seven to eight feet above the earth floor, resembled a logarithmic spiral. The wooden door, a rectangle made from vertical poles fastened together, had a spiral center. The door handle also resembled a snail's shape.

ABOVE: *Snail Cabin Exterior* by Wendell Beckwith, depicting Wendell's final home, burrowed into the land, only the door and window exposed to the weather.

The spiral doesn't relate to pi, but it is a lovely piece of art adopted from a small creature. Wendell said he no longer had the energy or time to chop the wood necessary to heat the other structures.

While we were on Best Island learning from Wendell, as a service project for him we cut, split, and stacked a cord or more of dead wood for him to use to heat his cabins. As more Outward Bound brigades like ours were stopping to visit, Wendell also wanted us to build an open-air latrine at the campsite we were using.

As we paddled away the next morning, Wendell stood on the beach waving goodbye. In my journal I wrote that "his gnomish appearance resembled a Daoist monk." I don't know why I wrote that; I'd never met a Daoist monk, only read about them living in the mountains and caves of China.

II. VISION

ABOVE: *Snail Cabin Interior* by Wendell Beckwith. COBWS staff and students assisted Wendell in building this cozy home.

> *People ask the way to Cold Mountain*
> *But roads don't reach Cold Mountain.*
> *In summer the ice doesn't melt*
> *And the morning fog is too dense.*
> *How did someone like me arrive?*
> *Our minds are not the same.*
> *If they were the same*
> *You would be here.*

—Han-Shan, No. 16, *Cold Mountain,* translated by Red Pine

After leaving Best Island, it took the brigade two more days to reach Scrag Lake, where the students spent seventy-two hours alone on solo. For most this meant fasting, meditating on spruce and birch trees . . . the granite of the

ABOVE: *Sleeping on Solo Under Mosquito Netting* by Lorne Tippett.

Canadian Shield . . . blue sky . . . fresh water drunk straight from the lake . . . forest birds and waterfowl . . . the primeval call of the loon . . . crawling and flying insects . . . caribou moss, hot sun, pollen in the air . . . sap flowing, summer coming, mayflies hatching . . . stars and moon at night . . . thoughts and emotions swirling . . . boredom, happiness, dreams of food, loved ones, regrets, and promises . . . life is amazing.

> *No two trees are the same to Raven.*
> *No two branches are the same to Wren.*
> *If what a tree or bush does is lost on you,*
> *You are surely lost. Stand still. The forest knows*
> *Where you are. You must let it find you.*
>
> —David Wagoner, from "Lost"

During the three-day solo, Kit and I checked on each student once every day. They were placed on islands or otherwise relatively far apart, but close enough for us to hear an emergency whistle blast. During the solo, if someone heard a whistle blast, they were also to blow their whistle, passing the emergency whistle blast down the line.

We also had a system where, if they were okay, they would wave as we paddled by. On the second day a student didn't wave, so Kit and I paddled in to see why. The young woman merely wanted some company, to talk. She had never been alone before like this. She felt vulnerable, awkward. Time was going slowly. Her memories at times were troubling. She shed a few tears, then she laughed. She eventually said she was okay. We spent maybe forty-five minutes with her. The following day, when we paddled by, she waved.

"Neither the love of man nor the love of God can take deep root in a child that does not know aloneness," wrote Kurt Hahn.

On the morning after the third night of solo, Kit and I took separate canoes and retrieved the students one by one. Their reunion with one another was special. Other humans—yeah!

"So good to talk with you again!"

"It wasn't really that bad! I'd do it again!"

Their smiles are what I remember. After three days of fasting, their faces emulated something special, angelic.

They wanted a bath; swimming was not allowed on solo. Using tent tarps and sleeping bags for insulation over a tripod of poles, Kit and I had built a small sauna. Later in the afternoon, after some food, three to four people at a time could sweat out the dirt and then jump into Scrag Lake. They also could soap up and rinse on the shore.

While the students were on solo, Kit and I had caught some walleye, and that afternoon we prepared a banquet of fresh fish, baked bread (using a reflector oven), miso soup, rice and beans, and rice pudding for dessert. As we ate, everyone sat around and talked and talked and talked, relating their solo stories to one another.

Their stories fed on others', solidifying our shared humanity and solo experience. For some it was difficult, for others blissful. We came as separate entities, a random group of individuals, each with a unique personal history and destiny. Yet we had created a tribe with a unified ethos. This was a highlight of the course for me.

During the remaining four days of the expedition, the brigade traveled on their own without their instructors (Kit and me). We were always a couple of hours behind them, but they didn't see us until the second-to-last day, when they put themselves in a dangerous situation on the Kopka River.

Reviewing the topographical maps we used, it's surprising to see how far they traveled in four days, from Scrag Lake to their pickup on Bukemiga Lake. Their route took them down the Slim River to Kenoji Lake and past the rapids of the Ogoki River, which they had been instructed to portage.

One of the rules for the final portion of the expedition was no whitewater. They were told to portage around all whitewater that produced standing waves that could swamp a loaded canoe. Riffles—Class I water—were permissible. The brigade was skilled enough by now to know and negotiate Class I water.

The Ogoki River between Kenoji and Wabakimi Lakes, however, had several major rapids with significant gradient drops, necessitating portaging. Human nature being what it is, on the final expedition students sometimes chose what appeared to be the most expedient way. ("That rapid doesn't look difficult! It would save us an hour of portaging!")

There are those who hate portaging, even though by this stage of the expedition the food was almost gone and the Duluth packs were light. Therefore, Kit and I followed closely behind to ensure the brigade observed the safety protocols outlined for the final expedition.

The Ojibwe had made these portage trails over centuries of traveling these interlinking waterways by birchbark canoe. This country was their home; we couldn't really call it wilderness, defined as uninhabited by humans. The lakes and rivers were their roads. But they, too, only portaged when it was absolutely necessary. Thus the portage trails would begin immediately—only a few feet, sometimes—above a waterfall or unnavigable rapid. Kit and I had taught the students to approach these hazards carefully, stopping well before a significant gradient drop. From shore one could often safely walk the loaded canoe—using bow and stern ropes, called lining—the few yards to the beginning of a portage.

II. VISION

Sometimes canoeists have capsized and lost their canoes—and sometimes their lives—when cavalierly approaching a rapid. You can hear a major rapid as you approach. If the horizon line running across the river disappears, you know there's a gradient drop in the river looming ahead.

Kit and I trusted this brigade. They had shown good judgment, listened to one another, supported one another, and made decisions by consensus (as we had practiced throughout the course).

After the rapids of the Ogoki River, they traveled through and camped on Smoothrock Lake. The beautiful granite rock of the Canadian Shield is prominent—thus its name, Smoothrock.

The students now navigated mostly flat water from Smoothrock Lake to cross the Canadian Northern Railway tracks at Schultz's Trail, another Ojibwe outpost on the rail line. The students continued south through Boulder Lake and then carried canoes and gear over a long portage into Kenakskaniss Lake. At the end of this portage, I spied a well-used hatchet stuck in a log.

Cross-country portage trails, such as the one from Boulder Lake to Kenakskaniss Lake, are often marked by blazes on trees—axe marks cutting off a patch of bark—which are signposts showing the way. If the trail is obscured by snow, for example, blaze marks are especially helpful. The hatchet in the log had probably been used for this purpose and then accidentally left behind.

The Kopka River flows through Kenakskaniss Lake. When they finished the portage, the brigade was only twenty-four hours away from their pickup on Bukemiga Lake. At the south end of Kenakskaniss Lake there is a long, two-mile portage around a series of rapids and waterfalls. The beginning of the trail is not well marked, however, and it can be difficult to find. The students hadn't found the trail and elected to slide down the first rapid, which was an easy one (Class I+). Maybe the portage trail was below it, they thought.

When Kit and I reached the same spot, and while we were looking for the portage, we heard what sounded like whistle blasts. We listened more carefully. Sure enough, they were whistle blasts coming from downstream—around the bend and out of sight.

We slid down the first rapid to a pool, then down another easy Class I rapid to another pool above a waterfall, where we found our brigade. They were stuck. They couldn't go back upstream, and the waterfall blocked their passage downstream.

Kit and I were overjoyed to see them safe and sound. It was getting late in the afternoon, so we decided to cook supper and relax for a while and discuss with the brigade their options. Kit and I had caught some fish that day, which we prepared with some soup.

After supper we began a bushwhack and found a trail around the several waterfalls—beautiful and exhilarating as they tumbled, mist rising in the early evening air. The terrain was steep, the weather beautiful, and we were energized from the food and being together again.

Just before dark, around nine, we reached flat water below the falls, where we made camp. A final four- to five-hour paddle would take us to Bukemiga Lake and our pickup at two the next afternoon.

After breakfast, the brigade shared with Kit and me their decision-making process at the falls the day before. Some had wanted to push on and bushwhack

ABOVE: *Supper Cooking on an Open Fire* by Lorne Tippett.

II. VISION

ABOVE: *Snow Goose Lodge* by Wendell Beckwith, the first building that Wendell built, with help from the local Ojibwe, who also lived on Whitewater Lake.

around the waterfalls, just as we had eventually done. Others wanted to wait and see if they could attract Kit and me with their whistle blasts.

Kit and I were impressed that the more gung-ho contingent had ceded to the more conservative contingent. Even if Kit and I hadn't arrived to offer some leadership, they would have eventually done the bushwhack on their own, probably nervously and on empty stomachs. What Kit and I offered was the wisdom to relax, take stock, and refuel before pressing on. The weather couldn't have been nicer, thus there was little fear of hypothermia or slipping on wet rocks.

Rereading my journal that I wrote those many years ago, I noticed that I had jotted down mostly objective facts—the weather, activities for the day, what we ate, and the like. I sometimes recorded, in a phrase or two, what I was feeling, but I didn't specifically record what I perceived individual students to be feeling. I now wish I had.

*   *   *

A smiling Rob Linscott was waiting for us at Bukemiga Lake Landing when we arrived on June 2. Rob had special homemade pastry treats from Bertha Bumchuckles and the Homeplace kitchen that he passed around to all of us. Such a grand feeling of accomplishment to fit a grand day! We ate our pastries. We laughed and smiled. We hugged. We unloaded our canoes and loaded everything onto the bus and canoe trailer. We said a final goodbye to Bukemiga Lake and the wilderness beyond. We said goodbye to the last fourteen days of the expedition.

The students still had a couple of days of rock climbing to look forward to, followed by a banquet at Homeplace with five other graduating brigades. My journal ended at Bukemiga Lake. As I conclude these words, that moment of being present from long ago lives on.

Sacred Sustenance—Alchemy in Action

Ginger Mason

This is why alchemy exists . . . So that everyone will search for [their] treasure, find it, and then want to be better than [they were] in [their] former life. . . . When we strive to become better than we are, everything around us becomes better too.

—Paulo Coelho, *The Alchemist*

All that you touch, you change
All that you change, changes you
The only lasting truth is change
God is change.

—Octavia Butler, *Parable of the Sower*

I have been asked to reflect on the role of food at Homeplace, where I lived and worked seasonally for the better part of a decade (1979–1989). My résumé after Outward Bound summarized my duties under the rather staid title of food services manager. That label accurately described the work expected of me in my tender and formative twenties, but I had to grow into it. Even a seasoned chef would have needed the help of the many Homeplace hands who made it possible to meet the daily necessity of feeding anywhere from 20 to 120 people. Accomplishing this was a true community feat, but as I look back at my role, I admit to being astonished by the scope of my part in it and the quality of my output.

While I don't recall applying for a position with a formal job description, I will never forget the flavor of my meeting with program director Wendy Pieh at Outward Bound's Yorkville office in 1979. (Victoria) Moon Joyce, a mutual friend, suggested to us both that we discuss a possible fit between my employment needs and the seasonal requirements of Outward Bound. Wendy had agreed to see me at the end of her working day, so there we were, chatting over a bottle of wine, and soon I was being offered the challenge of proving myself in a field—food service—where I had absolutely zero experience (unless you count a grim stint in a Schneiders meat packing plant!). However, Moon had testified to my enthusiasm as a vegetarian home cook, and I was clearly open to new experiences. I was also a floundering city dweller, a fledgling feminist, and a fiercely determined young woman in the throes of identity formation. The countercultural appeal of the back-to-the-land movement still had enough currency to put a shine on the idea of living in the remote northern Ontario wilderness, and my gut told me this was an opportunity not to be missed. I sensed that I might be getting in way over my head, but I was determined I would swim.

Little did I know, when I naively accepted the work after that very unconventional, after-hours job interview, that I would find myself inward bound with radical and profound lessons in Outward Bound service as well as Outward Bound schooling. When I arrived, the school was in its infancy, three years young. It was building on the legacy of Kurt Hahn's international educational innovation as well as Bob Pieh's ideals of service to others, self-discovery, sharing, and learning through direct experience and reflection. Bob's daughter Wendy facilitated a next-level, unique, and utopian iteration of an Outward Bound school and nourished the manifestation of community rooted in purpose. She believed wholeheartedly in the power of community, and she embodied her belief that everyone leads, everyone makes decisions together. The process of living, playing, and working together in backwoods isolation, with consensus decision-making baked in, served to magnify and expand our individual and collective consciousnesses.

And thanks to Wendy's commitment to ensuring staff had time together to work, play, and share, I had the life-changing opportunity to participate in staff training events. The outdoors as classroom, learning by doing! I attempted canoeing, portaging, rock climbing, rappelling, and kayaking, and I learned wilderness camping and cooking, compass navigation, environmental awareness and conservation, and first aid and safety protocols. But since my work was to oversee the food services while courses were running, the majority of my days were spent in camp.

Alchemy. It's the concept I like best to convey the magnitude and magic of what we pulled off together in the name of COBWS. There was a whole lot of alchemy going on by the shores of Black Sturgeon Lake! The alchemy of cooking for hungry hordes of students and staff; the personal alchemy of culture shock, adjusting to life in a remote wilderness base camp; the alchemy of experiential education, using the outdoors as a classroom; and the ultimate, interpersonal alchemy of creating a backwoods-but-oh-so-forward-thinking community rooted in compassion, connection, consensus, creativity, and collaboration.

And the role of food in all this? There would be no Homeplace, no wilderness canoe trips, no life without food. Food provides fuel and social ritual for our human bodies and our souls. The preparation of food—cooking as alchemy, and the offering of food as tokens of love and affection—is a sacrament. Physically, food supplies us with essential nutrients and is absolutely necessary for survival. A healthy, well-balanced diet allows us to think clearly and feel more alert, and improves our concentration and attention span. Being well-fed contributes to a sense of security, of belonging and enjoyment. One of life's greatest pleasures is sharing stories and laughter over a meal with friends and family.

At Homeplace, dining-hall food and trips food each had its dedicated area of storage and preparation, with both focused on a primarily vegetarian diet. We drew on the limited but rapidly evolving sources of the times, such as *Moosewood Cookbook* by Mollie Katzen. A revolutionary and best-selling publication was Frances Moore Lappé's complementary-protein bible *Diet for a Small Planet* (1971). My first few years, I also leaned heavily on *The Findhorn Cookbook: An Approach to Cooking with Consciousness* by Barbara Friedlander, from a remarkable community in Scotland. And over time the school developed its own trail food cookbook, *Trail Cookery*, published in 1982, which I believe Monica Bartman was responsible for getting started.

Densely caloric trips food had to provide essential energy for those who spent long hours on the trail in all sorts of weather, paddling, portaging, and setting up and taking down camp. Outward Bound staples included gorp (a trail mix of dried fruit, nuts, and chocolate), flapjacks (baked bars made of oats, fat, sugar, and syrup), and granola. These items were all assembled from scratch at Homeplace. Each group of students was given an orientation to trail food and received assistance in packing their course food.

Essential building blocks for Outward Bound course menus included peanut butter, tahini, jam, sugar, margarine, oils, powdered milk and eggs, hot chocolate mix, tea, drink crystals, textured vegetable protein (TVP), spices, dried onions and veggies, flour, pasta, rice, oats, cornmeal, legumes, beans, dried fruits, nuts, and Wasa crispbreads. Limited quantities of cheese were wrapped in vinegar-soaked cheesecloth to withstand the elements on canoe trips. Some instructors presoaked dehydrated beans prior to trips. Others brought their own pressure cookers to hasten the bean and legume cooking. Vienna Bakery in Thunder Bay provided dense loaves of rye bread. I'm sure I'm forgetting a lot, especially refinements and improvements over the years, but the main bits are described here.

Camp food, the dining-hall fare, was only slightly more exotic than trips food, with the addition of fresh eggs, a lot more cheese, yogurt (made from culture using powdered milk), fresh fruits and vegetables, and alfalfa sprouts grown in big gallon jars.

The kitchen, when I arrived in 1979, was rustic and basic, though commercially equipped with two massive Garland ranges, numerous refrigerators that ran on propane, and a Hobart standing mixer that was spacious enough to bathe in! Renovations and upgrades over the years brought in additional equipment, such as a double-door stainless steel refrigerator, new stainless steel sinks for dishwashing (the old one was installed outside for trips food), a freezer, and more. The first few years I was there, the entire camp ran off one very old and noisy diesel generator. There were set hours when it was on and strict limits on the power draw (nothing heat-producing like a toaster or a hair dryer). Honestly, the most important pieces of equipment in the kitchen were a radio and a cassette player, rigged to a car battery, so we could listen to the Canadian Broadcasting Corporation (CBC) and feel connected to the rest of the world or pop in a cassette tape with the music of the day. Sometimes there was unbridled dancing and singing. Great fun!

The week's supply of produce was usually unloaded from a van directly into the rather primitive root cellar (nothing more than a dirt hole in the ground). Without a constant temperature and due to ever-present moisture, food deteriorated quickly. The forty-pound blocks of cheese we stored in the root cellar fared slightly better because they were shipped shrink-wrapped in plastic. Fortunately, in the mid-1980s, Homeplace received a donated commercial compressor. At that point, the root cellar got a fabulous makeover with framing, insulation, and a proper roof to support the installation of the compressor. It marked a huge advancement in our backwoods food-storage capacity.

End-of-course banquets often included chicken, lasagna, Caesar salad, and dessert. Prior to sitting down to evening meals in the dining hall, a magnificent metal gong was struck to send reverberations throughout camp. This was the signal for everyone to gather together outside, where folks touched base and shared a poem, a song, a story. The dining tables usually had bouquets of fresh wildflowers, ferns, grasses, whatever was growing outside. The walls were decorated with recreated, painted versions of pictographs by Matty McNair, perhaps inspired by the famous Agawa Rock pictographs on Lake Superior.

Our remote location, one hundred miles northeast of the nearest supply center in Thunder Bay, Ontario, and the reality of a once-a-week town run to source not only food but also everything else that Homeplace might need fostered a make-do and can-do attitude. Not being able to dash to the grocery or any store inspired lots of resourcefulness and creativity, especially the day or two before the town run, when food supplies had dwindled or some critical piece of equipment had failed.

We had established suppliers and wholesalers in Thunder Bay, and they were often extending us credit. I was able to call in my orders ahead of time using the rustic radiophone that ran off twelve-volt car batteries. The first few years I was at Homeplace, we shared a party line with Kab Lake Lodge near Armstrong, Ontario. Eventually we were able to secure a second private line, and communication with the outside world became a bit easier.

I recall the annual food budget was around $80,000. It was adequate for a mostly meatless diet, and I found countless creative ways, most often involving root vegetables, to stay within budget. Although I was the only paid kitchen staff, the labor of producing daily meals and cleaning up afterward involved a great many volunteers over the years. And in my early days, when I was reeling with culture shock and overwhelmed by the tasks at hand, so many kind, resourceful, and supportive colleagues extended crucial advice or practical support, or both. It takes a village. And alchemy.

Weekly town runs began at first light, with road food to fortify us until we reached civilization. The two-hour drive to Thunder Bay involved a particular vigilance during the first half of it, along a gravel logging road that had potholes and washboards, where it was not uncommon to encounter fully loaded logging trucks hurtling toward us.

The other half of the drive, the final stretch, was a comparative sprint along the Trans-Canada Highway. First stop was usually the Hoito, a traditional Finnish restaurant established in 1918, for breakfast. The entire day was spent driving from supplier to supplier, packing the van to the rafters, then checking our post office box (a thrilling highlight, as it was always bursting with personal mail and care packages for staff), doing the banking, and often concluding the workday with dinner and a sauna at Kangas Sauna.

One of the rituals on the return trip to Homeplace was to place a collect call to the mythical Freda from the phone booth at the juncture of the highway and the gravel logging road. Folks knew not to accept the call and to start timing our arrival. If we didn't appear within the acceptable window of time, a search party would head out to locate and assist. Luckily, mishaps were infrequent, and only occasionally did a visitor arriving on their own get lost.

By the time the van rolled into camp, it was usually approaching dark, with all the cabins beaming out light. Sometimes a horn honk might be needed as a prod, but inevitably folks would appear like magic to unload the van. It was a real buzz to get out of camp once a week, and as the head chef, I really appreciated meeting directly with our Thunder Bay food suppliers to ensure we got what we needed.

A notable reality of living on-site and overseeing the food experience in our base camp meant I was embedded while everyone else came and went. There was an ebb and flow to life at Homeplace during the peak May–September season, with course starts staggered so as not to overload facilities. Staff would be on-site ahead of students, who, having been met at the Thunder Bay Airport, would arrive for a few days of orientation and preparation before heading out on seven- to fourteen-day canoe trips. Camp would bustle and hum with energy and excitement, and then it would fall quiet, only to have the pace quicken once again as groups returned for debriefing, cleanup, and the final banquet.

My experiences living and working at Homeplace illuminated possibilities beyond anything I'd ever imagined and gave me a starter kit for living an authentic life. It was there, during long periods of solitude, that I was able to confront existential angst. The life force energy surrounding and within Homeplace was a teacher, a guide, and a healer.

A final remembrance is of the unique fragrance of the air at Homeplace, with a sort of metallic tang blended with a citrusy hit. I didn't know then that my nose was sensing the hundreds of volatile organic compounds released from pockets in the leaf cells of trees. Trees also produce edible monoterpenes, fragrances that, when we inhale them, become part of our bodies, and so the forest becomes part of us. Alchemy, yes?

Yes! There was something in the air (and the water) there on the shore of Black Sturgeon Lake—an endless alchemy of humans' and nature's interactions that touched and transformed us all.

Pushing the Envelope of Outward Bound's Four Pillars

(Victoria) Moon Joyce

Homeplace was a hub of deep learning. We lived and worked to understand and achieve the four philosophical pillars of Outward Bound for the students, ourselves, and the wider Outward Bound community. The remote location provided us with a social incubator in which to discover and experiment with forms of communal self-management.

We heard rumors from local residents in the small towns of Hurkett and Dorion along the Trans-Canada Highway that we were a hippie commune in the woods. True, there was a lot of crunchy granola consumed. The early years of the school coincided with post-Vietnam North America and late-1960s and early-1970s social experiments in so-called free love and antiauthoritarianism. The desire for a better way of being together was reflected in our morning readings and lively conversations about how we would manage ourselves. Concepts like consensus decision-making, flattened hierarchies, and shared labor reflected what were considered left-wing politics at the time.

Physical fitness, craftsmanship, self-reliance, and compassion are the four traditional pillars of Outward Bound, educational theories that are similar to the five pillars[1] of the educational philosophy of Kurt Hahn (or Uncle Kurt, as he was affectionately nicknamed): "an enterprising curiosity; an indefatigable spirit; tenacity in pursuit; readiness for sensible self-denial; and above all, compassion."

At COBWS, the four pillars of Outward Bound were reconceptualized into a less-regimented, more soft-skills and touchy-feely approach to accomplish the pedagogical goals of an Outward Bound experience. For example, the physical

---

1. Outward Bound mimicked Kurt Hahn and also used the word *pillars* to describe their principles, which can be confusing for a general reader. —Ed.

fitness pillar expanded into a holistic concept of well-being of the whole person, and emotional safety is one example of what became an essential component of leading a course.

In the late 1970s and early 1980s, the topics of personal power and empowerment became central to our understanding of personal growth. The pillar of compassion morphed into discussions of power: who had it and who didn't. While the larger society was increasingly talking about systemic racism, sexism, and the other forms of oppression, this discourse was also coming into our discussions as an educational body. Compassion included service and concepts of egalitarianism and social relations of power. Ideas around equity and power sharing could be found in deep conversations at community meetings and during off-duty times. We heard William Sloane Coffin Jr. speak about this shift at an Outward Bound International Conference when he encouraged Outward Bound to resist allowing charity to take the place of justice.

Specific community courses evolved from this recognition that life is not a level playing field for many, and the Native Canadian and Women of Courage programs in the early 1980s were attempts to begin addressing social inequities and abuses. The Native Canadian program brought primarily non-Indigenous brigades into the First Nation community of Gull Bay for what were termed service projects. Over time it was clear it was the staff and students who benefited most from these cultural exchanges. We soon learned the Native Canadian program instructed by non-Indigenous staff was lip service. Attracting Indigenous staff and envisioning a better approach eventually led to a stronger program by and for Indigenous people, which was called Giwaykiwin.[2]

Feminism gave us language to understand that the personal *is* political. How we are socially positioned, by birth or circumstance, does impact our access to resources, opportunities, and well-being. COBWS started with a gender parity that was not prevalent in other programs at the time; it attracted many talented women instructors, resource people, and administrators. It was inevitable that conversations about societal inequities based on gender would arise in conversations among staff and adult students.

---

2. *Giwaykiwin* is an Anishinabe (Ojibwe) word meaning *coming home*. You can watch the three-part 1998 CBC series *Strangers to the Land*, featuring Terry Swan and Ray Katt, online.

Self-reliance was confronted by concepts such as challenge by choice. Rugged individualism that was historically lauded in the culture of early Outward Bound was tempered with advanced group facilitation focusing on teamwork, healthy interdependency, and the need for learning how to give and receive support.

Craft was taken very seriously in our desire to create the best courses and advance our skills and knowledge as outdoor adventure educators. Staff training trips were rigorous; we took the kind of risks we would not likely take with students, all in service to the maxim, "We get good judgment by doing things we wouldn't have done if we had good judgment." On another level, staff took on projects on a shoestring budget, such as beautifying buildings; carving our own paddles; illustrating our homegrown publications; publishing *The Journal of COBWS Education*; designing T-shirts and outdoor clothing; and reveling in wildly creative staff celebrations, which included belly dancing and circus acrobatics. We celebrated imagination, innovation, and excellence.

In addition to gender parity, from the earliest years at COBWS we discussed sexual identity and orientation. Personally, I found a safe space to explore my own identity as queer (now LGBTQIA2+) and a deeper sense of self and self-acceptance. With all our daily readings about authenticity, taking risks in order to grow as a person, and being your whole self, I took that to heart. The outdoors is such a great equalizer. I found a healing place where to be lesbian was acceptable. This was at a time when it was certainly not acceptable in the outside world. Those early years at COBWS, facing a multitude of challenges and discovering capabilities I didn't know I had, led me to adopt the name Moon for myself—an act of self-empowerment that resonates still.

Musically, I learned how powerful the act of singing together could shift the energy of a group and be a vehicle for group bonding, enhancing community, individual healing, and social justice dialogues. Like so many of my COBWS peers, my experiences during those years blossomed in later life into deeper work. My master's and doctoral studies allowed me to formalize knowledge gained from living and working at COBWS and to apply it later in diverse educational contexts.

COBWS was a mirror reflecting movements in the wider world, and while I was able to grow and find self-acceptance, not all my fellow staff members were comfortable with the repercussions of this societal shift within the COBWS community. I recall one male staff member expressing that he felt there were "too many lesbians" in the organization. In another example, at a diversity training workshop addressing issues of inequities and violence based on positions of racialization, gender, sexuality, class, and more, the topic of male privilege resulted in a number of men choosing to avoid acknowledgment of their gender, instead staunchly referring to themselves as humans.

These were examples of growing pains in the maturation of COBWS as a learning institution. In time, great advances were made in embracing and respecting differences in wider discussions of systemic disadvantage and oppression. This in turn challenged and helped transform traditional understandings of the Kurt Hahn and Outward Bound pillar of compassion, which we also interpreted as service to others. Community programs were born of these early and often difficult conversations.

In the beginning, Bob Pieh was the founder, driving force, and visionary for our community. I often reflect on what he would think of the roads we have traveled since then. Homeplace is now only a beloved memory, but I still draw inspiration and strength from a poem Bob wrote and used in the early years of the school:

> *Be tough yet gentle*
> *Humble yet bold*
> *Swayed always by beauty and truth.*

May it always be so.

Wendell Beckwith

Wendy Pieh

Wendell Beckwith was a close friend of mine. I first met him when my father and I flew in a floatplane to his home on Best Island, on Whitewater Lake in northern Ontario. At the time he had just recognized the central focus of everything that existed: the number pi. He had spent years sitting at the edge of the lake, watching the water, sky, and land, looking for, and measuring, patterns that could make sense.

A little background on Wendell. He was an indifferent student of organized learning, yet had a tenacious interest in how things worked and came together. After failing at several different colleges, his family sent him to the University of Alabama, figuring that would be easier for him. He lasted one year. He later joined a research team at the Parker Pen Company. At the time they were trying to develop a ballpoint pen where the ink would not skip; the company was struggling with its unreliable ink. Six companies had teamed together. Wendell created ink that would write for a mile without skipping. He helped create a successful ballpoint pen. I suspect there are many other patents under his name, all of them innovative and creative.[1]

After leaving the Parker Pen Company, he once again found himself at loose ends with little sense of what to do next. He lived with his family in Whitewater, Wisconsin, but he felt strongly that his answers lay in the far north and began walking north. When asked where he was going, he would respond, "I don't know, but I'm making good time."

Harry Wirth, a San Francisco architect and developer who owned Best Island and used it for a retreat, hired Wendell to be the caretaker, and he settled into his final home. At the time, the Ojibwe still lived year-round on the lake, and they became his friends and support as he created his own cabin

---

1. There are fourteen patents listed under Beckwith's name in the USPTO database. —Ed.

on the island. He helped them develop their own cottage industry creating beautiful beaded-leather clothing and various items that they could sell. He was saddened when they moved away, but he understood that living on the lake was no longer viable for them.

I visited with Wendell regularly and would stay for several days. One time he decided that the big cabin needed a skylight because it was quite dark inside. So we cut a hole in the roof, covered the opening with thick plastic, and thoroughly secured it with wood. As we finished it began to rain, and Wendell said, "Our noses were just long enough."

He had a notion, from watching everything around him, that it would be ideal to build a small house that would be burrowed into the earth on three sides and in the shape of a spiral, like a snail. COBWS students would regularly visit him on their long canoe trips and do service projects for him. He sent me his drawing of his house, what he called the Snail, and many of us from Homeplace also came up to help him build what would be his final dwelling.

The Ontario government eventually got wind of this interloper in the northern lakes region and ordered him to come to Toronto to verify his permanent residency in Canada. He was insistent that he was a citizen of the world, not of any one country, which made it fairly hard for them to figure out how to support his presence on the island. After some deliberation, they said if he would sign a statement saying who he was and where he lived, they would find a positive solution. He said he needed to walk and think about it. After some walking, he decided that he could not sign the document, so he just plain went home. He pulled out an old rifle and prepared to defend himself. Of course, that was not necessary, as the Ontario government decided to let him stay.

The local bush pilots kept an eye on Wendell, and one year they found him weak and in bed. They flew him to a hospital, where he turned out to be malnourished. In discussing this with me, he said that all he had eaten all winter had been old, moldy oatmeal, wanting to keep all his other food in case he needed it. After that we at COBWS made sure that he had plenty of food on hand and regular company. Like many of us, chocolate seemed to be his favorite, as he quickly put it into a special, hidden place.

Wendell did go out to visit family occasionally. One year while he was watching the Tournament of Rose Parade on TV (Rose Parade), he discovered

ABOVE: *Dew Drop Inn* by Wendell Beckwith, Wendell's home for many years on Whitewater Lake.

that his twin daughters were Princesses of the Rose Parade! Didn't he get a tickle out of that.

In terms of his scientific studies and recognition that nature revolved around pi, Wendell explained that he watched the movement of everything around him, particularly the rhythm of the waves. He had many pages of notes that showed his progress, and even drew a model of our solar system on a parabola that supported his theory. I can close my eyes and still see it hanging in the window.

One spring day Wendell greeted me with the announcement that he had discovered the mate for pi. I think it was a number that began with 1.77; it seemed to me that it might be the square root of pi. He had also decided that it was time for him to bring in students to learn his theories and spread them to others. He began to focus on making his discoveries and outlines clear in his writing and hoped some like-minded students might join him.

On a day in August 1980, Wendell passed away on his beach of a heart attack. He was a gift to all of us who knew him. I treasure my memories of him. We were so lucky to have him as a part of our COBWS story. The sauna at Homeplace on Black Sturgeon Lake was built on Wendell's Snail design.

From Skepticism to Fervent Belief

Ian Yolles

Nothing can be created outside until it is created inside first.

—Ilarion Merculieff

I was an Outward Bound skeptic.

My first memory of Outward Bound came via a 1973 television documentary. In it, an Outward Bound student was about to rappel off a cliff. Although they were securely roped in, they were frightened. Rather than calming and encouraging the student, the instructor physically forced them closer to the precipice of the rockface. Apparently, that was his preferred method of nudging them over the edge. I was not impressed.[1]

Therefore, when a friend told me about her plans to take a summer course at the now-defunct Texas Outward Bound School, I tried to dissuade her. She went anyway, returning with tales of a flash flood that swept down the canyon they backpacked in. To escape the wall of water, they climbed a tree. One student didn't make it. They spent two days searching for the body.

There were also the stories about early morning cold showers at Gordonstoun, the school in Scotland that Kurt Hahn founded before he started Outward Bound.

* * *

---

[1]. Decades later, during the writing of this book, I learned from my colleague Alistair McArthur that this depiction was a "media stunt" created by the filmmakers for dramatic effect. It was in no way condoned by Outward Bound or reflective of Outward Bound's practices. Alistair worked at the Outward Bound school depicted in the film at the time the film was made. I was relieved to hear the backstory about the making of the documentary film.

So what propelled me to apply for a job at Outward Bound?

When I attended Antioch College in Yellow Springs, Ohio, I became part of a cohort that was passionate about the outdoors. We whitewater kayaked and climbed together. Many of them worked with Outward Bound. I didn't hold that against them; they were kindred spirits. Their values, passions, and worldviews aligned with mine.

But why would such great people choose to work with an organization that appeared to be so off the wall? I couldn't reconcile the tension between who they were as people and the tenets I assumed informed the Outward Bound way.

I decided to find out for myself. Or at least I thought I would. The first time I applied to work at Outward Bound, I was rejected. Fortunately, the second time around, in 1978 when I applied to work at COBWS, Wendy Pieh hired me as an intern. Welcome to Homeplace.

To my surprise, the minute I arrived I knew I was home.

To get to Homeplace, the most remote Outward Bound school in the world, I took the train from Toronto to Nipigon in northern Ontario. From there I hitchhiked to Hurkett, where Christo Grayling, a megaspirited Aussie, picked me up. Meeting him, I knew I was in for a ride. A couple of months later, I instructed my first Outward Bound course with Christo. We became lifelong friends.

Kurt Hahn said the aim of education is "to impel young people into value-forming experiences . . . to ensure the survival of these qualities: an enterprising curiosity, an undefeatable spirit, tenacity in pursuit, readiness for sensible self-denial, and above all, compassion." Those are the qualities that Outward Bound sought to evoke in its participants.

What made COBWS unique is the way it went about fostering those qualities, not only in its students but also in its staff.

I could cite many contributing factors, beginning with the school's founders. Bob Pieh and his daughter Wendy explored new directions in the way they interpreted the Outward Bound philosophy. They deepened the impact of Outward Bound by valuing reflection on the experience as much as the experience itself. Their leadership was based on a fluid hierarchy of responsibility and a willingness to try new things rather than conform to rigid definitions based on job titles, seniority, or the bureaucratic inertia that usually accompanies top-down, command-and-control management.

There was also the remote location of Homeplace and the wilderness that we expeditioned through. Just getting to Homeplace wasn't easy. The physical journey also involved a psychological, even mythic, dimension. Joseph Campbell described it as the hero's journey—a narrative archetype that involves a person going off on an adventure, finding allies, learning lessons, winning victories of sorts with their newfound knowledge, then returning home transformed. As Campbell notes, the first step in the journey requires leaving the familiar world behind and entering a special world. In physical and psychological terms, turning north off the Trans-Canada Highway and driving fifty miles up the long, twisty dirt logging road to get to Homeplace embodied both the experience of departure from the familiar world and the sense of arrival in a special place, that being Homeplace, situated on the western shore of the pristine, magnificently beautiful, even sublime Black Sturgeon Lake.

When I arrived at Homeplace for the first time forty-four years ago, it was a place ahead of its time.

Men and women shared equally in all aspects of running the school. Many women were in significant leadership roles, and in an environment that required physical effort, nothing seemed to separate the genders (including the two-seater, side-by-side outhouse).

In today's world of Impossible Burgers, vegan diets, and kale salads, we take healthy food choices for granted. Bertha Bumchuckles (Ginger Mason) and her chef-in-waiting, Tentfly (Rick Cotter), were pioneers at Homeplace. Thanks to them, we ate delicious, incredibly nutritious vegetarian, or vegetarian-leaning, home-cooked meals that at the time weren't considered typical fare.

And then there were the monthly community meetings. They employed a form of deliberative dialogue that enabled a functional form of consensus decision-making. The meetings were deemed to be so important that the entire program schedule was structured to enable all staff to participate. At times these often marathon meetings were hilarious, frustrating, exhausting, and stimulating, but always generative because decisions and outcomes reflected the collective intelligence of the entire community. From an implementation perspective, buy-in was exceedingly high given all voices had space to be heard.

But to me, there was something more fundamental at work that made COBWS unique and unusually effective in delivering its mission. It's been referred to as holographic participation.

As staff, we were there to deliver Outward Bound experiences and all the associated learnings to our students. But as staff, we were also part of a living organization, taking part in the thinking and interactions of the whole.

Just like an Outward Bound course, by design, as staff working and living together, we'd get all the voices in the room to ensure people knew their viewpoints were heard and that all perspectives were comprehended prior to decisions being made. In effect, we were a living microcosm within a larger system, modeling a different way of approaching problems and discovering how best to work and live together.

That modeling dynamic set something in motion that had a rippling impact on the courses we were delivering to our students. It can be described as holographic participation because an organization is holographic to the degree to which its behaviors and actions reflect a healthy and congruent set of values that all staff hold in common. The result was a Homeplace community that ran very effectively with internal congruence and lived experience that directly connected to the student experience we were orchestrating.

For me, a profoundly personal example of the holographic participation principle in action took place between courses in the summer of 1979. It was my second summer season at COBWS, but this one was different.

When I arrived, I was fresh off an attempted winter ascent of Mount Rainier during which two members of the climbing team were killed in an avalanche. One was my teacher, Willi Unsoeld. Willi was the director of the Peace Corps in Nepal, pioneered the first ascent of the West Ridge on Mount Everest, had a long association with Outward Bound in the United States, and ultimately became a professor at The Evergreen State College. The other was my classmate Janie Diepenbrock.

II. VISION

The experience on Rainier catapulted me into an existential crisis. Confronting death and one's mortality at a young age has a way of doing that. Intuitively, Wendy knew I was fragile, still trying to make sense of what happened and my place in the terrible events that led to the deaths of two remarkable people, one of whom was my mentor. I was also self-conscious, knowing that all my fellow Outward Bound colleagues knew something about those events. A gray haze of grief and shame, not to mention deep feelings of survivor guilt, washed over me.

Wendy oh-so-sensitively suggested I consider sharing my story with the entire community of Homeplace staff. She pointed out that the very act of telling the story in a safe place with trusted friends and colleagues could, in and of itself, be a catalyst for healing as well as a deep bonding experience for the entire community. As usual, she was right.

We gathered one evening in the Cow Palace, one of the many buildings at Homeplace that housed staff. In exceptionally close quarters, I told my story, beginning with why I chose to travel across the country to study with Willi and ending with our descent from Rainier following three days waiting out a storm at Camp Muir, a climbing hut that we retreated to following the avalanche. As I recall, what followed was an astonishing stream of moving reflections, supportive comments, and probing questions and insights shared by many in the room. We communed late into the night.

That was forty-four years ago. Since then, I have never told the story to another large group. In fact, I've only shared it with my wife and, on an individual basis, with close friends—no more than two, possibly three times. But telling it that evening, in the safe and rarified atmosphere that permeated the Homeplace community, was indeed, as Wendy suggested it might be, healing.

It's also exactly what we would have done with students following a significant moment while on an Outward Bound expedition.

When a hologram is divided into pieces, each part still contains the entire image within it, although each new image is from a slightly different perspective. The analogy to COBWS holds true. Each individual staff member embodied the learning that we aspired to create for our students, albeit from a slightly different perspective. We all shared responsibility for the whole, not just our individual piece of the whole. But our component pieces weren't identical. Each of us held the whole picture from a different point of view. The result was greater intensity, deeper learning, enduring friendship, and a more visceral sense of aliveness. As we grew, our students grew.

III. HOMEPLACE

Home. Place. The home of the Canadian Outward Bound Wilderness School was originally a spruce budworm research station built in the 1950s by the Ontario Ministry of Natural Resources (MNR), located on the western shore of the magnificent Black Sturgeon Lake. The closest neighbors lived in the Gull Bay First Nation community (Kiashke Zaaging Anishinaabek) about thirty miles north, and the tiny town of Hurkett, located about fifty miles south along the Trans-Canada Highway; both communities were accessible to Homeplace via a dirt logging road. All program staff lived at Homeplace in wood buildings heated by woodstoves. It was a community, in the wild.

Home. The importance of a home lies in its provision of comfort, stability, and security. It provides for the safety and health of those inhabiting it. The abandoned MNR research station that became Homeplace for COBWS contained approximately two dozen buildings: an industrial kitchen and large dining room; an office with several rooms (one became the Map Room); a shop with several outbuildings, the outbuildings transformed into trips food and trips equipment; a couple outhouses that periodically had to be moved; some larger houses for families; and many bunkhouse buildings for single men and women.

There was also a diesel generator, which ran during the warmer months to provide electricity. Someone would sign up to turn it on in the morning and turn it off in the evening. It was connected to the main site by a trail through the woods. On starless and moonless nights, if the generator custodian didn't

OPPOSITE: *Outward Bound from Homeplace on Canoe Expedition* by Lorne Tippett.

carry a flashlight, they sometimes lost the trail and stumbled around for a bit after turning off the generator, which extinguished the lights. At least once, the custodian didn't make it back home and slept in the woods.

In the summer a water line running from Black Sturgeon Lake to the kitchen supplied its water. In the winter, however, the residents kept a hole in the ice open and carried the water from the frozen lake to the kitchen. By midwinter the hole in the ice would be three to four feet deep and would require someone in the hole handing buckets up to others to carry.

The MNR did not build the site and its structures for winter use. The buildings were without insulation. Temperatures often reached minus 40 degrees Celsius and Fahrenheit. Thus, during the winter months, only a couple buildings were used as staff housing; the barrel woodstoves would burn 24/7, except when the stovepipes needed the creosote removed. Creosote fires were a constant worry. In winter, the summer dining hall became student coed housing, with bunk beds for twelve students. At all times of year, but especially in winter, those at Homeplace were left to their own resources to survive.

Place. Homeplace sits on the Canadian Shield, a height of land composed of igneous and metamorphic rock, some of the oldest rock on earth, dating back four billion years. The surrounding ecosystem is boreal forest and encompasses a vast region of northern Canada, from Labrador to the Yukon. The forests are mostly composed of white and black spruce, tamarack, and pine, with thousands of riparian corridors, water highways of rivers and lakes created by the continental glaciers, which covered and scoured the land fifteen thousand years ago.

North of the height of land, the water flows north to James Bay and Hudson Bay. The Canadian Northern (CN) Railroad tracks passing through Armstrong, Ontario, fifty miles north of Homeplace, generally follow this height of land. South of the CN tracks the water flows to Lake Superior. Wetlands of bog and muskeg cover much of the topography. The common fish are northern pike and walleye. During the summer months blackflies and mosquitos feast on the warm-blooded animals, such as Outward Bound students and personnel.

Homeplace was also synonymous with its people—those who followed Bob and Wendy Pieh to this remote location to build an Outward Bound school from scratch. Survival as an Outward Bound school also depended

III. HOMEPLACE

on creating a healthy community of equal partners focused on supporting and teaching the best Outward Bound courses they could imagine.

In Alistair McArthur's "The Early Days: Late 1970s to Early 1980s," he describes the tone set by the first generation of leaders at Homeplace, as well as the financial challenges that beset the school and a tragic drowning that deeply affected the entire community.

"Board Member Perspective" by Biff Matthews, the first board chair, outlines how an exceptional group of volunteers were assembled to support the birth of the school and their steadfast support in its earliest, often challenging days.

In "The Big Map," Charlie Orsak describes, well, the big map! It hung on a wall in the administrative office building. Here instructors planned expedition routes through the immense wilderness area that they explored with their students: Black Sturgeon River Provincial Park, Kopka River Provincial Park, Obonga-Ottertooth Provincial Park, and Windigo Bay Provincial Park on Lake Nipigon, all south of the CN tracks; and Wabakimi Provincial Park, Whitesand Provincial Park, and Albany River Provincial Park north of the CN tracks.

"My First Summer at COBWS: Memories, Friends, and Community" by Bill Templeman is a beautiful remembrance of the informal mentor-mentee relationship that defines course-instructor pairings. He also reflects on the quality of friendships that permeated the community of staff and the focus on learning to live together and how best to serve students.

In "Ramblings" by Christo Grayling, we get a glimpse of an adventurous young man arriving at Homeplace and seeing his life expand exponentially as he was given more and more responsibility under the watchful eyes of capable women leaders.

In "Tentfly," Rick Cotter describes how he got his nickname and the melting pot of different lifestyles, experiences, and backgrounds that were more than the sum of the parts.

"Homeplace" by Eric MacDonald whimsically portrays the lifelong friendships that emerged out of his time at Homeplace.

Will Pooley's "Five Things from My Time Living at Homeplace" describes the lessons he learned during his time at Homeplace that still prove valuable today.

"Black Sturgeon Lake" by Homeplace's poet laureate Ken Victor is a lyrical ode to a sudden storm overtaking the lake.

In "Visits to Homeplace Since 2004," the year Homeplace closed, Rob Linscott works to maintain a place he still loves.

This collection of essays brings to life some of the more intangible and idiosyncratic qualities that defined the Homeplace community and the role it played in animating the student experience. —Ed.

The Early Days: Late 1970s to Early 1980s

Alistair McArthur

*A society grows great when old men plant trees whose
shade they know they shall never sit in.*

—Greek proverb

A defining feature of COBWS in the early days (mid-1970s) would be program director Wendy Pieh's infectious laugh. Her warm, generous personality affected everyone who came within her orbit. Her emotional intelligence was of a very high order, her organizational skills were exceptional, and her innate leadership qualities were second to none.

Deeply imbedded in Wendy's psyche were the founding principles of Outward Bound that went back to World War II. She had very firm ideas of what her educational goals and objectives were, and she had the ability to attract young, focused, articulate, and energetic staff to assist her in realizing her goals. Wendy embraced this quote from Kurt Hahn, cofounder of The Outward Bound Trust: "We are all better than we know; if only we can be brought to realize this, we may never again be prepared to settle for anything less."

Another defining feature of COBWS in the early days was a strong commitment from a group of young, idealistic educators to immerse themselves in the guiding philosophies of Outward Bound. The jobs list pinned on the wall of the kitchen at Homeplace on Black Sturgeon Lake in northern Ontario was symbolic of Wendy's leadership style. If a person thought that they could do a specific job, they put their name beside the job and got on with it. This empowered individuals, and they felt that they were contributors to the community.

Chuck Luckmann and Ian Yolles, who followed Wendy Pieh as program directors, also had deeply held and well-founded educational philosophies, which meant that COBWS continued to be highly regarded for its outstanding programs. Chuck and Ian were also skilled and experienced outdoor professionals, so the school was in safe hands. Staff were warmly welcomed and embraced by the COBWS community. It was a happy place with much laughter.

Homeplace was a group of buildings (a former research station built in the 1950s) situated in a very remote setting in northern Ontario, approximately eight hundred fifty miles northwest of Toronto. A long gravel logging road through approximately fifty miles of dense forest led to an open clearing beside the lake. Many wooden buildings were scattered around the site, proving more than adequate for our purposes. This self-contained community took on a life of its own, organizing and running sophisticated Outward Bound courses in the vast wilderness areas west and north of Lake Nipigon, now part of Wabakimi Provincial Park. The area was ideally suited to extended canoe journeys.

COBWS was founded in 1976 by Bob Pieh, the previous director of MOBS and Wendy's father, while he was still working for Queen's University in Kingston, Ontario. After the first two summers (1976 and 1977), Bob and the board of trustees decided that the school needed a full-time executive director and appointed me in January 1978. I was moving from the Colorado Outward Bound School, one of the largest Outward Bound schools in the world, to the smallest Outward Bound school in the world.

Within days of my arrival in Toronto, I received a phone call from a creditor asking me to pay an outstanding invoice for a substantial amount of money for new canoes that had been purchased before my arrival. For me, this was the beginning of an ongoing battle with our creditors and the bank.

The precarious financial situation of COBWS in the early days caused considerable personal stress for me as well as for the other decision-makers at COBWS. We were struggling to find sponsors for scholarships and major capital items. I became adept at being very frugal on many fronts; however, I was determined not to compromise safety.

A major positive feature of the early days at COBWS was the culture of support among all the staff in the organization. This was discussed on many levels, particularly between the field staff and the administration. A lofty concept, indeed, but at COBWS it was active and worked.

III. HOMEPLACE

Despite the severe lack of financial resources, the active notion of reciprocal support between Homeplace on Black Sturgeon Lake and the Outward Bound office in Toronto, eight hundred fifty miles from the program area, was sustaining, energizing, and uplifting.

The concept of community was discussed and acted upon, and it worked. It was a defining feature of COBWS in the early days. Community meetings at the end of a course were legendary. Everything was discussed—logistics, food, programs, students, staff, site needs, and the like. There were no time limits. The meetings were not over until consensus had been achieved. Often meetings would last for three to six hours. People were valued for their opinions, not for their gender, title, or position.

The influences of Biff Matthews (corporate lawyer and inaugural chair of the COBWS board of trustees) and Peter Green (corporate CEO and second chair of the COBWS board) were profound. They both were practical, level-headed, pragmatic, and committed. Importantly, they embraced our objectives, had no self-interest, and were influential, energetic, efficient, and easy to work with. COBWS was very lucky to have them guiding the school in the early days.

Fundraising and marketing were ongoing and relentless exercises. I have a clear memory of scores of meetings with potential donors in Toronto when I was required to wear a suit and tie while trying to convince a potential donor to give money to Outward Bound rather than the local hospital or another worthwhile charity. The board of trustees was pivotal in making these connections, and the members proved to be up for the task.

Summer courses included canoeing, rock climbing, rappelling, kayaking, campcraft, navigation, solo excursions, environmental awareness and conservation, group dynamics, first aid, safety, search and rescue, and expeditions. Winter courses included cross-country skiing, snowshoeing, winter camping, and dogsledding.

At the peak of the summer season in the early days (for example, July 1979), there would be approximately one hundred co-ed participants on a canoeing course supported by approximately thirty staff members (e.g. executive director, program director, course directors, instructors, interns, and office manager; plus specialist staff who were responsible for vehicles, food, logistics, rock climbing, whitewater, kitchen, site, and equipment). Innovations at COBWS included a strong focus on student involvement in menu planning and uses of specific food (for example, pulses and beans) that could be taken on fifteen- to eighteen-day expeditions without resupply. In 1979, COBWS was the first Outward Bound school in the world to introduce dogsledding. Students drove the dog team, and this program component proved to be a thoroughly worthwhile activity in winter courses.

A major traumatic event in the early years was the drowning of a fifteen-year-old student. Mark Bateman was a quiet, reserved young man who was a known nonswimmer. It remains a mystery how he entered the water. He was alone, on solo at the time, aside from daily checks by the two instructors. This tragedy occurred in summer 1979 at a remote lake in northern Ontario. I was deeply involved in the aftermath of Mark's death. Dealing with the next of kin, staff, trustees, media, police, lawyers, the inquest, and many other details took its toll on me and on many others.

His mother, Irene Bateman, had been assisting in the Toronto office as her contribution to the scholarship that we had provided for Mark. Many of us were deeply traumatized by his drowning; the effects were significant and continue to this day.

The early days of COBWS were marked by deeply held and well-founded educational principals coming from Kurt Hahn and a fragile and precarious financial position, which meant that the early days were like riding a roller coaster. Operating on a shoestring budget bonded everyone who had any connection with COBWS during that time. It was a heady mixture of high ideals mixed with surviving under challenging circumstances.

By the early 1980s, enrollment had improved, and the budget had increased from about $150,000 per annum to around $300,000 per annum. We also achieved an operating surplus, which was quite remarkable. Peter Green convinced his firm, Andrés Wines Ltd., to donate approximately $90,000 to the school; this proved to be an absolute breakthrough in dealing with our delicate financial situation.

Looking back, COBWS was indeed an extraordinary place. I was privileged to be part of this energetic, purposeful, innovative, and creative institution.

Board Member Perspective

Biff Matthews

Bob Pieh founded COBWS in 1976. For reasons not known to me, Bob arrived in Toronto from MOBS with a view of starting an Outward Bound school in Ontario. (There was already a school in British Columbia.)

Bob was greatly assisted in this by his daughter Wendy, a wonderful person and fine outdoorsperson. I cannot recall how Bob found Homeplace, but it was a brilliant initiative. Bob somehow recruited at least one highly prestigious board member—Omond Solandt, the chancellor of the University of Toronto and an experienced wilderness canoeist. Bob also recruited for the board a couple of prominent and experienced businesspeople, including Peter Green of Andrés Wines Ltd. and Alan Paterson of Selco Inc.

Bob also approached Jack Godfrey, a Queen's Counsel (later a senator) who was senior partner of the law firm Campbell, Godfrey & Lewtas (now known as Fasken). Jack's reaction was that he had no interest in wilderness canoeing, but his daughter, Anne, had a boyfriend who lived for that sort of thing. That was me, a newly minted lawyer. Bob asked if I would be willing to join the board of this new school, and I jumped at the chance.

Later, Bob asked Omond if he would be the chairman. He declined—as did every other director. So by process of elimination, I, in my late twenties, became the first chairman of COBWS.

The next stage was to hire an executive director. I'm sure Bob was directing things from the wings, but it fell to me to interview candidates. Based on both the résumés received and the interviews, the obvious choice was Alistair McArthur, an Australian of about thirty-five who had traveled widely, had Outward Bound experience in Colorado, and amazingly, in his early twenties, had served as a magistrate in the wilds of Papua New Guinea, then an Australian protectorate.

Alistair turned out to be a fine choice and became a good friend. Among other non–Outward Bound activities, Alistair and I took a terrific one-week canoe trip on the Groundhog River—a far wilder river than the name would suggest—in northern Ontario with two other friends.

At the time, I lived in a second-floor apartment at 165 Admiral Road in the Annex area of Toronto, and that became the first office of the school. I would leave for work at nine in the morning, just as Alistair, Wendy Pieh, and anyone they had hired would arrive. Within a month or two, Alistair found space on Yorkville Avenue for a proper office.

In the late 1970s I spent a week or so at Homeplace, rappelling and learning how to use a river kayak in rapids. I never did manage to master the so-called kayak roll. Homeplace was warm and friendly. I remember the wonderfully supportive staff and holding hands for grace before meals. Being that far away from the rest of the world helped make it special.

After two or three years, Peter Green agreed to take over as chairman of the school. I remained on the board. One morning when Peter was out of the country, a tragedy occurred—a student, the son of one of our office workers, drowned while on an Outward Bound trip during his solo. I received a call from Alistair at about six o'clock in the morning, and the two of us immediately drove to the basement apartment on O'Connor Drive where the boy's parents lived to tell them the terribly sad news.

It was one of the worst moments of my life and one I will never forget.

I returned to Homeplace in February 1988 for a ten-day winter camping trip—cross-country skiing, with the supplies transported by dogsled—with my friends Tom Heintzman, Ramsay Derry (by then both ex–Outward Bound board members), and Gary Girvan. Other participants were Tom's friends Bill Harris and the two Moffat brothers. One of our guides was Matty McNair, who was both fun and extremely capable. A great trip.

Homeplace definitely had a special magic. It's sad to know that it is no more.

The Big Map

Charlie Orsak

COBWS was the right time, right place—a sweet spot, for me at any rate. Don't mean to sound like one of those "In my day . . ." geezers, but here is what I mean. In the early 1980s, we were still in a time when the paddling possibilities were endless. We had Wabakimi and thousands of other lakes all to ourselves, with few restraints, rules, regulations, or field support, for that matter. We didn't need any, really. We had our ethics and judgment, honed by experience.

How many hours—looking for new routes—we spent studying the big map! It covered one entire wall of the office building. "Any brigades been to Webster Lake? No? Well, let's go, then."

What a gift.

At the same time, with help from others, I came to understand how to add the beauty of relationships and personal learning into the adventure mix.

My First Summer at COBWS: Memories, Friends, and Community

Bill Templeman

I came up to Homeplace in May 1979. Wendy Pieh hired me, a most courageous decision on her part and one for which I am still grateful. Given my phobia for commitments, her description of the intern program sounded ideal: "Try it and see."

Back in the fall of 1978, I was getting ready to go trekking in Nepal and so was reluctant to apply, as I might have been too late for staff training.

"Oh, go to Nepal, then come up north when you get back," Wendy said.

So off I went. I came back four months later, enriched by memories of the Himalayas and weakened by a bout of dysentery. I had lost twenty pounds. I recall that sitting on wooden benches during my first community meeting at Homeplace was a very acute pain in the butt; I had to use a cushion. I was almost spectral. But Bertha Bumchuckles's cooking worked its magic, and I revived to the point of being able to go out on the trail as an assistant instructor in August.

If I try to channel the spring 1979 version of myself, a very blurry image emerges—a gaunt, tentative, searching, preoccupied character whose mental world was tied up in ideas, theories, and words. The preceding years had set me up as an ideal candidate for the experiential teachings of the boreal forest. University, books, reading, words, and trying to sort out the meaning of it all had been my main preoccupations for years, as I searched in vain for a clear path through a profusion of cognitive clutter.

This mess, alas, was my psychic default. What was I going to do with my life? A question that lingers still. Learning experiences that forced me out of my head were new. I was obsessed with words and caught up in never-ending conversations with myself. The gods on high must have looked down at that magical little settlement on the shore of Black Sturgeon Lake and chuckled. They must have smiled at each other when one of them said, "*Just look at that one. Pitiful. He's completely lost in his head. We have the perfect instructor for this case. Let's send him out on the trail with Greg Logan.*"

Now Logan, for those who never knew him, was undeniably the slowest native speaker of English on the planet. He was highly sensitive to language and put a lot of reflection into everything he said and everything that was said to him. He spoke slowly, but he thought deeply about his words and the lives around him. Logan did not do small talk. He did not do gossip. In the time it took him to thoughtfully answer one of my questions, I'd thought of twenty additional questions. I took a careless, shotgun approach to conversations. More was better, or so I thought. I spoke quickly and offered many haphazard ways of saying the same thing. Instead, Logan patiently released carefully aimed, single arrows. Very . . . slowly. He made me think. And listen. He was the most thoughtful person I had ever met; he was thoughtful in the literal sense of the word. Everyone called him by his last name; somehow it was more intimate and friendly than Greg. Some called him Logie.

The two of us were a study in contrasts. I had grown up as an urban animal in Montreal; Logan was from small-town Iowa. During the 1960s, I had demonstrated against the Vietnam War; Logan had been drafted and served with the US Army. He seldom talked about Vietnam. To the credit of the community, none of us ever asked. Logan had been a competitive wrestler in college; I had been a competitive malingerer in libraries. He was the consummate wilderness athlete. I was the consummate beginner. I was an overly righteous vegetarian; Logan was a hunter, who while living in northern Minnesota for a few years after his discharge from the army would only eat meat he killed himself.

Our students were a group of educators. They were a diverse, eager collection of contrasting individuals who wanted to learn as much as possible from the course. Logan was the model of humility and understanding. He could see into the motivations of people with a clarity that helped him identify the essence of what each student needed to achieve. He respected boundaries and led by example, then got out of the way.

That course with Logan opened up my definition of what Outward Bound could be. Within COBWS, Outward Bound morphed into a huge portfolio of possibilities. Until I had worked that course, Outward Bound was a theoretical construct, an experimental approach to education. A bunch of ideas. That summer, I learned more about goals, confidence, integrity, and being alive than I had learned in my years of academic incarceration at university.

What I recall most of all, looking back over the decades to that summer of 1979, are the friendships, the sense of belonging, and the mostly pristine wilderness around us. I remember paddling on Smoothrock Lake with Paul Landry in September of that year and saying to the students in the next canoe, "Welcome to the North. There's nothing between us and Hudson Bay."

Back then it was true.

Another memory from 1979 has to be the ineffable sense of community and shared power at COBWS. Everyone had power, but some of us didn't really know it. Yes, there was a decision-making hierarchy, but it was permeable and based on real things instead of bureaucratic requirements. Specialization existed. For example, the rocks coordinator was in charge of climbing, and that was fine. But everyone took ownership.

Who is responsible? Look in the mirror. Difficult decisions that affected the community were made by consensus, sometimes with protracted difficulty. I remember the creation of a safety policy during a series of community meetings. It took forever, and the process was thoroughly tedious. But at the end of it all, it was our policy because we had created it. Compliance was not an issue. The most stunning thing about the COBWS community seemed to be our collective celebration of our largest challenges: figuring out how to live together and how to best serve our students.

I would love to see all those people again, but I also want to see Kopka Falls, Whitewater Lake, and Cliff Lake again, and so much more. Or would I want to see all those places now? Is that countryside still there in the way I remember it? Maybe forest fires, clear-cuts, logging roads, and development have changed the land. Attachment to vivid memories can be an impediment to seeing what really is in front of us. Perhaps I don't want to see the development of the land north and west of Lake Nipigon. Perhaps I don't want to see what is really in front of me.

Maybe I'll hold on to those attachments. Life moves on whether we want it to or not. Greg Logan, Deb Cooke, Guy Lacelle, Diana Meredith, Nancy

III. HOMEPLACE

Suchman, Magnus Flood, and Mary Morgan were all at COBWS; they were an integral part of the COBWS tableau, but they are no longer with us. We carry them in our hearts.

We cannot live in our memories. But can we try for a few minutes?

Ramblings

Christo Grayling

I arrived at COBWS in early May 1977, a month before my twentieth birthday. I had hitchhiked from Boulder, Colorado. After spending my first night in Canada at the single men's hostel in Thunder Bay, I got a ride to Hurkett and eventually up the gravel road, arriving at Homeplace. This quickly became one of the most significant times of my life.

My road to Outward Bound and Homeplace began in 1972 at Scotch College in Adelaide, Australia, where I met Campbell Whalley, a mate of Alistair McArthur's. He introduced me to climbing, kayaking, and a different kind of teamwork, and got me excited with his tales of being an Outward Bound instructor. Then along came Colin Bolton, and that was it! I shadowed and followed him vigorously until I hit the road in 1976 to follow the plan he had basically mapped out for me. Colin regaled me with stories from Outward Bound worldwide, and I remember vividly his passion for the Minnesota Northwoods and the desert of Keremeos, British Columbia. At this stage I had no idea of the connections: McArthur and Campbell, Bolton, and the whole Pieh family.

After six months of climbing and skiing in New Zealand and a season at Outward Bound in Australia, Alistair fantastically got me into the Colorado Outward Bound School in Leadville, Colorado, for a winter course in February 1977. I met Don Kafrissen, who was the maintenance guy there; at the end of the course, he told me about COBWS and suggested I check into it.

I went to Boulder to hang and climb. Somehow I got a phone interview at a pay phone in Eldorado Canyon. I was late for the call with Wendy Pieh; I bailed and rappelled off the wrong climb. Got the job, and the very next day stuck my thumb out and headed for Canada.

* * *

COBWS was unique for me, for sure. In no particular order, the following are some highlights and important insights and wonderful memories that contributed to directing and informing my life to this day.

I met my closest friends there: Michael Hendrick, who became my best man; Barb Hertell, my life partner; Greg Logan, my spiritual advisor; and Ian Yolles, held in love and awe by our kids. The kicker was getting to work with Colin Bolton one summer, something we had joked about back when I was seventeen and a student at Scotch College. At that stage COBWS did not exist.

At COBWS you were trusted for who you were. You were encouraged to be the best version of yourself and expected to show up as who you were, and at the same time nudged to develop and explore and muddle out who you were to become in the next version of yourself.

As young and inexperienced as I was, I quickly became aware of a kind of leadership I had no idea existed. Bob and Wendy Pieh appeared to seamlessly influence and build commitment with grace, honesty, and ease. Transparency was abundant and at times unsettling, and yet I was profoundly shifted and jolted by it. As they say, the books were open. Alistair McArthur was the ever-frugal example of getting it done. To this day I well remember Alistair, the director of the school, hitching from Toronto to Homeplace.

This has been etched in my mind since: Do your very best at what it takes to get it done and show up!

During the winters of 1978 and 1979, when I was at college in Toronto, I regularly visited the office on Friday afternoons. I am grateful for that opportunity. It was like a family visit, and it gave me a view into how it looks to lead and implement from a distance and on a fucking shoestring. Fun times with Gayle Goldhart and Greg Siren! Occasionally, I got to interact with board members, which was hugely eye-opening and encouraging. I always enjoyed their visits to Homeplace, and I became much more aware of different ways of belonging and contributing.

I think it was in the summer of 1980 when Homeplace and the surrounding area were seriously threatened by fires. A very tough, important, and wise decision was made to evacuate Homeplace, while still running the programs.

I'll hold off on the details of the evacuation, as others will share more eloquently. I learned once again about the power of a common, well-understood vision and shared values and the determination to get the job done, doing whatever it took. This guides me to this day.

About a month later, between courses, Alistair McArthur was up from Toronto for the community and leadership meetings. It was during that visit that I discovered my all-time favorite Alistair line, which became legendary after the fire evacuation. During dinner, Alistair rose to say a few words. With a big, wide, generous, and genuine smile on his face, he began, "You guys fuuucking amaaaaazzze me."

He has a way of drawing out a word, and you listen in for it. I always loved and was comforted by Alistair's pretty raw Aussie accent.

The death of Mark Bateman has been present with me since that day. I had not been around death like that before. I did not know Mark; however, I was instructing and leading another junior brigade on the same course. I was at the inquest. Wow! What an eye-opener for a young wannabe outdoor educator.

I quickly became a very nervous instructor, and for years I think I was hesitant and overly cautious in letting go. I wanted our students on a tight leash; I was terrified of an accident. I believe I was a very safe outdoor instructor, but after many years of holding on tightly, I became more comfortable.

It was at COBWS that I became more aware of women in leadership roles, and collectively, women providing leadership who influenced me. I had spent my life with a strong and capable woman: my mom. As a kid I did not see her as a leader, however. I later proudly learned what a leader my mum was (and is to this day, at ninety-four).

It was not surprising for me to be around women getting it done. I had just not been around *so many* women getting it done, and certainly not in the New Age style of the times. Many of my fantastic COBWS reflections and memories are of wonderful women who really helped me grow and learn at a powerful personal level. This was and still remains huge for me.

* * *

COBWS West was a very cool time. It started with the migration of a few COBWS instructors to Calgary, Alberta, to work for Enviros Wilderness School, and from there it blossomed. At one point, I reckon there were twenty to thirty COBWS folks in and around southern Alberta.

Group homes, Enviros, Project Trust, University of Calgary, the Rocky Mountains, and ranching brought us together in the same place. Community was one of the drawing cards. Around 1985, about twenty of us lived within a four-block radius of each other in Calgary. Jim Bell and Wendy Talbot and their household were our next-door neighbors. We had backyards that we shared. We all branched out in different directions, but at the same time remained a tight community.

This was the launching pad for Barb Hertell and me, and many of our dear friends, for our individual and collective work. Thanks, COBWS!

Tentfly

Rick Cotter

I first came to Homeplace in 1980. I had just finished university with a degree in English literature. Ha ha. The real education began with my experiences working at COBWS. I quickly discovered that I could do anything that needed to be done. There was so much to learn . . . from starting the generator to driving a school bus to patching aluminum canoes to vegetarian cooking.

It could have been overwhelming; there was such a diverse cast of characters on staff, and everyone had different skill sets that were shared openly. This is what made COBWS unique: a melting pot of different lifestyles, experiences, and backgrounds, all working together toward the common goal of creating the best experience possible for its students.

My personal story begins with my nickname of Tentfly. I was asked to drive a brigade to the expedition launch site, and I didn't know until the last minute that it was an overnighter. Someone tossed me a tent bag as we were about to depart. Later that night, I opened up the bag to discover only a tent fly inside. It was a clear, starry night, so I climbed on top of the bus, onto the roof rack. I rolled up in the tent fly and slept there. I woke up as Tentfly.

A few years later, I was walking in downtown Toronto at the corner of Yonge and Bloor. I heard someone yell, "It's Tentfly!" Two former Outward Bound students recognized me as the driver for their excursion.

Other fond memories include bringing Hawaiian shirts to the land of lumberjack plaid, assisting in creating the Scourge of the Black Sturge pirate ships, daily visits with the sled dogs, town runs to Thunder Bay, and explaining to locals that we were not a commune.

Certainly Outward Bound instilled in me a sense of community and belonging. For that I am forever grateful.

Homeplace

Eric MacDonald

There is a cadre of folks that I seem to be tag-teaming through life. They serve as mentors, sounding boards, inspirations, co-adventurers, and bastions of memory. I commune with them on a daily basis. They are brothers and sisters. They hail from those days at Homeplace: days of passion, purpose, fellowship, and wonder.

Homeplace came to me at a time in life when I was, what can I say . . . malleable? A liminal space of sorts? I've got this theory. There's a homing device embedded in these grand experiments of human enterprise, calling those who need to heal. I was no exception. I took that highway: Frontier College and Katimavik.

I railed against the storm. I sought the source. And eventually it found me on a bus en route from London to Athens. I was on my way to Crete, to find a power spot. I was taking the Magic Bus, sitting at the emergency door, when the bus got entangled in an eighty-vehicle collision on the German Autobahn outside of Prien am Chiemsee.

The door was ripped open as the bus slammed into the median and I was catapulted over three lanes of the Autobahn highway. I regained consciousness over a month later.

I woke up in restraining straps in the ICU in the Grosshadern University hospital in Munich.

I didn't know who I was, I couldn't read, I couldn't focus. I couldn't recognize my two sisters who came to see me. Eventually my mother came with Gordon Lightfoot tapes and pictures. The Kaleidoscope started to patch itself together.

I was badly broken. Two inches shorter. Fused discs in my back from the impact. And everything else. Eventually, when the brain scans showed some easing, my mother somehow managed to get me flown back to Canada in a body cast. That began a ten-year odyssey to put Humpty back together again: hospital bed, wheelchair, walkers, crutches. According to the doctor I should prepare myself for a sedentary life.

My memory was shattered, my body broken, my emotions in tatters. It would be a decade of wanderlust until the pieces stopped quivering. My first canoe trip down the Magnetawan River was in a torso cast. I was in a frenzied fever to find sparks, reclaim shattered memories. I recreated the person I imagined myself to be. It was at the start of this journey that I got a call from Ian Yolles inviting me to join the COBWS merry band of pranksters.

My memory and healing began to consolidate in the grail of uncommon, rare souls at Homeplace. What an assembly! My memories came in a flurry. The canvas of the Homeplace era for me was laughter, singing, and play. Forgive me if these fragments are disjointed—they weave a tapestry for me that still leaves me longing to find a way back.

There were the personalities.

At the start, Peter Morgan, who I could swear had just walked off a yacht, was my bunkmate. When a question would come to me in the middle of the night, he would bolt straight up from a dead sleep to help me ponder the issue. The Thomson brothers, Ian and David, who instilled confidence at the Claghorn bluffs, were skilled, thorough, and rock solid. John Mordhorst, meister of dogs, told unbelievable stories of his Arctic odyssey. Jonathan Golding. Robin Harrison, also known as Sara. Tentfly, Rick Cotter, with his Caribbean shirts. Bertha Bumchuckles . . . I always wondered how she got that name. There was the warden, Ian Yolles, a sly wizard in his Hobbit hovel. Matty and Paul Landry. The maniacal cackle of Ken Victor, who in those days would get me howling wolflike and I'd drop laughing to the ground.

And the time Lorne Tippett and Wade Campbell, with their prototype mountain bikes, newly released, rode like banshees through the boreal glades that surrounded Homeplace. The time I built a high ropes course with Geoff Murray and instructed my first course with Marian Flammang. That time when Grant Wilde donned horn-rimmed glasses and feigned the yokel, pranking his brigade at the course start. How about when Rod Taylor staged a coup against the macrobiotic crowd? The all-day community meetings: epic and sacred.

And the moments.

I remember just being with one another in the lounge, laughing and singing. And the stories! We sang Stan Rogers's tunes the summer he died. And standing outside Marge Lachecki's cabin as she sang the song that I still sing today. Could Marge sing! Do you remember after the life choices workshop, we summarily excused ourselves to the lounge to earnestly throw the I Ching to figure out life, after the season ended? I remember hanging on to what it revealed like a lifeline.

And the journeys.

Flotillas down Black Sturgeon Lake, canoes lashed and sails unfurled; Diane Lemire swimming across Black Sturgeon Lake. Or that time we all went down to Madawaska Kanu Camp, and the trailer unhitched and rolled into the lake. We laughed until we cried.

Not so many courses that year. A gang of us took a climbing trip to Carlton Peak and Shovel Point, which savaged my hands. Bill Templeman and I cleaned out the bottom of the post-trip food barrel and journeyed down the Pukaskwa River. Bill famously asked me what he should think about on our long paddle back to the car. Or our reconnoiter down the Albany River, when we did a wind ferry over to Fort Albany, scaring the bejesus out of me.

And the courses.

I remember the alumni course, canoeing the Kopka River with Lorne Tippett. On the trail with Jill Bennett. And what was that crazy portage with mud up over the knees? The educators course with Andrew Orr and Daniel Vokey is where I met S. L. N. Swamy, which opened the doors to India for me. I tried out guided imagery with the brigade—everyone so open to everything.

* * *

And the years afterward.

Life intersects in Asia, with Wade Campbell and Peter Morgan, which changed the course of my life.

I find myself still outward bound. Writing this leaves me with a longing to find a way back to Homeplace.

Five Things from My Time Living at Homeplace

Will Pooley

Every time I look at Homeplace pictures, I am transported there. The place and time, what we did, the people—all put a smile in my heart. My gratitude is beyond measure. W. B. Yeats nailed it:

> *Think where man's glory most begins and ends,*
> *And say my glory was I had such friends.*

Dozens of episodes occur to me to offer to our collection. The following vignettes and some reflections are just a beginning.

RETURNING THE GIFTS

In 1986, Paul Landry, the program director, and Phil Blackford, the director of program development, asked me to coordinate COBWS's fledging Native Canadian program. Their ask proved to be a lifelong gift. For the next three years, I spent much of my time introducing COBWS to many Indigenous elders, community leaders, educators, and young people in Thunder Bay, Ontario, and in other Indigenous communities. I put a few thousand miles on my old Chevy station wagon, took advantage of virtually limitless VIA Rail tickets, and visited remote tribal communities by bush plane.

Our initial efforts were aided tremendously by several elders with substantial stature among Indigenous communities, who saw our efforts as sincere and agreed to serve as an informal advisory council. The late Walter Linklater explained traditional beliefs and customs, offered sweat lodges, and along with his wife, Maria, opened his home in Thunder Bay to all who wished to learn or were in need. During a COBWS spring staff training, they made the trip from their Thunder Bay home to Homeplace, gave a presentation, and offered their friendship.

Maria and other women opened the first shelter in Fort William for Indigenous women and children needing a safe place to stay. The late Richard Lyons was central to teaching Indigenous young people traditional drumming, singing, and dancing. Richard was one of many elders who were encouraging young people to learn their native language. Typically, the grandparents were fluent in their natal language and spoke little English; their children, my generation, knew both English and their native language; the grandchildren, however, were usually only fluent in English, knowing just a bit of their grandparents' language.

A vital and early supporter of the program was the resourceful and always energetic Marlene Pierre, director of the Thunder Bay Indian Friendship Centre and a leader of the Ontario Native Women's Association. Marlene's passionate support for COBWS started early, largely because in the early 1980s one of her sons participated in a COBWS course. Marlene encouraged a collaborative and cooperative programming model of COBWS partnering with Indigenous organizations. In 1988, Marlene helped us arrange the first partnership between the Friendship Centre and COBWS: an all-Indigenous course for Indigenous teens at a Thunder Bay school.

Eddie Benton-Banai, a well-known and respected American Ojibwe author, teacher, and cofounder of the American Indian Movement, offered additional literature and advice. And Indigenous instructors, including Ray Katt, Kirk Crowshoe, Hepsi Barnett, and after my time at Homeplace, Terry Swan, among others, were essential and enriched our collective efforts.

From the feedback I received, word was out among Indigenous communities that COBWS was offering respectful, unique, and worthwhile experiences. Participation of Indigenous men and women grew from about a dozen in 1986 to over sixty in 1989.[1]

From coordinating this program, I offer five perspectives from my time at Homeplace.

---

1. (Victoria) Moon Joyce and Chuck Luckmann taught the first Indigenous course with eight Ojibwe students in August 1979. —Ed.

III. HOMEPLACE

First, the effectiveness of collaboration. The stories of Indigenous people are theirs to tell. And COBWS's sincere efforts gained trust and benefited greatly from input by Indigenous staff and elders, critical in the early days of the original Native Canadian program as it evolved into what later became Giwaykiwin, Ojibwe for *coming home*. A beautiful and powerful documentary film about an all-Indigenous course out of Homeplace was aired on CBC in 1998 entitled *Strangers to the Land*, featuring Terry Swan and Ray Katt.

Second, some of the stories I listened to from many Indigenous people kept me awake at night. The predominant historical treatment of Indigenous people by national governments in Canada and the United States was blatantly destructive. Traditions, languages, and families were literally defined and treated as worthless.

Third, I also learned firsthand the distinction between guilt and responsibility. Although my generation is not guilty of this gut-wrenching record, my generation, my children's generation, and my grandchildren's generation are responsible. Responsible to actively do whatever we can, as often as we can, and for as long as we can to learn about and correct thoughtless ways. We must teach our children well.

A fourth takeaway is the importance and vitality of active compassion. Emerson wrote that success is to leave the world a bit better than you found it, and "in the woods, we return to reason and faith." Homeplace will forever be a spiritual center for those of us who lived there and for those who visited. When each of us returned to the world where people were often messing things up, we returned more generous and better able to roll up our sleeves and make a positive difference.

Finally, I suggest that every so often each of us tap ourselves on the shoulder and say, "Remember what you did with COBWS. Good job. Now today, contribute something . . . live this day with hope."

One COBWS board member seemed to have an endless supply of train passes, so I made many rail trips. One such trip in 1987 was for several days to the Spanish River Reserve, located on the north shore of Lake Huron in the Sudbury area. After this visit talking with parents and the community council, the next couple of years found several young people signing up for COBWS courses.

It was a windy November afternoon with light snow. Three friends picked me up at the train station. We stopped at McDonald's and then drove to the reserve itself. After a couple of hours, we pulled up to a small tar paper–covered cabin.

"This is where you'll stay," said my friend. And we went in. A small woman greeted us with a wide smile and gestured to the coffee pot and a small table. She and one friend chatted in Ojibwe.

"She has no English," my friend said.

"I have no Ojibwe," I responded.

For the three days, I would return there in the evening. At night we enjoyed playing cards on the small kitchen table. She insisted I sleep in the only bed while she slept on a couch. In the morning, we shared toast, bacon, and eggs. A smile . . . a nod . . . a gentle touch were plenty to let me know I was welcome. Like the coffee pot, her kindness was bottomless.

Chi-miigwech! (Thank you very much.)

JOHNNY CASH VISITS HOMEPLACE

As we all know, sometimes neighbors unexpectedly drop by for a visit. Our closest neighbor at Homeplace was the Gull Bay Reserve on the western shore of the huge Lake Nipigon. In the 1980s, what connected them to us was a sometimes dicey hour-long ride over the always challenging Hurkett Road, an old logging path, and then the recently paved Armstrong road, Highway 527.

By the late 1980s a few friendships were established and blooming between Homeplace and Gull Bay. Often brigades on a course would choose Gull Bay as a location for a service project, usually entertaining and playing with the kids there. And several Gull Bay men and women participated in a COBWS course or two during the mid- to late 1980s.

In the summer of 1988, my friend Patty Nawagesic and a few other Gull Bay residents and I began to talk seriously about a social visit at Homeplace for our two communities. One evening in mid-August, Homeplace staff members were in the dining hall, wrapping up a gorgeous day that was warm and clear with a light breeze, and, treat of all treats, the bugs were somewhere else! The dining hall was packed with summer staff when a small caravan of cars, pickup trucks, and one large, black flatbed truck rolled in. Our friends from Gull Bay had decided the time was right for a visit.

Our surprised group quickly organized into smaller groups: A few folks began putting together snacks of fruit, peanut butter and jelly sandwiches, and pitchers of water and Kool-Aid; a few agreed to show our neighbors around Homeplace; a few offered to give canoe rides from the northern beach up and down the shoreline; and a few offered to introduce the sled dogs.

Soon Patty took me aside and, with a wry smile, explained, "One of our guys likes to sing. And he loves to do Johnny Cash. That's what this flatbed is for with the speakers and microphones tied down." She nodded to the back of the big flatbed. So we moved a few school vans from the parking area, backed in his flatbed truck, and plugged in a couple of extension cords.

And so on that evening, as the sun set and for a few hours later, Homeplace was full and joyful because about twenty-five of our nearest neighbors decided to get better acquainted with those people who were tucked away on the shores of Black Sturgeon Lake. Adults and kids mingled casually in the dining hall, the sled dogs reveled at the extra attention, a few kids played basketball while many of us lingered in the parking area, and a few danced to, among other crowd favorites, "I Walk the Line," "Ring of Fire," and "Folsom Prison Blues."

JOHN BOY FIGURES IT OUT

It was one of those rare and brief stretches at Homeplace: hot and still. The place was packed with summer staff and students. About midnight, the dogs went crazy . . . intense barking and howling. John "John Boy" Mordhorst, in charge of the dogs, was living in the Zoo (a staff residence) and would holler every fifteen minutes or so. Immediately after, the dogs would quiet down for no more than two minutes before starting up again. This dance went on all night. About dawn it ended. At breakfast we found out that two bear cubs had wandered into the dog yard and were frightened, so immediately escaped up a tree in the yard. At first light, John and a few other staff moved the dogs so the cubs could climb down and run away.

WINTER RESCUE

Paul Landry thought it would be a good precaution, especially during the winter, to monitor the Homeplace radiophone if we knew someone would be traveling up or down the road, just in case. It was fifty miles from Homeplace to the Trans-Canada Highway. Especially in the deep winter, not much traffic was on the road.

Fortunately, the phone was on when I started out in a red pickup after supper, on my way to Thunder Bay for a presentation the next day about our Native Canadian program. I was sipping a cup of coffee when the old truck decided it had gone far enough . . . thirty-eight miles was it.

I finished my coffee and started walking. It was minus eighteen degrees. Keep moving, I told myself. Actually, though, it was truly a beautiful night.

After twelve miles, I spotted a small cabin on the north side of Dorion, a small village close to the Trans-Canada Highway. I knocked on the door, explained what happened, and was invited in.

I called Paul, waited, ate cookies, and drank more coffee.

All's well that ends well.

GUY AND THE SWIM

Early August 1983 was unusually hot for a couple of weeks. One evening at dinner, folks at our table began chattering about swimming across Black Sturgeon Lake. Before the dinner dishes made it back into the kitchen, Guy Lacelle, Donna Clark, Diane Lemire, and I shrugged. *Why not*?

The next morning, Guy and Diane started swimming from the southern beach while Donna and I each paddled a support canoe. The plan was for Guy and Diane to swim to the far shore and then for Donna and me to swim back.

Guy was an amazing athlete . . . but he swam like a rock. Muscle-bound, he just had no buoyancy at all. He made it about halfway and got in the canoe. That evening we all celebrated at dinner. Guy, forever the good sport, laughed at the day.

That was the last time I saw him. Charlie Orsak called me in December 2009 to say, "I'm afraid I have some sad news. Guy died in a climbing accident." He was at the Bozeman Ice Festival in Montana simply waiting his turn on a ledge when a small pocket of ice above him pulled out, caught him, and took him down the cliff.

Guy was one of the world's finest and most graceful ice climbers. He simply loved climbing, accumulating world-renowned and groundbreaking first ascents in the Canadian Rockies, the United States, and Europe. Soon after his death, his wife, Marge Lachecki, also a former COBWS instructor, reflected, "Guy's athleticism is not the story people are telling, however. They are telling the human stories about the lovely human being he was, and that just says it all to me."

Black Sturgeon Lake

(for Ian Yolles)

Ken Victor

The lake a plowed
meadow, wind

turning it over,
black water

white foam,
air

ripe with moisture, then
a sudden

calm . . .
low clouds

unravel their rain
like strands of loosened hair.

Visits to Homeplace Since 2004

Rob Linscott

Rob Linscott was a Homeplace site manager and Outward Bound instructor for four decades, from the 1970s to the 2000s. Outward Bound Canada closed Homeplace in 2004 and moved its field operations to southern Ontario to be closer to Toronto. Subsequently, most every fall since then, Rob Linscott has returned to maintain the site and buildings. These are some of his email reflections about those visits. —Ed.

Last fall when I was there, loggers were cutting across the road from Homeplace. Not many trees were left standing heading west to Suzie Creek from Homeplace. However, the Black Sturgeon Road was in excellent shape, with a monster road grader shaping and smoothing the surface five days a week.

Lots of local people who were camping stopped by to walk the site. The place was in good shape, with fresh plastic bags lining the garbage cans in the dining hall, just waiting for the next rental user. Some shingle roofs have leaked a little, causing small areas of ceiling to cave in but no serious deteriorations. The site continues to get more overgrown.

I had an unusual experience while doing some work on Southern Comfort house that sort of involves Ken Victor. Some fellows started calling "Hello" by Buckwheat cabin. I called back, "Down here!" and went to meet them. We met in front of Pink Flamingo. One fellow about my age was a prospector looking to rent a building so he could boat to the east side of the lake and do more exploring. He said he had proven deposits of several minerals worth $300 million in the hills on the far shore and needed a base camp to do more exploring. He thought Outward Bound still owned the site. I had to disappoint him with the news that the province owned the place. The jaw-dropper for me was that the second, younger fellow was the twin of Ken Victor in appearance and voice when Ken was a young man and lived and worked at

III. HOMEPLACE

Homeplace in the 1980s. I was stunned and did not think to take a picture. Both fellows live in Nipigon.

The missing forest to the west of Homeplace is a different scene, although you do not see anything while at Homeplace. I doubt if the prospector will be able to bring his deposits to the mining phase for a long time yet. The forestry industry used to have a deluxe log cabin lodge on the east side of the lake. Perhaps lights will once more glow at night on the far shore.

Most of the local people who stop by think Outward Bound still owns the site. I tell them it isn't so and to organize a coalition of users in the area to take it over. I am loath to see Homeplace fall into disrepair and get torn down. It is now part of Black Sturgeon River Provincial Park. A decision was supposed to have been made two years ago on its future. Its beauty is its isolation. It is also its curse.

I still love to see the waves march in rows up or down Black Sturgeon Lake or when the lake is mirror smooth. The gently worn hills on the east side make an interesting and pleasing horizon. Looking up or down the east shore of the lake with its series of curving points and sweeping bays calms me. The triple rainbows over the lake following an afternoon shower still inspire me. These things remain at Homeplace. Best of all are the memories of the people I got to live and work with and the vibrant community that once flourished here.

IV. COMMUNITY

Located on the shore of Black Sturgeon Lake, Homeplace was born in 1976. Some of the buildings were in need of repair, the generator had to be convinced it had a job to do, and the kitchen had to have running water and propane for cooking and cleaning, all in a tight time frame before students arrived to participate in their first Outward Bound course.

A significant group of volunteers and staff went to work. Everyone pitched in and rotated the various daily tasks, such as cooking and cleaning. During recess breaks, the school's director, Bob Pieh, would structure small group learning experiences for the staff. A small group challenge might be how to get the group over the twelve-foot-high wall in the newly constructed ropes course. Sometimes the learning exercise would be to share something about yourself with the group. Or it would be an initiative game, such as how to construct a bridge with very little equipment.

Individuals felt safe enough in these groups to share of themselves, particularly about who they were deep inside, about their hopes and fears. The support given each other in these small groups carried forward into personal reflection and growth for the individual, building Homeplace into a community of individuals where everyone was living Outward Bound collectively. This openness also fostered a community of people working together with humor and energy into a shared mission of establishing a new Outward Bound school, regardless of the task, even including the building of a four-seat outhouse.

OPPOSITE: *Ropes Course Challenge* by Lorne Tippett.

A sense of pride and commitment evolved, and an appreciation of the time and effort that everyone was putting in to be ready for courses to begin.

From the beginning there was an emphasis at Homeplace on working together, learning through experience (experientially), and making decisions based on consensus. The instructors took this emphasis into their brigades; the courses they facilitated positively impacted their students, who then took that learning home.

Students arrived wondering, *What have I gotten myself into*? as the bus kept going farther and farther away from civilization, traveling along a bumpy dirt road to a remote destination—Homeplace. Everyone was on a list to join a specific brigade. Each brigade had two instructors; they were the guides through this new experience. The instructors were open, friendly, and encouraging as they introduced themselves and began to get to know their students. A vibrant, thriving community began to evolve in each brigade, through learning new skills and the conscious effort of their instructors, inviting them to be themselves, even when the going got rough, like carrying a canoe or food pack over a long portage, or feeling like you wanted to cry.

The instructors made time for brigade check-ins or meetings. These brigade meetings allowed students and instructors to assimilate learning, both as individuals and as part of a small, self-reliant community. The veneer of who you project you are slips away when you are confronted by fears of what is coming next, or the fear is right there in front of you. Fears were shared, followed by encouragement, and individuals grew in self-esteem and inner strength. What mattered was a belief in each person's ability to be authentic and to support their fellow brigade members and instructors to be themselves as well. As the courses progressed, the brigades began living Outward Bound.

At graduation at the end of a course, students had a new lift in their steps, a broader smile on their faces, clearly showing new physical, mental, and emotional strengths as they transitioned into their future. Many have stayed in touch over the years; some students returned later to work with COBWS.

Staff also cherished the opportunity to be themselves, to support one another, and to enthusiastically attend and actively participate in the monthly celebration at the end of each course. A huge meal was prepared for the evening. Over supper instructors shared their experiences with one another, full of excitement about how their brigades came together and began to live

Outward Bound. The evening wrapped up with singing, dancing, and unwinding with a cup of tea or their favorite beer.

The next morning staff arrived for breakfast and preparations for the community meeting began. The agenda was up on the blackboard, including debriefing the courses: What went well? Where could we make improvements? What should we change before the next group of students arrived? Anyone could add an agenda subject, such as how to better care for the sled dogs during the summer months. The program director chaired the meeting and opened the meeting with some positive observations and congratulations on the safe, successful Outward Bound courses just completed. The community required everyone to attend. Frequently administrative staff from the Toronto office had arrived the day before so they too could attend the community meeting. One time Greg Logan did not appear, and Bill Templeman went roaring out the door, "I'll get him!"

Community meetings also involved important aspects of living together with differences of opinion regarding keeping the community healthy (physically, mentally, and emotionally), which sometimes involved discussing personal behaviors. Decisions were arrived at through consensus. Consensus decisions take time. There is no hierarchy. All thoughts are brought into the conversation, discussed, digested, and usually decisions are unanimously agreed upon. If differences continued, the discussion continued until a solution arose that everyone could agree upon. This often took many hours. While not everyone participated in every discussion, it was often someone who did not have a strong opinion about the issue who would come up with a solution that everyone could live with.

(Victoria) Moon Joyce, in "Community and Creativity," discusses working together, evolvement, and inspiration. An accomplished singer, she also discusses the role of music in her work.

In "Inclusion and Influence," Philip Blackford writes about COBWS's relationships with the larger worldwide scope of Outward Bound, and COBWS's impact on it. He concludes with an interesting recipe.

Juliet Westgate (Duff), in "Reflections," celebrates a community that was greater than the sum of its parts. She writes about a caring and dynamic community in the wilds of Canada's North. She shares her thoughts about the spirit of love.

In "Fire Evacuation," Charles Luckmann remembers a wild forest fire approaching Homeplace and what staff did to try to save the site before evacuating to the Claghorn bluffs and later to Thunder Bay. In two days another series of courses were about to begin. The survival of the school hung on a decision they would make.

Ian Kilborn, in "What Made COBWS Unique," muses about group decision-making, the Homeplace community he witnessed, the positive effects of working with women leaders, and the continuing effect of the Homeplace community on his life.

In "Women of Courage" and "Women of Courage Program Is the Opposite of Abuse," Ruth Goldman and Louise Karch, respectively, share their experiences of seven-day courses with women who have experienced violence. They describe a model of courage and strength as these women confront their fears within a community of support.

Peter Morgan, in "What Matters," describes his experiences with staff, working and playing together and living Outward Bound all over the world. He describes various adventures and their impact on him.

COBWS evolved into a safe community where anyone—students or staff—could change and grow into who they wanted to be. There was a real sense of *I'm safe. I can be myself here.*

    Caring for one another
    Open-minded to challenges and new ideas
    Moderate in opinion, even when feeling extreme
    Magic of love permeating the entire community
    Uplifted by the support and kindness of others
    Nonjudgmental when listening to others' opinions
    Involved in every aspect of community life
    Trust that this community accepts all of me
    Yes instead of no.

That spells *community*. —Ed.

Community and Creativity

(Victoria) Moon Joyce

COBWS gave us an opportunity to experiment with community. Due to our isolation and the residential nature of the school, we trained together, worked together, lived together (cheek by jowl), and self-governed as a school *and* as a community. This is a rare thing for young people to be allowed to do, and most people did so with heart, imagination, and devotion.

Homeplace was a welcoming place. Everyone who managed to make it up the fifty-mile logging road from the Trans-Canada Highway would be greeted and shown around and invited to meals, and often invited to stay. Occasionally, visitors stayed on to volunteer. Everyone was expected to pitch in and help with all manner of tasks to make the place operational. This leveling of the hierarchy of work created a space of communal interdependence, which in turn created cohesiveness, closeness, and a sense of ownership for how we would be together, not just how we would do our jobs as outdoor adventure educators.

In those first years we were definitely a motley crew. Many American instructors were recruited until there were enough Canadian instructors trained. We were mostly in our early twenties, young and eager for adventure. And if an Outward Bound course wasn't adventure enough, having the opportunity to turn an old spruce budworm research station into a functioning wilderness school was a grand adventure in creativity. Housing, an industrial kitchen, a dining hall, outhouses, trips food, and equipment facilities all had to be made serviceable.

Housing was particularly fun to create out of existing buildings: the icehouse, a large two-hole outhouse, storage sheds, and of course Wendell Beckwith's snail-shaped sauna. With meager resources we learned to be resourceful and innovative, if not always entirely legal. There were a few sinks and light fixtures that owe their plumbing and wiring to materials scavenged from abandoned logging camps and dumps.

How many of us learned to use power tools and service vehicle engines, trailers, and the old diesel generator? How many learned to cook, even as grand as a three-course banquet for eighty people in a tiny kitchen, where the nearest grocery store was over sixty miles away in Nipigon? How many learned carpentry? Repairing aluminum and fiberglass kayaks and canoes? And plumbing! So many skills were gained through the tutelage of people like Rick Tait and Rob Linscott, our two multiskilled site managers. Both were excellent course instructors as well as wonderful teachers of all kinds of practical skills. Homeplace ran autonomously in a very remote location, and whatever crises arose had to be dealt with by whomever was in camp.

Instructors and other workers came (and went) for various reasons, and many found inspiration from working at COBWS that led to lifelong pursuits. There was Daniel Vokey, a deep thinker who went on from his COBWS time to reflect upon his experiences and complete a doctorate in the philosophy of education, which examined in enormous depth the question "What is a value?" As a result, his work has contributed to the field of values education.

Ruth Goldman and Louise Karch went on to graduate school and pursued questions that arose from the Women of Courage program that they collaborated in creating at COBWS. From my own experiences using singing with women on those courses, I too spent a number of years understanding the role of music in healing, learning, and growth and how, collectively, we use music to build community—all stemming from my experiences at COBWS.

A key person was our energetic, mercurial head cook, Bertha Bumchuckles (born Cindy Butcher, now known as Ginger Mason). She worked with everyone who came through Homeplace and lived there basically year-round for several years. The dining hall was the social hub (and heart) of Homeplace. Bertha had endless patience with all the people who helped cook and clean. She reigned with patience, humor, a high level of organization and logistical skill, and extraordinary culinary talent. I'm told she chose the name Bumchuckles after adopting a vegetarian diet heavy in beans, bulgur, and pulses.

* * *

Many people gave of their talents far beyond what was required to run courses. I often reflect on the Outward Bound philosophical pillar of craftsmanship and think that we exemplified that in so many wonderful ways. People brought many gifts that were generously shared. Over a number of seasons, Lynn Peplinski hosted clothes-making sessions for outdoor gear to make it affordable and appropriate to the conditions of a northern climate. John Martin (aka Jean-Luc Martin) was a rock climbing lead instructor, and his growing interest in acrobatic clowning became a much-loved recreational pastime for a number of staff. Jean-Luc later went on to become a full-time acrobat with the world-famous Cirque du Soleil.

Lorne Tippett was a multitalented instructor with a passion for art. His artwork has appeared in numerous school publications and on bandanna designs, and it even adorned the sides of the yellow school bus used to transport students, canoes, and expedition equipment. Lorne's illustrations grace this publication. He now works as a stained glass artist.

Matty McNair's appreciation for Anishinabe pictographs, found painted on cliffs in various locations north of Lake Superior where brigades traveled, led her to paint reproductions of these images on the walls of the dining hall. As Matty prepared to do an extensive Arctic journey by dog team around Baffin Island, Nunavut, she designed and made polar clothing and gear for Arctic dogsledding with fan hitches and an Arctic-style sled called a komatik. Following this expedition with husband Paul Landry and fellow staff Rosemary and Geoff Murray, Matty, Paul, and their children, Sarah and Eric, relocated permanently to Iqaluit, Nunavut, where the whole family built careers as polar explorers and expedition leaders.

There were many more people who went on to make contributions in extraordinary and creative ways, inspired by their associations with people in the community in those early years and supported by long friendships.

Professionally and personally, the impacts of COBWS have been deep, extensive, and long-lasting. Collaboration with other instructors resulted in highly creative courses, as we learned how to capitalize on our different strengths and support one another in addressing our growing edges with compassion, courage, and humility. I learned lifelong lessons about starting with people where they are, listening and looking for the gifts they bring to a group, and engineering teachable moments for individuals to discover their own capacities for living an authentic life. I also learned the essential need for creating and maintaining an emotionally safe space for people to work, especially when the challenges are stressful and people are pushing their own limits.

Stretches of off-duty time for personal and professional growth were another gift of the remoteness of the community. With nowhere else to go, we were able to take personal trips to push our own skills and knowledge. An expression often heard was, "We get good judgment by doing things we wouldn't have done if we had good judgment." We used these opportunities to take risks that would result in better judgment. We had all the equipment (and leftover trips food) at our disposal and the very best companions for adventure. We had time to talk, debate, and challenge each other in our thinking as educators. This was possibly the most fertile period in my life.

Inclusion and Influence
Philip Blackford

Only connect! That was the whole of her sermon. Only connect the prose and the passion, and both will be exalted, and human love will be seen at its height. Live in fragments no longer.

—E. M. Forster, *Howards End*

By the mid-1980s, COBWS's reputation was spreading. Some of the school's original guiding lights were either gradually pulling back or had already moved on. Others, though, were being drawn to the school because of what had been created.

When Ian Yolles became executive director, the program expanded and diversified dramatically. By the late 1990s, our student base had grown tenfold. But more importantly, the program had become far broader and more inclusive. By then, more than a quarter of our work was in our Community & Health Services Programs,[1] and as I remember Ken Victor pointing out, the participants in our Professional Development Program (known then as the Centre for Change) were far more reflective of Canada's diverse population than our open enrollment students or, at the time, the staff itself. When Hepsi Barnett and Terry Swan arrived (in 1985 and 1990, respectively) and quickly took on leadership roles, they not only helped us establish trust and credibility within the Indigenous community but also

---

1. COBWS's Community & Health Services Programs included:
    Giwaykiwin—Indigenous participants
    Youth Challenge—at-risk students
    Women of Courage—women who had experienced violence
    Access to Adventure—participants with known disabilities

had a significant impact on the school at large. They influenced how we saw ourselves and how, in turn, we were seen in the broader community. The following are three very short stories from this chapter in COBWS's history.

COBWS was always a welcome guest at Outward Bound USA National Safety Committee meetings. At one meeting, Wendy Talbot presented our most recent incident and accident statistics, using a form we had redesigned to include emotional safety protocols (ESP).[2] When she was done, there was total silence in the room. Finally someone said, "Boy, it sounds like you folks are dealing with some tough stuff up there." Thankfully, a couple of staff from the North Carolina Outward Bound School delicately helped make the point that the reason other North American schools weren't yet reporting ESP incidents was because they weren't looking for them.

The opportunity to earn high school credit was a way to involve young people who might not otherwise consider or be able to afford a course (including Youth Challenge and high school retention students). In 1988, Bob Couchman (who chaired our program committee at the time) led a group of staff and volunteers in the development of a thirty-two-page curriculum document tied to the Ontario Ministry of Education's new personal life management course. The final step in approving the curriculum and accrediting the school involved an inspection of the program by a Ministry of Education official. The fellow chosen to conduct the review didn't say much on the drive up from Thunder Bay, but did spend four or five hours touring Homeplace and talking in depth with staff and students. The guy was even quieter on the drive back to town, until about halfway down the Black Sturgeon Road he slapped his thigh and shouted, "Shit!"

When I asked what was wrong, he explained that he had grown disenchanted with his work and with the direction of education in general over the past few years—so much so that he had pretty well given up altogether and

---

2. Emotional safety protocols (ESP) are ways of interacting that acknowledge the potential to feel unsafe emotionally as well as physically. Themes include active listening, accepting personal differences, promoting challenge by choice, and respecting personal boundaries.

was just counting the days to retirement. When he had climbed into the van that morning, he hadn't thought there was a hope in hell he would approve the program. However, what he had seen and heard at Homeplace had shaken him. We had renewed his faith in education, and he was struggling to integrate the shift in perspective. We were approved.

In 1995, the Outward Bound Trust in Rugby, England, was forced to undergo a major restructuring, and because the Outward Bound trademark resided with the trust, Outward Bound International (OBI) was worried it would be at risk if the reorganization was unsuccessful. Consequently, Bill Phillips, the chair of both OBI and the international advisory board, "undertook to find a new home for the Secretariat."[3] The two largest and most powerful Outward Bound organizations at the time were Outward Bound USA and Outward Bound Australia, and both wanted to bring OBI into their organizations. However, many of the other thirty-plus Outward Bound member countries around the world weren't happy with the idea of either of them having control.

By this point in our evolution, COBWS had developed strong, respectful relationships (even formal mentorships) with a number of the other schools. Our reputation for inclusivity, innovation, and consensus was also widely established, in part due to our participation at international Outward Bound gatherings and conferences (including Cooperstown in 1988, Aberdovey in 1991, and Hong Kong, China in 1994). So we invited Phillips to spend a few days at Homeplace to see if there was a way Outward Bound Canada could help. It was a short but fruitful visit: Five months later, OBI set up shop in Vancouver with Outward Bound Western Canada, which generously offered to share office space, and Bart MacDougall (a member of the Outward Bound Canada board of trustees) stepping into the role of volunteer treasurer.

When I moved into the Toronto office on a full-time basis, I started a rainy-day paper file. It was for special notes and letters from people thanking us for their course or for their child's or client's course, or for helping them or their organization in some other way. I used to pull the file out when I was feeling

---

3. Outward Bound International, 1996 Annual Report.

discouraged or somehow disconnected from what we were working so hard to achieve. It always made me feel better. When I left COBWS in the fall of 1998, the file was several inches thick.

I think about what was created on the shores of Black Sturgeon Lake in 1976 as being like a spectacular loaf of sourdough bread. Everyone who experienced COBWS came away with a nub of starter dough. Every time a fresh loaf is made from one of those nubs, a little something new is added. That initial loaf fed a lot of people. It's feeding people still.

Reflections

Juliet Westgate (Duff)

So much more than a typical Outward Bound school, Homeplace was for me a beautiful place immersed in nature where a wonderful group of adventuresome, talented, and skilled people worked and played, stretched their capacities, and eventually learned to cocreate a community that became much more than the sum of the parts. After each season I would leave Homeplace feeling more whole and fulfilled than when I had arrived—and it was so much fun!

Students and courses, staff, experiential education, consensus, group process, active listening. Wendy Pieh and fellow head honchos facilitated the expansion of our personal and professional potentials by using a holistic, dynamic process that we all invested in to keep us as healthy, effective, and happy as we could be. It was up to each of us to do our part; everyone was included, and we were going to make it as beautiful and radiant as we could.

Giving the highest quality experience to our students was our raison d'être, and I have no doubt that the vast majority of our students expanded beyond their expectations due to the extraordinarily resonant school that was COBWS. Ahead of its time, it was subtly about raising consciousness, for both the individual and the collective.

There is a much broader vocabulary to capture some of the less-defined concepts that flourished there. I think love—nonpersonal and unconditional—was the key component at a time when it was not so experienced, or even comprehended, in most people's realities.

A spirit of oneness extended beyond the human domain to our environment—animals and plants (Gaia)—and gave me a euphoric experience of being at one with all that is.

We had the freedom to stretch our potential as part of staff enhancement activities. This required trust from the head honchos, and I deeply appreciated and respected that. Not only did it enhance my own skills and abilities but it also integrated and committed me at a deeper level into the whole experience. I remain grateful for the expanded understanding of leadership that it instilled in me.

Experiential education and group processes (debriefing, active listening, consensus) were the bases of the courses we ran and the life we lived there. Effective staff training instilled these values, along with other useful skills, and it was no mean feat, as it was so different from the education model of the day.

These were the key foundations. It took so much more energy than just orchestrating or teaching Outward Bound courses. In my experience, COBWS was unique in succeeding so well in this endeavor.

I have a plethora of wonderful memories from those days that have served me well in life. Going out on a three-day fasting solo in the nearby wilderness was always a highlight during a summer season there. Taking very little with me, I could experience melding into one with nature. This truly was an exceptional possibility offered to everyone at COBWS.

The camaraderie and oneness, within a caring and dynamic community, served a higher purpose. And we were doing it highly effectively and having so much fun. There was so much to learn from such an exceptional group of open-minded and openhearted, generous colleagues.

Homeplace was a place where all the *sy-* words could manifest. Synergy, syntropy, symbiotic relationships, and synchronicity abounded and were part of our teachings about life, for the school was grounded in a higher consciousness than most people experience in their worlds. A place where things just seemed to come together and work in harmony, possibly despite ourselves.

The setting was magical—in the wilds of Canada's North.

Sending these reflections with love, big hugs, and heartfelt thanks to all of you who shared a slice of life at COBWS.

Fire Evacuation

Charles Luckmann

Fires nearly destroyed Homeplace during unseasonably dry weather following the May 18, 1980, Mount Saint Helens eruption. Without the usual rainfall, dozens of fires raged throughout northern Ontario.

I don't remember exactly when the fires crossed the Canadian Northern Railway tracks, forcing the evacuation of the small community of Armstrong, but I do remember that three days before students were expected to arrive for the July program, Ontario authorities ordered us to evacuate Homeplace. We were asked to leave in one hour even though it was almost dark. We could smell smoke, and some people said they saw flames in the distance.

In a rush, we sank aluminum canoes in the lake, loaded equipment and food into every available vehicle, said a couple of prayers, left a few amulets, and drove in a long, dusty caravan into the night down Black Sturgeon Road to the rock climbing site, a few miles north of Hurkett and Highway 11, where we piled the equipment and food and pitched our tents for the night. At the time, I thought I might never see the buildings at Homeplace again.

The next morning, at first light, I drove to Highway 11, and from a phone booth at the Dorion Inn & Store, I called Alistair McArthur, the school director, and told him the news. He paused for a very long moment before asking, "Can we run the courses?"

I told him our course area was closed, our equipment in a heap, and we had no base of operations to receive students.

"We can't refund the money," he said. "We've already spent it. We'll go tits up for sure this time. The school phone is ringing bloody awful—the fires play every night on the television screens, and people are worried about safety."

Alistair also was worried the public would not tolerate another outdoor program disaster. He cited the Saint John's School of Ontario, remembering when thirteen died from hypothermia two years previously, in June 1978, when their canoes capsized in a windstorm on Lake Timiskaming.

"If we can't guarantee reasonable risk and safety, we close the school," Alistair emphasized.

Trying to offer a glimmer of hope, I told Alistair, "Let's see what the staff have to say. Let me confer with them before you cancel the July courses. I'll get back to you in a couple of hours."

Alistair agreed, but he said we needed to decide within twenty-four hours. The July courses were to start in two days—our situation looked bleak. I drove the several long miles back to where everyone was eating breakfast and playing Hacky Sack. Really? Playing Hacky Sack? This impressed me, how nonchalant they were with our situation.

Everyone gathered around. I summarized my phone conversation with Alistair and then asked, "Can we meet students in forty-eight hours and run safe Outward Bound courses?"

The consensus was, "Hell yes!"

Someone suggested we contact Lakehead University in Thunder Bay to see if they had space for us. Someone else suggested we contact MOBS for emergency assistance. Maybe they would let us use their program area— the Boundary Waters Canoe Area (BWCA)—on the American side of the US-Canada border, not far from Thunder Bay.

Lakehead University quickly agreed to allow us use of their gymnasium as our base of operations. Within six hours we were there, sorting equipment and food. The time was frenzied but also joyful.

I remember Tentfly (Rick Cotter), trips equipment manager, walking around the gym with his inventory sheet and ubiquitous smile. The pay phone outside the gymnasium became our twenty-four-hours-a-day emergency center. Someone always slept nearby. That night everyone else slept on the gym floor.

I had phoned Alistair and told him we could safely run our July courses. "Bring on the students," I said. "We'll use the BWCA as our staging area, which MOBS agreed to share with us."

When the July students arrived in Thunder Bay, they were soon on their way to the United States for their Outward Bound experience, the fire a hundred miles away. A yellow school bus and several blue vans carried scores of anxious and excited students south to the US-Canada border and beyond. The vehicles towed canoe trailers with paddles and life jackets. Duluth packs filled with food, tents, sleeping bags, and other camping supplies were loaded in the storage racks atop the bus and vans. We were tired but walking on clouds. We had accomplished what appeared undoable a couple of days earlier.

The school survived the 1980 fires. For the August and September programs, we returned to Homeplace, which now felt even more special to all of us.

The attitude of our community saved the school from bankruptcy, not only in 1980, but in subsequent years as well. The power of positive thinking was evident. Our collective action to give our best to the world and each other was more powerful than a fire—which miraculously had stalled a mile from the school (prevailing winds had shifted by 180 degrees).

What Made COBWS Unique

Ian Kilborn

I went to school to be an engineer. I worked for five years in my first job in the nuclear industry. Sensing that I needed a big change in culture and values (and fun), I left my job in the late 1980s, was lucky to be hired by Paul Landry based on my technical outdoor skills, and came to Homeplace. I learned so many life-changing things there in a short period of time.

COBWS was much more consensus-based than anyplace else I'd been, and I learned the true meaning of consensus decision-making. There was a hybrid model—some decisions would be made by consensus alone, some by leadership after soliciting input—but when done properly, it was transparent and we could see the process.

Another thing that made the COBWS culture unique was experience working with confident and capable women. There were so many strong women. Interactions with them informed my relationships with women for the rest of my life. Attitudes that many men my age are just now starting to grapple with and understand were taught to me by these women way back then.

I have never duplicated the sense of community that I felt at COBWS. People were genuinely caring. People authentically reached out to me, a new hire from a different background. I felt supported and cared for. The COBWS version of community remains the standard by which I measure all other communities. When I can influence my current communities a little bit, I do it with values and wisdom I learned from COBWS.

I've never owned a digital calendar or organizer that could show the whole picture of a complex logistical operation as well as the big board at Homeplace, with its calendar dates, cardboard cutouts of vans representing drop-offs and pickups, and so much more. Brilliant! Just like the people who created it.

Women of Courage

Ruth Goldman

Dedicated to, and in memory of, Diana Meredith (March 25, 1954–January 27, 2018), first Women of Courage (WOC) instructor, COBWS cook, instructor, mentor, and beautiful woman sorely missed and loved by all.

> *We will laugh again and be whole again; and in time,*
> *we will be the person we have always been inside.*
>
> —Cathy Price, WOC Alumnus 1988

Why Women of Courage? Violence against women is perpetrated against the body, and while emotional and psychic healing are essential, reconnecting with the physical body, making oneself whole again, can be incredibly powerful and a crucial part of the healing process. Women of Courage courses were designed to support the final stages of a woman's therapeutic journey of self-recovery and growth. As the old brochure articulated, the courses were a time "for participants to explore perceived limits and expand capabilities, and for each woman to experience her physical self as strong and competent."

How did WOC come about? The courses were initiated in 1987 by Philip Blackford, COBWS's director of program development, in close consultation with Family Service Toronto, which was looking to augment its group therapeutic work with women survivors of violence. It was initially called the Violence Against Women program. Counselors from partner agencies accompanied the eight to ten participants on the courses, all of whom had successfully completed a therapeutic program. Later there would be courses without counselors, and finally, open enrollment programs for any woman who identified as being a survivor of violence. To our knowledge, COBWS was the first to initiate such programs but not the last.

What did it take to become a Woman of Courage? First of all, one had to sign up. This, in and of itself, was often a feat. Most women had never camped in the outdoors or traveled in the wilderness. Many had to overcome the legacies of abuse—depression, anxiety, chronic illnesses—and the stresses of everyday life, often leaving behind young children to embark on a seven-day wilderness journey. Social service agencies encouraged and promoted the program, but it was the inner strength of individual women that had them saying yes to the unknown and making their own healing a priority.

For women who have experienced violence and criticism in their everyday lives, opinions and put-downs often frame how they see themselves. On a seven-day trip in an environment of complete acceptance, immersed in the beauty of nature, with the slow movements of water, sun, rain, and wind, women were offered a break, a crack in their lives to breathe, to put their shoulders down, to be themselves, or as one woman put it, "To be the people we've always been inside."

The classic Outward Bound course was modified, with shorter routes, more time for individual check-ins, and typically, longer daily debriefs. Yet the core components were the same: canoeing, portaging, rock climbing, solo, and camping. Hoisting five Grumman canoes and gear to the end of the portage; climbing a rock face and trusting a belay partner; spending every night in a tent sardined among two or three other women—facing fears and overcoming obstacles transformed negative self-perceptions into celebrations of self.

On a WOC course, some of the simplest tasks were the hardest. One participant was terrified of water; she could not swim and feared drowning. At the start of the course, she refused to get in the canoe. With coaching, and with the group's support, she inched her way to the canoe's bow and picked up a paddle. One stroke: A milestone was achieved. On day six, after her solo experience, she decided to immerse herself chest deep in the water; she put on her life jacket, held a rock, and slipped into the water.

Most telling was the way participants looked at the end of the course. Physically transformed, their faces were softer and more open, their shoulders down, and their steps more confident. In seven days, the program offered respite, tools, learning, community, and support, enabling these women to discover who they were and what they were made of.

Every course component was amplified in intensity on a WOC trip. The seven days typically felt like seven weeks given the excitement, stress, and ferocity of emotion. Activities that were usually uneventful on regular Outward Bound courses became unexpected moments of joyful celebration. On one of the few courses to take place at Homeplace, a paddle through the culvert (a long, low steel tunnel) at the north end of the lake became an experience of rebirth, with loud shouting and singing as every woman hooted and hollered while pulling themselves through the culvert, some even crying with exhilaration. Conversely, ho-hum activities could quickly turn into crises, with emotions running out of control and women feeling triggered by water, lightning, or the confined space of a tent.

The rappel was always the crux, metaphorically and physically. The transformative moment was when women stepped off the edge, into trust and into themselves. Sometimes it took moments, and many times hours. After four or five days of paddling, camping, portaging, pooping in the woods, and often deep and moving campfire conversations, some women were already fearless and ready for the moment; others needed a little more time, a bit more confidence, another summoning of courage.

Singing also became an incredibly powerful component of a WOC course. "Finding your voice," "giving voice," and "breaking silence" are all embedded in therapeutic language that addresses violence and abuse. Singing is risky; it requires confidence in oneself and faith that the rest of the group will join with you, no matter how good you are. It requires withholding judgment and leaning into the joy and release of voice. The women took on singing with full-on voices and a delight in making music together as play and as deep expression.

It doesn't matter what the song is; the act of singing takes courage, and once you have experienced that glorious feeling of making something beautiful from your own flesh with the support of others, it has a deep and lasting impact. The song is a safe container; it has a beginning, middle, and end. In a group, it is both an individual act and a collective act, and everyone together is creating something they could not do alone. People feel a sense of us-ness, and for women who have been abused, silenced, and isolated from supportive family and friends, this can be part of a healing experience.

On one course, a woman was stuck at a crux on a climbing wall—piano fingers and shaking legs. As her energy was draining and she was clearly frustrated to the point of being distraught, she called down to her belayer (a fellow participant with staff backup) and asked if anyone who was free could sing out the lullaby that the group sang every evening. Voices rose across the climbing site. She gathered herself, gave a roar, swung out to grasp the hold that had eluded her, and scrambled up the climb to the top. Once back down at the bottom, exhausted and emotional, she expressed her gratitude amid tears, and everyone at the cliff was changed a little bit in that sweet moment of her success.

As instructors, WOC courses were a gift to ourselves and to the greater endeavor of our collective consciousness as women in a world that is not always kind to us. Just as each participant's gifts were honored and celebrated, we instructors leaned into our own strengths, and these were often the most magical and powerful parts of a course. We learned from each other and from the participants, and like all courses at COBWS, each of us brought something uniquely a part of ourselves—our superpower—as well as our own fears and hopes.

As instructors grew more experienced and built up a legacy of WOC wisdom, we discovered that simple activities such as singing, laughter, silence, holding hands, or an elementary art exercise could elicit important growth or help transform a challenging moment. As an example, the traditional solo was occasionally modified into quiet reflection time, as the early instructors instinctively knew that a night alone was beyond a reasonable challenge for some women and could even feel abusive. The reflection time could be done alone or in pairs, and some women requested to stay in camp, as instructors endeavored to make the time meaningful for a range of needs. One woman even referred to the anticipated quiet reflection time as "getting the silent treatment." Creativity, flexibility, and listening to the women were our guiding principles.

We also came to realize that who we were as women instructors—how we held our bodies, exuded confidence, celebrated our strength, took up space—was an essential part of the course, as were our relationships with each other and with the women in the group. There was an intentionality and deliberateness in every aspect of the course and our relationships with each other, as well as with the social workers who accompanied some groups and were also having their own Outward Bound experiences. As instructors, we universally found these courses deeply moving, incredibly challenging, and requiring levels of emotional and facilitative skills well beyond any courses any of us had ever worked. They were always the most rewarding of Outward Bound experiences and the most exhausting.

WOC also had a profound impact on the COBWS community at large. Such a deep dive into women's experiences of violence—physical and emotional—does not leave a community or the instructors untouched. Women at COBWS began reframing their own feelings about of a range of misogynistic experiences. Trainings were done at COBWS to make staff aware that participants on all courses could be survivors and that we had a duty to create safe environments, especially when it came to issues with other students. COBWS staff were also invited to other Outward Bound schools to offer trainings on sexual assault and working with survivors of violence.

To my knowledge, Outward Bound never did an evaluation of the program; however, I know that several master's theses and papers were inspired by the program, including my own. In 1994, I completed a final project that involved qualitative analysis—using participatory research and grounded theory practices—of interviews I conducted with WOC alumni. I demonstrated that therapeutic milestones, as articulated by feminist theory of the time, were achieved during the seven-day program, as expressed by the women.

No one helped articulate and inspire us as WOC instructors more than Diana Meredith. She urged the formation of this program, consulted on the early design, instructed the first and many of the early courses, and most importantly, mentored and supported many of us as instructors. She helped us manage and put into context the power and liberatory act of Women of Courage.

Many thanks to Sandra Van Ruymbeke, (Victoria) Moon Joyce, and Sheila D'Amore for their encouragement and contributions to this essay.

Women of Courage Program Is the Opposite of Abuse

Louise Karch

Abuse is a profound violation of safety. WOC programs put safety first, always. When abused, women have little power or control. WOC programs support challenge by choice. Choice equals empowerment. *No* is celebrated as much as *yes*. When a woman who has been hung from a twelfth-floor balcony starts to rock climb, she is facing and reducing the past's hold on her life. Each step, whether she reaches the top or not, is celebrated. Healing can happen in a single tears-streaming-down-the-face, rapid-sewing-machine-leg-pumping, brave step on a craggy rock face.

With violence, when a woman says "Stop," the perpetrator doesn't care. WOC programs are highly responsive. When a woman asks to be rescued, like from a high ropes course, it happens, and it happens quickly. A rescue is done with compassion and without judgment. Asking for help is heroic. WOC provides power in the present, which gives hope for the future. Put that on a T-shirt!

With abuse, experience and meaning-making are violently separated. Whether children, teens, or adults, some survivors dissociate to cope. Being able to detach from horror is a helpful mechanism. It temporarily severs the connection between the body and mind. WOC programs are the opposite. WOC programs are embodied. Program instructor Ruth Goldman explains:

> Ultimately, abuse happens to the body. WOC is about deliberately moving women into their bodies so they can experience pleasure, the "good" pain of a hard day's work, the taste of food, getting dirty, and doing physical things that never seemed remotely possible. Through the power of the body, women make many other connections. Participants come face-to-face with

fears, take control, lose control, and all within the emotional and physical safety of the course. Women are most taken with the strength and "body-ness" (and bawdiness) of the instructors. The positive ripple effect of WOC can be seen as concentric rings with the woman's body at the center, moving out through emotional energy, then to the mind and spirit. The integration is huge, but it begins and grows out of the connection to the body. After all, for many survivors, the loss of bodily self is one of the most alienating aspects of abuse.

Abusers silence. Shame is the result. In abusive environments, many topics are taboo. In society, talking about violence against women is taboo. WOC participants are free to talk about anything, or not. Like all courses, women are invited to speak about their Outward Bound experiences, to think about what they mean, and to contribute their insights. Reflection happens privately in journals, one-on-one, on solo, and more publicly during group debriefs. Reflection is designed to deepen women's insights. Whether using Kolb's learning model or the simpler "What happened? So what? Now what?" women are asked, "What does this mean to you? How do you see yourself now? Who are you becoming?" Conscious processing helps women make meaning in the moment. It reconnects their bodies, minds, and hearts. On WOC courses, processing is the protocol. Pride is the result.

While the media has made post-traumatic stress disorder (PTSD) well known, the surprisingly more common phenomenon is post-traumatic growth, according to Martin Seligman, author of *Flourish: A Visionary New Understanding of Happiness and Well-Being*. To maximize growth and minimize trauma stressors, WOC instructors understand that the choice to disclose trauma belongs to the woman. Only she knows what constitutes a safe and sensitive environment for her disclosure. Creating opportunities for processing that allow for reflection without any pressure to share is paramount. This gives women power over a realm where they were formerly powerless. Lorraine Greaves, coeditor of *Making It Better: Gender-Transformative Heath Promotion*, suggests this choice be instilled as a trauma-informed best practice.

Abusers set women up for failure. Life is unpredictable, and information is withheld. Women are exhausted by the constant vigilant monitoring of their worlds. Fear of change, violence, and betrayal are constant, unmanageable forces. WOC courses set women up for success. WOC instructors explain what is happening and what will happen. Knowing what is coming is comforting. When women get triggered, as they inevitably do, instructors (and we also had counselors on courses) help women process what comes up so they can name it, reframe it, claim it, and continue.

Abuse is power over others. WOC facilitates power from within. Abusers make sure women never know whether they are doing the right thing or the wrong thing. Women are made to feel that they are making mistakes or that they are a mistake. WOC courses value each woman, period. Instructors know mistakes are the price you pay for progress. When women zigzag from one side of a river to the other as they learn their J-stroke, they are never criticized or condemned, ever! I will always remember one woman's reaction to being allowed to learn without judgment, blame, or shame; my afternoon of patience and lack of anger were astounding to her. She had never experienced that in her life. WOC provides judgment-free learning, which fosters competence and accomplishment.

Abuse makes a woman's world small. Partners often limit and control social connections. Isolation fosters depression and anxiety, helplessness, and despair. WOC courses create community. Members of this survivor clan share a unique bond. They discover they can achieve more than they thought possible because of the group, and they have fun along the way. WOC provides opportunities for women to reestablish trust, build relationships, and start to dissolve doubt.

When abused, a woman's very skin can be a battleground. The external natural world is inconsequential. With abuse you look away. With WOC courses you look closer. Women find themselves in the middle of the wilderness, face-to-face with nature's power and beauty. I remember stopping and pointing out the tiniest green tree frog, a new bloom of an almost hidden wild orchid, and a turtle laying its eggs on a riverbank portage. Being in the now means not being consumed by the past or fearing the future. Japan's Dr. Qing Li, author of *Forest Bathing*, calls this *forest therapy*. We didn't have that expression in the 1990s; however, our First Nations elders may have said being with Mother Earth and Father Sky is healing. WOC courses give the gift of the present moment.

Abuse is the opposite of equality. WOC courses are predicated on equality. One person is just as valuable and important as another. Statements of racism and homophobia and any form of inequity are recognized as opportunities to discuss and embrace inclusiveness. Not always easy or comfortable, but absolutely necessary for this living lab of equality.

Abusers don't care about women's stories. WOC knows your story matters, and this course is the turnaround chapter. It was cliché in the 1990s to say, "From surviving to thriving," but dear reader, that's what it was all about! Women wrote letters from their best WOC selves to their future selves. Their letters were mailed back six months later. The WOC program was seen as an intentional catalyst for growth and an opportunity for women to reclaim their lives, their full lives: powerful, purposeful, joyful, and exuberant. I remember one woman saying, "WOC was like vitamins for the soul."

Sometimes abusers want women dead, literally or metaphorically. Their abuse is exhausting. WOC programs are curated to maximize impact without draining a woman's vitality, which is often already compromised. Time is set aside to reflect, process, and play. The canoe routes are not as arduous as those in standardized courses. That's because the emotional lives of participants add a rich dimension that require instructors' attentiveness. There needs to be time to process issues with compassion and wisdom. WOC courses teach women how to manage their vitality.

Abusers care how women look. On a WOC course, image is irrelevant. If a woman happens to look good in an Outward Bound red life jacket zipped over a yellow Outward Bound raincoat with fingerless purple gloves, blue polypro long underwear, and a Canadian Tire toque, then a collective whoop of "Look at how fabulous you look" might be spoken. Or not. There are no mirrors, makeup, or image monitoring. The only thing in vogue is fabric function. *Hot stuff* means staying warm and dry.

Abusers cultivate worthlessness. WOC courses assume brilliance. Instructors share their gifts—singing, music, comedy, photography, yoga, you name it. Instructors encourage women to share their talents. Physical stretching, massage techniques, dancing, cooking skills, watercolors—whatever they bring is welcomed. I loved doing courses with (Victoria) Moon Joyce. She is a gifted musician, and her singing provided a rich modality for healing. Research backs this up. We knew women couldn't sing and worry at the same time.

You can't laugh and worry at the same time, either. Abuse is not funny. WOC courses are hilarious. Pooing in the woods provides organic comedy.

That and farting from freeze-dried onions. I would employ comic characters in my repertoire to provide edutainment. Every time instructor Sheila D'Amore unleashed her massive guffaw, you couldn't help but feel washed anew with joy. I think it was her T-shirt that said, "She who laughs, lasts." Laughter just might be the best medicine. If there isn't laughter on a course, you are probably moving too fast.

WOC courses were some of the most meaningful work of my life. My co-instructors were role models of skill, talent, and compassion. "Powerful medicine," as First People would say. Many women would ask me why I liked doing these courses. I would point to my own scarred cleft lip and say, "Scar tissue is the strongest. What we survive gives us strengths that few people understand." But I could and did. I understood what it was to live as bravely as you could bear.

I also knew that as an instructor I had to be very careful and conscious of my role as a leader. The inherent authority in the position had to be managed with grace and thoughtfulness.

Special thanks to past COBWS staff (Victoria) Moon Joyce, Ruth Goldman, and professional editor Janet Money.

What Matters

Peter Morgan

*The best things that happen in our lives or the moments
we treasure most are those when we don't consciously
understand ourselves.*

—Ai Weiwei, artist and activist

A year or so before I was hired at COBWS, I sat in a converted barn with a dozen others who had opted to take the Outdoor and Experiential Education certificate in addition to their Queen's University teaching degree. We listened in awe as Canadian author and adventurer Jim Raffan, one of Bob Pieh's successors at Queen's, gave a slide show of a recent Arctic canoe trip down the Thelon River. After the presentation, I asked Jim how to do such a trip—it all seemed daunting, from gear to flights to skills. Jim said matter-of-factly, "Just find a group." The advice seemed commonsensical, but I thought there must be more to it than that.

I'd already been a student at Keremeos, British Columbia, the Canadian Outward Bound Mountain School. The course I took was full of adventure. We students got lost on the first immersion trip, but then so did the instructors, prompting a search. On the next trip, a student developed pneumonia. He had to be evacuated off the side of a mountain by helicopter. And there were more conventional moments. Ken Madsen, one of the instructors, epitomized what I would learn to call the "Let the Mountains Speak for Themselves" approach. The instructors trailed discreetly as we cycled through the stages of group development toward competence.

Still, the notion of being an Outward Bound instructor seemed remote.

Ian Yolles, I later realized, had a genius for hiring a diverse and motley crew—as unconventional a mix as I have ever worked with. My first bunkmate in the narrow lower cabin amid the pine trees and overlooking Black Sturgeon Lake was Eric MacDonald—some guy who'd worked at Katimavik and in northern mines before being injured in a bus accident on a quest to the Greek island of Crete, and who thought I was a blue blood.

After a couple of summers I worked a winter at COBWS. My first course was with Ian Thomson. Our immersion trip started with hours of magical skate skiing on Lake Superior and a staff ice-climbing day with Guy Lacelle, followed by a course Guy and I co-instructed. I remember we were camping out on Lake Nipigon, and I noticed Guy's Therm-a-Rest would be deflated each morning. "Leaks somewhere," he said casually. Nighttime temperatures were consistently minus forty degrees.

There was a September course with Wade Campbell in Algonquin Provincial Park somewhere amid those years. Monica Bartman sorted the logistics and support competently, and Grant Wildi led the climbing. Mostly what I remember of our drive from Homeplace to Algonquin Park was the laughter among the four of us. And Grant peeling off on his motorbike from the campsite after the day of climbing was finished. It was as if we'd witnessed Jack Kerouac's departure on Route 66.

There were also trips after the summer courses. One fall Roo Whetstone and I took a driveaway car from Toronto to Vancouver, and then I took a Greyhound bus to Moab, Utah. A week before, I'd agreed to meet Eric MacDonald, Diane Lemire, and others at the Moab post office, which none of us had ever been to, at noon on the seventh day and every day thereafter if one or another didn't show. That was in the almost inconceivable days before mobile phones. I missed the first day by an hour. Sure enough, we met the next day.

At the end of another summer, Paul Landry indulged in a staff trip down the Albany River to scout a possible course to hone whitewater skills.

Toward the end of one season, Rod Taylor suggested paddling the Back River, in the Northwest Territories, the following summer of 1986. Suddenly I had Jim Raffan's group! The next summer, six of us left Homeplace for the Back River: Bill Templeman, Pam Ramage, Rob Grant, Daniel Vokey, Peter Morgan, Rod Taylor, and me. We traded turns on a Greyhound bus and in Daniel Vokey's van. The van had three Old Town Tripper canoes on the roof, and we had over 650 pounds of food and gear in duffel bags in the baggage bay of the bus to Yellowknife.

IV. COMMUNITY

Each of these trips spins into its own stories. For instance, on the Back River, the only other group on the river that year included the singer-songwriter Gordon Lightfoot. One morning while we were breaking camp on an esker, Lightfoot paddled by, strumming and singing "Canadian Railroad Trilogy." At the end, at the mouth of the Back, our pickup was five days overdue and food was running short.

The last season I worked at COBWS, Rob Grant suggested hiking in Auyuittuq National Park on Baffin Island. He had an inexpensive film camera with him and said he would try his hand at photography. Eight months later, sitting on the ramshackle balcony of the only guesthouse in Kendari on the island of Sulawesi in Indonesia, I got a package in the infrequent mail. There was news Eric MacDonald would be visiting. And Bill Templeman had found discarded Indian music cassette tapes on the mean streets of Toronto. He recorded his stories over the jingling songs as he drove north to see his future wife, interspersing the remaining music and anecdotes with reassuring bits of *CBC News*. But most remarkably, in the post was a magazine. The cover of *Up Here* had a shot of yours truly in the pale-blue polypropylene of the day, posing in front of a vast glaciated stretch of Pangnirtung Fjord. Rob had entered his sure-not-to-win photos and won first prize.

I calculated I spent more than 180 days camped out some of those years.

It's been a long time since then, but the trips haven't stopped. Cycling the Indian Himalayas with Eric MacDonald. Paddling down the Berens River with Ian Yolles. More Arctic rivers, even the Thelon. Sharing stories with Chuck Luckmann over beers in Singapore.

But there was more. Several people have recently mentioned how determined I am. How much of who I am now is due to Outward Bound? I can't be sure. But the portion is undoubtedly significant. The simple lessons one learns with a group and a wall. Or observing the quietest or most junior member of a brigade early on proposing a solution to a problem facing a lost group and how long it takes for people to seize the advice. How many times in my career have I thought to look around the room for that insight? I think of Homeplace as a kind of utopia. But I think we were fortunate not to try too deliberately to be more than an Outward Bound school in a remote location. The mountains (and rivers) continue to speak.

I think of how our philosophers-in-chief, Daniel Vokey and Andrew Orr, applied the mysticism of William James's *The Varieties of Religious Experience* to the outdoors. I still recite *Winds from the Wilderness* quotes, like the one from French surrealist René Daumal's *Mount Analogue* about those who have been above and being able to see what is below. But even from the middling heights of my Mount Analogue, COBWS enabled me to see much more.

If we were now revising *Winds from the Wildness*, I'd want to include Ai Weiwei's words about the best things occurring when we don't understand ourselves. He continues, "Maybe that not understanding or a lack of consciousness opens the opportunity for those things to happen."

What matters? The people.

V. WINTER

Sleeping on snow under a flimsy flysheet (a large piece of plastic or nylon material) at minus thirty to minus forty degrees certainly tested the mettle of students and staff on winter courses leaving from Homeplace on Black Sturgeon Lake. How to get fresh water, cross-country ski, drive a dog team, keep warm, survive an overnight solo, and learn what and how to cook and eat at subzero temperatures were key components of the winter program.

The idea of adding a dogsledding program to a winter course was a stretch. No Outward Bound school in the world had devised and implemented a dogsledding curriculum in their winter programs before COBWS. Alistair McArthur, executive director of COBWS from 1978 to 1982, who had gained dogsledding experience on a two-year expedition in the Antarctic (1967–1968), discusses "The Evolution of a Dogsledding Program" at COBWS and how he recruited John Mordhorst as the official dog musher.

How to devise a program that would involve students in actually driving a dog team was the important question that John Mordhorst considers in "The First Winter," describing the many trials and tribulations of that first year.

Pamela Ramage-Morin, in "Winter on Black Sturgeon Lake," reminisces about the difficulties of adapting to the extreme temperatures.

In "Winter Reflections," David Thomson writes about his eight profound years on staff and provides an intimate understanding of how winter courses were taught.

OPPOSITE: *Dogsledding on Frozen Black Sturgeon Lake* by Lorne Tippett.

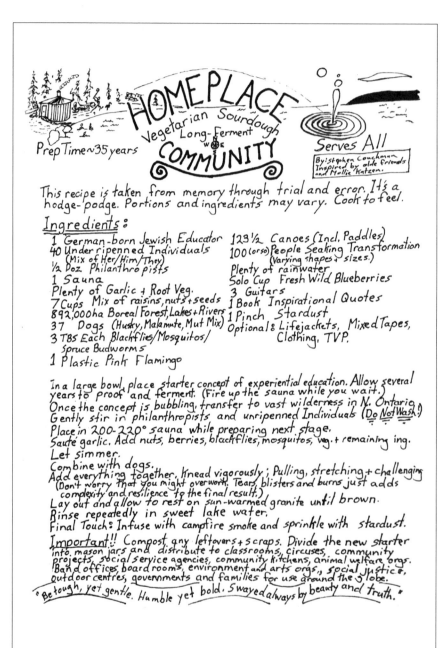

ABOVE: *Recipe* by Stephen Couchman.

Geoff Murray's "Overheard in the Dog Yard and on the Trail: Imagined Thoughts and Conversations from Sled Dogs" is a wonderful exploration of what sled dogs might say to each other when involved in an innovative outdoor education program.

In "Homeplace, Me, and Baffin Island," Paul Landry considers his ten years at COBWS and the establishment of Outward Bound courses on Baffin Island. He describes winter courses at Homeplace on Black Sturgeon Lake, the variety of activities, and how everyone adapted to living and working in an extreme environment. He also discusses his family and the impact this remote location had on his young children.

In "Sled Dogs Fly Free: Baffin Island 1987 Reconnaissance Expedition," Sara Harrison writes about Baffin Island as a potential course site and how this trip profoundly impacted her life.

Winter courses at COBWS were special and unique. In this extreme environment, safety was uppermost in the minds of staff. To the credit of everyone involved, there were no major incidents throughout the duration of the winter programs.

It was a steep learning curve for everyone involved. Staff and students were stretched to their limit from time to time. Yet the educational outcome was evident: Students learned how to adapt to winter without the buffers of modern life; they learned that camping outdoors in winter can be fun; and they participated in a mythic Canadian experience with sled dogs. —Ed.

The Evolution of a Dogsledding Program

Alistair McArthur

The idea of dogsledding with students at COBWS captured my attention immediately. It had the possibility to be a strong experience-based learning program due to the combination of humans and animals that required nurturing, resilience, skill, a potentially harsh outdoor environment, and considerable enjoyment.

In January 1978, I arrived in Toronto as the new executive director of COBWS—a new country, an unfamiliar program, new people, new environment. I had come from the Colorado Outward Bound School, which was in serious mountain country. I faced a very steep learning curve.

No Outward Bound school in the world had developed a dogsledding program. We were in new territory. We had the right ingredients: long, cold winters with plenty of snow in northwestern Ontario in the Lake Nipigon area. Cross-country skiing programs in the area had considerable appeal. We had the potential of putting together a viable dog team. Curriculum development would be ongoing.

My main concern was whether a dog team would respond to different dog drivers during the course of a twenty-three-day winter program.

I'd driven a dog team for two years in the late 1960s when I worked for the British Antarctic Survey in Antarctica. I was the base commander at Station E on Stonington Island, in charge of a thirteen-person scientific team with a focus on mapping and geological and geophysical surveys. We had over one hundred huskies, nine dog teams. I spent more than ten months in the field over two winters and two summers during 1967 and 1968.

I traveled over fifteen hundred miles with my own dog team, the Komats. Each team of nine dogs had its own driver. It took many months for the dog team to get used to a new driver. We drove the team on voice commands—turn left, turn right, start, stop, pull harder, etc. The attachment between a driver and the specific dog team was close, emotional, and bonded. Driving my own dog team in Antarctica over that two-year period was an incredible experience.

In Antarctica, each dog responded differently, depending on the driver. And each dog team performed differently too. Some teams were well-disciplined, able to travel in a straight line on a compass bearing and carry a decent load on the sled (six hundred to eight hundred pounds). Some dog teams were ill-disciplined, fought each other on a regular basis, would not respond to commands, performed poorly as the lead team, and could not carry a decent, respectable weight on the sled. Dog drivers were of mixed quality. During the two years there was much discussion about dogs, their merits, abilities, personalities, and breeding capacity.

In Canada, I was keen to see whether we could run a dog team as an educational exercise with students as drivers. I pondered whether a variety of student dog drivers could get control of the team and have an appropriate wilderness experience. I also pondered whether we could maintain the dogs through the summer, what the costs might be, and whether we could find staff willing to take on this brand-new concept of outdoor education within the Outward Bound context.

John Mordhorst had worked with me previously, in Hawaii in 1975, when I was a consultant for a new outdoor education program called Hawaii Bound. John was skilled and competent in the outdoors. He joined us at COBWS in 1978 and showed early interest in the potential of a dogsledding program. He had some experience driving a dog team on an expedition in the Northwest Territories and was keen to work with dogs at COBWS.

Through Robert Common, who had worked with Bob Pieh at Queen's University, we created the nucleus of a new dog team consisting of huskies that had originally come from Greenland, Alaska, and northern Canada. Robert agreed to loan his dog team to us as a trial for the first winter.

We had advice from experienced dog team drivers and slowly built and trained a decent team of seven dogs. We used a classic Canadian dogsled, which was quite different to the Nansen sled I had used in the Antarctic.

Dogsledding at COBWS was often in sparsely forested areas or on frozen rivers and lakes—very different from glaciers, sea ice, and the polar plateau in Antarctica.

What amazed and surprised me was that the dogs responded to various drivers and different voices. Students and staff were exhilarated with the experience of actually driving the dog team and having a close interaction with a variety of dogs. Students often would cross-country ski ahead of the dog team to break the trail for them, so navigation was much easier than my experience in Antarctica.

The terrain suited our curriculum. Students and staff slept under a rudimentary and large bivouac sheet. Temperatures around Homeplace on Black Sturgeon Lake have lows below minus twenty-five degrees; however, fierce storms and high winds are rare. In Antarctica we slept in two- and three-person, double-walled pyramid tents with rigid poles capable of withstanding extremely strong winds, blizzards, and temperatures to minus forty degrees.

John became a highly skilled manager of our first dog team. He was assisted at times by various staff members, who adapted to the idea of having animals as well as humans on our winter courses.

After considerable experimentation and trial and error, we established a stable dogsledding program that was based at Homeplace. Many staff and students had their first tastes of backcountry travel by dog team and skis. Much was learned about looking after animals and humans in a harsh and unforgiving winter environment.

The First Winter

John Mordhorst

An out-of-the-blue phone call from the father of a Barren Grounds trapper changed my life and led me to Black Sturgeon Lake in the winter of 1978–1979. This unexpected call was an offer to rent a dog team during the winter months of a canoe expedition I helped organize that crossed the Northwest Territories. Our small group of six men planned to overwinter in a cabin in the Thelon Wildlife Sanctuary. This dog team would prove to be the highlight (except for a Russian satellite, but that's another story) of our winter.

No one in our group had ever mushed a dog team . . . but so what? Six dogs and gear were flown in to our winter location with food and supplies. The trapper scribbled a one-page note of instructions that ended with, "Remember, you run the dogs. They don't run you!" The dogs were patient teachers and helped us learn—by experience.

Robert Common, one of our team, had worked with Bob Pieh at Queen's University and was familiar with the start-up of COBWS. He wrote Bob repeatedly that winter, urging COBWS to start a winter program. Robert planned to buy our dog team, transport them south, and establish a dogsledding program at Homeplace. Unfortunately, Robert's letters had lain unread in Bob's office as the school searched for a new executive director to succeed him. After not getting a response, Robert took a teaching job and brought the dog team south to his new school. Later, after Alistair McArthur was hired, COBWS decided to move ahead with a winter program, and Robert kindly lent the team to the school.

Several years earlier, I was lucky enough to have met the new executive director, Alistair McArthur, at an Outward Bound adaptive program in Hawaii. By chance, Alistair and I both landed in Boulder, Colorado, a year or so later, after I'd hatched the idea of the Northwest Territories trip.

His thoughtful guidance helped me navigate the ups and downs of planning a fourteen-month expedition.

That is the backstory for how I ended up as the musher that first winter of 1978–1979. My friendship with Alistair and my experience with Robert's dog team led to my hiring. I appreciated the many back-and-forth discussions in the Toronto office that fall. How could a dog team fit into the curriculum of a new winter program? Could the dogs adapt to being around new people in a new place? After my experience with six novice mushers in the Northwest Territories, I felt confident that the dogs could well adapt to being around new people and that we would figure out a way to effectively integrate the dogs into the winter ski expedition program.

Robert put the dogs on a train and traveled with them to Armstrong, Ontario, where he hitched them up and drove them south on the road to Homeplace. He then caught a ride with Nick the Grader to get back up north to Armstrong. I arrived via a more conventional mode of travel by flying into Thunder Bay, where I was picked up by Sheila Hendricks. Immediately we hustled around town picking up various supplies. That was my very first town run. I spent my first night sleeping on the floor of a low-rent motel and then getting introduced to breakfast at the Hoito.

That first winter seems like a blur to me now. After that fifty-mile drive up a snow-covered logging road, we found the staff busy winterizing Homeplace by stapling plastic over the windows, insulating cabins, building wood-burning stoves, punching a hole through the lake ice for water, and of course splitting firewood. I was excited to see the dogs again, who were chained to trees next to the office. In addition to Sheila, I soon met Wendy Pieh, Greg Logan, Olivier LaRocque, Greg Wiggins, and Rob Linscott. (Burt Hyde and Matty McNair also instructed courses that winter.) I was quickly accepted into the crew and joined the flurry of work.

During the first winter staff training, we explored overgrown logging roads on the east side of Black Sturgeon Lake and deemed it our course area. We broke trail through heavy snow and hacked through thick, overhanging willows. The dogs labored behind, struggling through deep, soft snow that was so different from the hard-packed snowy surface of the Barren Grounds, their former home. The dogs endeared themselves to us, as they were friendly and hardworking, each with their own unique personality and character. At night they got their one meal of the day, and then curled up in tight balls of fur to insulate themselves from the intense cold.

We had four courses that first winter. At first I was the musher in charge of running the dogs and went on each expedition. It wasn't long, though, before students took turns behind the sled, shouting commands to the dogs as if they'd been mushers their whole lives. It seemed everyone had a favorite dog and would give them lots of attention. As time went by we gained confidence and entrusted the students with the feeding, harnessing, and untangling of the traces (the dogs liked to roll on their backs during rest stops). Back at Homeplace they also scooped the poop in the dog yard. I stayed behind at Homeplace during the final course, as we had learned that instructors and students could responsibly run the dogs without the head musher being there. I remember feeling like a nervous mother sending her children off to school, as the group set off across the lake without me. Once again, however, the dogs proved to be understanding, tolerant, and capable teachers.

At the end of that first winter, Olivier LaRocque and I drove back up to Armstrong, loaded the dogs in a baggage car, and headed for Montreal. In Montreal, we rented a van and drove to Sherbrooke, Quebec, where Robert was teaching. We got in late and slept on the football field with the dogs tethered to the goalposts. Robert appeared the next morning, eager to see his dogs again. I set off hitchhiking to Toronto, wondering how we'd find a new dog team for the next winter program.

I spent the following several years developing the dog-mushing program in fits and starts. COBWS was especially hard-pressed for funds, and there was little money available to buy and outfit a new dog team. I used just about every bit of ingenuity I had to locate and train dogs, build sleds, make the traces, and somehow come up with the various components that go into establishing a dog-mushing program. We were fortunate to have had a trained dog team loaned to us for the first winter program, but after that we had to create our own from scratch.

Finding good sled dogs wasn't easy. Luckily, there were a few dog-racing kennels in the Thunder Bay area with experienced owners who were willing to help and tutor someone mostly inexperienced in developing a good dog team and dog yard. In addition, I made friends in the dog-mushing community of northern Minnesota—the Ely and Grand Marais areas. Dog racers are always trying to find and breed the fastest dogs possible. Through buying and trading with other racers, they would build up their kennels. Sometimes a dog wouldn't work out for them—too slow, usually, but it also might not fit in with the personalities of their other dogs. They can't afford to keep dogs that don't fit in.

Slowly I found some of these castoffs and they became the nucleus of our team. Nancy and Sandy came from a racer in Ely. Nancy had been trained as a leader but just wasn't fast enough. I scraped $200 together to buy her, and the owner threw in Sandy as part of the deal. We got Chip from a Thunder Bay racer. He just couldn't get Chip to run very hard. We also got Blue from him because Blue was touchy and didn't always get along with the other dogs in his kennel. I hoped I could get Chip to run harder and find an easygoing dog that Blue could tolerate running next to. I was given one dog that was fast but so skittish he was too difficult to handle. As soon as we brought this dog back to Homeplace, he jumped out of the van and refused to come close to anyone. We left food out for him, but we still couldn't gain his trust. Finally, I set up a trap for him by hanging a piece of meat from a rope hanging from a rafter in the shop. When the dog grabbed at the meat it triggered the door to close. That dog went back to his former owner on the next town run.

I learned about running dogs in tandem (side by side), which was different from the single-file system Robert's dogs had been trained in. This meant using different harnesses and traces to attach the dogs to the sled. From the racers I learned how to make the traces from hollow polypropylene rope. Some racers gave us old harnesses that we used to get by with at first. Someone donated a broken road cart to us that we repaired and used for road training in the fall. I built our first sled, modeled on a lightweight racing design. Luckily we were given a mold for creating the upturned shape of the runners. I had to learn how to steam thin, twelve-foot-long strips of oak that I'd press into the mold. They would dry into the upturned shape and then I'd glue them together for strength and durability. I found three-eighths-inch sheets of plastic that I'd cut into ten-foot lengths, about thirty inches wide, to attach to the tops of the runners to make the bed. I'd use the same plastic to sheathe the runners. The uprights and handlebar in the back were oak.

A strong steel claw was tied to the rear of the sled, which the musher stomped into the snow to anchor the sled.

The dogs endeared themselves to staff. And in typical Homeplace fashion, many folks pitched in to feed and water them, walk and exercise them, and of course scoop the poop.

We ran some very successful winter programs with dogs at COBWS, so the experiment worked.

Winter on Black Sturgeon Lake

Pamela Ramage-Morin

Winter at COBWS was a challenging but extraordinarily special time. I have fond memories of the winter I worked a course with Marge Lachecki. It was so incredibly cold that one needed to be constantly moving quickly enough to stay warm but slowly enough to never raise a sweat.

I think that it was Dave Thomson who reported that while we were on the trail the thermometer at Homeplace dipped below the lowest mark of minus forty degrees. The students were on their solos that night. Marge and I did a final check on them, who were all deep in their sleeping bags and likely wondering why they hadn't chosen a summer course, and then a final visit to check on each of the dogs. All but one were buried in the snow, curled up tightly with noses covered by tails. You know it's cold when you slide a hand down to tickle a belly and there isn't the slightest inclination to uncurl. Popcorn seemed to have given up on any hope of staying warm—he was sitting up, shaking, and looking forlorn. When we brought him into the tent, he headed directly for our sleeping bags. Marge and I spent a good night with Popcorn snuggled between us.

That was the same winter that Nahanni's eight pups were born and Marge introduced us all to puppy breath, that sweet smell exhaled by young milk-fed puppies. And Guy Lacelle came to visit. I remember him cutting wood and splitting a winter's worth of kindling. In true Guy fashion, he just kept chopping at a steady pace, relishing the work and the cold. Always on the lookout for ice, Guy took Tim Morin to a climbable piece that had formed along the gravel road to Homeplace—a first ascent of Bits, as named by Guy. Marge and I, meanwhile, started knitting mittens in the morning and were still knitting when Tim and Guy finally returned.

V. WINTER

Winter at COBWS had a way of stripping life down to the necessities: staying warm, cleaning chimneys, and keeping the fires going, then gearing up to help students share some of the magic. Caring for the dogs was a highlight. They really came into their own in the winter, with thick, healthy coats and unbridled enthusiasm for visits, meals, and being hitched up for a run. And they weren't just a pack of dogs; they were a complex group of different personalities, each with their own idiosyncrasies. What they did have in common was their generosity; the joy they offered was a huge part of the magic of COBWS in winter.

Winter Reflections

David Thomson

Now I see the secret of making the best persons; it is to grow in the open air, and to eat and sleep with the earth.

—Walt Whitman

One gift of age is being able to look back on your life journey to see and appreciate how a single decision or moment or connection decades ago profoundly affected every aspect of your life, and continues to manifest each day, and to appreciate how deeply fortunate you are that certain magical stars, in the forms of people or circumstances, just happened to align to start and guide every step of the journey. This is how I have always, and increasingly, seen my relationship with COBWS that started in 1980: not as an experience back then, but as the defining thread that has been present throughout my whole life, every day, such that I can't imagine the life I would have led without it.

My first exposure to COBWS immediately revealed two core qualities: inclusiveness and creativity. I was in my second year of studying commerce at Queen's University in Kingston, Ontario, and feeling disillusioned about the prospect of three more years of accounting, finance, economics, marketing, etc. A friend introduced me to Sue Clarry and Dave Gibson, who were studying in the Faculty of Education at Queen's and who had worked at COBWS. They graciously introduced me to COBWS founder Bob Pieh, who was a professor in the Outdoor & Experiential Education program (OEE).

Amazingly (to a nobody business student), Bob agreed to meet with me. I was hoping he would encourage me to quit commerce and make the decision for me, and I was also partly expecting a "Sorry, but you don't meet our standards." But instead, Bob had one simple, unexpected piece of advice: "Don't quit your business studies, because Outward Bound needs people like you." Bob's words threw a whole other level of possibility—and challenge—at me, which in hindsight was so in the philosophy of Outward Bound. Immediately I felt inspired and seen by Bob and impressed with the creativity in seeing how I might contribute. I tackled my studies anew, but hedged my bets with some courses in Queen's Outdoor program.

I applied to be an assistant instructor at COBWS in 1982, but was told that I was a bit too young, and instead, Ian Yolles offered me the office manager job at Homeplace that summer. Bob's advice had paid off!

Arriving at Homeplace in May 1982, I immediately saw I was indeed a youngster amid people vastly older—in their late twenties or even thirties. But what struck me even more was the incredible diversity of backgrounds, worldviews, nationalities, and sexual orientation of the other staff (racial diversity in the outdoor world in the early 1980s was very low). I had grown up in the white-bread Toronto suburb of Scarborough, so I felt like a fish out of water, and over the first summer at COBWS, I continued to have my small world exploded in so many ways. I was grateful to have as my cabinmate the amazing Bertha Bumchuckles, who welcomed "Davey boy" and blew open my whole sense of food and gender. It was during that summer that I continued to experience COBWS's inclusiveness and creativity. The office manager job took about one day a week, and program staff quickly and eagerly had me supporting students at the Claghorn climbing site, or amid the whitewater on the Black Sturgeon River, or on the ropes course, all where my real passion and experience lay.

After my first summer at COBWS, I went back to my last year of business studies. After graduation, I started working at Deloitte, one of the big global accounting firms. My office was on the sixtieth floor of a Toronto skyscraper, and the suits and corporate world were a world away from the shores of Black Sturgeon Lake and the COBWS community. It all came to a head one dreary, early winter day when the decision that would change my life became crystal clear: *This isn't for me.* Several weeks later, I was at winter staff training at Homeplace, mushing sled dogs across a frozen lake. I honestly can't remember now how that even happened.

Over the first years at COBWS, I came to appreciate my timing; it was clear the school was in a transition from its early, founding years. There were still staff around from the start of COBWS, and their stories of the creativity, hardship, freedom, uncertainty, and magic of the first few years were captivating and inspiring. I felt fortunate to get to know and learn from this amazing group at the same time as new staff like me were arriving with more traditional backgrounds and the real world was slowly creeping up Black Sturgeon Road in the form of more rules, standards, funding, technology, clear-cut logging, and so on.

It also became apparent that Homeplace was far more than a base camp for courses; instead, it was clearly a living experiment to create a home for progressive and provocative ideals around community, equality, personal growth, justice, anticorporatism, sustainability, and more, all while trying to run an outdoor school with limited money—all of which generated a dynamic tension that was always present to varying degrees. Community meetings were daylong affairs that painstakingly, and sometimes painfully, combined philosophy and pragmatism and a wide range of opinions to explore questions ranging from the roles of personal dogs or meals with meat at Homeplace to whether we should have corporate types on the COBWS board, run courses for corporations, or pay everyone the same. A series of financial crises, coupled with rapid growth and courses for underprivileged students, impelled the school leadership to beef up the capacity and role of the board of directors and form relationships with donors and corporations, decisions that weren't universally embraced. Those first few years saw a lot of changes as the school pursued more financial stability, diverse course offerings, and better pay for staff.

For me these were giddy years—with amazing new friendships formed, skills learned, and responsibilities increased. My worldview was broadened with adventure travel. Some great trips, big and small, happened: climbing trips to Minnesota, where cooking pots were beer cans over fires; traveling to Argentina with Paul Landry, Rod Taylor, and my brother, Ian Thomson, to climb Aconcagua; joining other staff at Association for Experiential Education conferences in New England and Colorado.

There were also sobering reminders of how our adventures always carried real risks, sometimes in the midst of the most exciting and powerful moments. For example, while returning from a weeklong staff trip to Madawaska Kanu in southern Ontario in a school van with kayaks and canoes on the trailer,

V. WINTER

a middle-of-the-night pee stop almost turned tragic. Somehow the parking brake didn't fully engage, and the van, loaded with sleeping staff, rolled off a steep embankment straight into a lake. Later, the police said the only thing that had stopped the van from plunging into the depths was a large rock—the only rock on the entire shore. I'll also never forget sitting in a staff training, listening to the instructors of a course several years before talking about when a young student had drowned while on solo. The impact on those instructors, the family, and everyone who had been involved was so palpable and wrenching; from that I carried forward a deep sense of responsibility for people's lives in the outdoors that still is with me today.

A winter spent working in the Everglades with the North Carolina Outward Bound school (NCOBS) deepened my appreciation for COBWS—going from sleeping in a snow cave on Lake Nipigon to sleeping on a plywood platform constructed each night on seven Grumman canoes tied together and anchored in mangrove swamps. But the biggest contrast was experiencing another base camp—NCOBS at Table Rock—and appreciating how COBWS's remoteness, newness, diversity, and commitment to intentional community made it so unique and dynamic. I left NCOBS grateful for the experience but even more grateful to be heading back to Homeplace.

The winter program at COBWS, and Homeplace in winter, was like another world but with familiar faces. Homeplace in summer was a fast-paced, ever-changing carnival of experiences: staff coming and going, visitors, large crowds (often eighty or more people), daylong community meetings, students around a lot, board members and safety inspections, many trips into town, relaxed days off, and frequent drives to Armstrong to drop off trips.

Winter, however, was an intimate, slower-paced immersion where everything we took for granted in the summer—opening a tap for water, starting a vehicle, flipping a switch for power, packing food, safety, taking off for a quick trip to town or a day off, going on a solo trip—was profoundly different and required so much more energy and attention. Pipes froze and burst on a regular basis, vehicles wouldn't start—no end of problems. I remember one fateful, frigid day when I was to pick up Geoff Murray in Thunder Bay. It took a couple of hours to warm up the car oil pan with hot coals and a generator.

Finally underway, I took a turn too fast six miles down the road and went into a ditch. In the summer, you could just wait for someone to eventually come along, but in winter the road was deserted. A long walk back to Homeplace, heating up another vehicle, pulling my car out of the ditch, and making it to Thunder Bay many hours late—this was winter at Homeplace. Nothing happened easily or quickly, and something always went wrong.

Getting ready for winter took many weeks: chainsawing ten cords of birch trees a local logger would dump in the yard, then splitting and stacking them by hand; winterizing pipes and cabins; cleaning and fixing winter gear; and putting away summer gear. As soon as the snow started to pile up, an old friend would appear: Nick the Grader, a wizened, cheerful man, who would park his massive road grader at Homeplace after plowing the road from Hurkett many hours south and drink coffee in the kitchen, filling us in on local gossip.

The sled dogs—variously known as doggies, furheads, and goofballs—were the heart of the winter program and Homeplace. They were a motley collection of mostly mutts and the occasional purebred, gleaned from mushers across Canada and the United States. Usually around twenty-five dogs, they had names like Sam and Buddy (brothers), Sandy, Blue, Chip, Pang, Perusie, Yukon Jack, Logan, Buster, Wiggins, Kopka, Kazan, Chopper, Whiskey, and Tanner. We became deeply attached to them. They were the responsibility of a head dog person—Guy Lacelle, Geoff Murray, Tim Morin, Jeff Wilson, and others—who took on incredible responsibility with a steep learning curve and little support (the closest vet was hours away).

In the summer the dogs appeared in a sorry state: thick winter fur hanging in patches off them and strewn around the dog yard, the waft of dog poop, relentless swarms of biting insects, bored faces. But each fall the homemade, wheeled training road cart (one person would stand on the back and control the steering and brakes while another would sit for ballast) would get pulled out, and in an instant the dogs' passion to pull anything elicited a chorus of excited barks and rapid circles back and forth on their chains as they all barked, *Pick me, pick me!*

Hours every day, more certainly in the winter, were dedicated to training dogs, cleaning up their shit, preparing their food and water in huge pots on propane burners outside the kitchen back door, looking after their health (worms, sores, wounds from frequent fights), and fixing their harnesses and gear and chewed-up doghouses.

V. WINTER

Feeding the dogs always presented multiple challenges. The twenty-five or more dogs needed a *lot* of food and water every day. At temperatures that could go to minus forty degrees, the mere task of boiling water and soaking or cooking food was a multihour logistical juggle. And dog food was expensive. For a while we were able to get a dog-food sponsor, which was great. But lean times called for creative approaches.

This is how the Daisy Chainsaw Massacre came to be. One of the farm families at the bottom of the road in Hurkett, whom we knew through summer service projects, called us one early winter day to ask whether we could use their dear pet cow, Daisy, who had died and was now frozen solid in their yard. Dog food! We quickly formulated a plan and were soon driving down the road, pulling the utility trailer with chainsaws and axes in hand. The very large Daisy was loaded onto the trailer by a tractor, and quite a while later we were at the end of a clear-cut spur far off the road south of Homeplace. The chainsaws (drained of oil) were soon at work, and the wisdom of our head-to-toe rain gear, helmets, and face shields became apparent when Daisy chips flew in all directions as we carved and chopped Daisy into chunks. Those chunks of Daisy were cooked up in a brew to feed the thankful furheads for many weeks.

Only in hindsight is it clear how unique the dog program was. Very few of the dogs had much mushing experience, nor did the staff, and it was a constant trial by fire. The dogs had a range of wildness, and when they were hitched to a sled it was never certain what would happen despite all the training. We always struggled to find and train good lead dogs, which were critical because the lead dog's role was to follow directions (*gee*, *haw*, *whoa* . . .) and to keep the lead to the sled tight. We had many times when a lead dog would just suddenly stop, all the dogs behind would pile up, and suddenly a full-on dogfight was at hand. This put the dogs at risk, as well as us when we waded in to break up the fight. I remember one trip when a nasty dogfight the first day left a large flap hanging off one dog's face, which we had to patch up the best we could to last for the next five days (the dog seemed much less upset than we were).

The sleds were heavily loaded with food for people and dogs, all the dog equipment, a large canvas Yukon tent with a collapsible woodstove, and tarps for sleeping under. Even though the dogsleds had a place for the musher to stand, most of the time the student musher would run behind the sled, pushing it and frequently having to wrestle it back upright in deep snow. It was exhausting.

The dogs were incredibly tough. They would pull a heavy sled all day long, helping to pull it out of snowbanks when it tipped over. At the end of the day they'd receive a bowl of warm gruel before curling up, all stretched out in a row on the cable and chains, and fall asleep in temperatures that could drop to minus forty degrees. Some of the dogs had impressive winter coats, but others were rangy mutts who didn't have an ounce of fat. After a snowy evening the dogs were nowhere to be seen the next morning, buried under snow, noses tucked under tails, but their heads would pop out of the snow at the sound of food being prepared. And then they would excitedly bark as they were harnessed for another day of pulling.

While the rawness of winter was always present, the beauty was often breathtaking: northern lights tugging a multicolored dancing mosaic across the sky; stars and constellations so sharp and clear it felt like you could reach out and touch them; frozen lakes singing their creaks and moans; a pack of wolves silently creeping close to our camp and then breaking out in a chorus of howls, making the hair on the backs of our necks tingle and the dogs go very quiet.

The physical and mental challenges of instructing in the winter were also unique: warming toes and fingers on your bare stomach and in your armpits; getting out of a sleeping bag and getting dressed in the open during a blizzard; bare hands on the dog hardware; pushing sleds out of deep snowbanks over and over; navigating tricky waterways while fearing going through the ice. And always having to look after yourself first so you had a margin to draw on if needed.

One part of every winter course that we didn't look forward to was the ice rescue simulation. Early in the course students would learn how to rescue someone who fell through the ice, and then were told there would be a real simulation sometime in the next several days. At lunch one day, near open water or a quickly chopped hole, an instructor would quietly slide away out of sight, then minutes later would start yelling for help. All hell would break loose: students running for rope, sleeping bags, pads, tarps, and other equipment. Just before the students came into view, the instructor would slide into the water and start thrashing around. The students would haul the instructor out (quickly, we fervently hoped), strip them down to their underwear (or less), and stuff them in a sleeping bag burrito with two other similarly clad students. This was always an initiation rite for new instructors.

Only looking back now can we appreciate how radical and unique those early days at COBWS were. Graduates of OEE were just emerging, and many of the staff had backgrounds as poets, blacksmiths, teachers, artists, writers, welders, Vietnam vets, or dog mushers, who also happened to have some outdoor skills and a passion for teaching and sharing a love of the wilderness. Safety technology in the form of satellite phones, emergency beacons, or even handheld radios was nonexistent. To reach someone with a medical emergency meant either paddling for a day or two or a long day of skiing or sledding. I remember a two-week winter expedition on Lake Nipigon in a howling blizzard with -112-degree windchill, feeling very far from anywhere and very vulnerable to anything that could go wrong.

Just a few years ago I had the great fortune to visit Alistair McArthur in Melbourne. He'd been the executive director my first summer at COBWS and was now an internationally recognized outdoor program safety expert. After decades working in outdoor programs around the world, Alistair said that COBWS was the most remote program anywhere; we were literally and figuratively on the edge, though at the time we just accepted it.

A hallmark of each day at Homeplace was the gathering of the whole community, including students, before dinner. Greetings were given, announcements would be made, and then we would close with the words of a poem or reading by a staff or student, often from the COBWS-published book *Winds from the Wilderness*. One reading that has stayed with me my whole life, which perfectly captures the gift of COBWS, will be familiar to many:

> *You cannot stay on the summit forever; you have to come down again ... So why bother in the first place? Just this: What is above knows what is below, but what is below does not know what is above. In climbing, always take note of the difficulties along the way, for as you go up you can observe them. Coming down you will no longer see them, but you will know they are there if you have observed them well. ... There is an art of*

> *conducting oneself in the lower regions by the*
> *memory of what one saw higher up.*
> *When one can no longer see, one can at least still know.*
>
> —René Daumal, *Mount Analogue*

Leaving the rarified peak of COBWS after eight profound years was hard and yet necessary. Not surprisingly, it was Wendy Pieh who planted the seed for what would become the next thirty years of rich work. She told me one day of Pepperdine's master's of science in organization development and encouraged me to apply. How fitting that Wendy set me on the next stage of the journey that Bob Pieh had started!

Especially now, the gifts and influences of COBWS continue to be central to every part of my life, every day: my wife, whom I met because of Outward Bound; my children's love of the outdoors; my ongoing outdoor adventures; and my deepest friendships. It is hard to imagine what my life would have been without COBWS.

Overheard in the Dog Yard and on the Trail: Imagined Thoughts and Conversations from Sled Dogs

Geoff Murray

Sam: *Oh! My favorite thing, a group of people. Gotta be a snack in someone's pocket . . . or at least someone to pee on. They sure come in all shapes and sizes, but they all smell the same, like smoke or garlic or something.*

Nancy: *It's always nice when a group of people come around. Lots of petting and talking. It breaks up the long, buggy summer days.*

Kazan: *Round and round and round I go, just moving, gotta move, gotta run, round and round and round!*

Chip: *Here they come to see me. I'll just sit here on top of my house, raise my head a bit so they can see the big, strong weight-pulling champion.*

Ten: *Chip, you were the strong one one time! Did you tell them about the time you hid in the dog trailer at Gull Bay and the trip left without you? No one noticed you were gone until they got back to Homeplace!*

Chimo: *Oh boy. Here they come to see me. I'm the true husky. They make nice with the others, but I'm the one they like best. Oh yeah, right there, right behind the ears!*

Sam: *Hey, Pretty Boy! I'm looking forward to showing you a thing or two about pulling like a sled dog. You look like a sled dog, but when they load up, who is at the wheel?*

Blue: *Please, no! Please just walk around on the other side of my circle, just— no, please don't come close, don't try to pet me.*

Ten: *What's with Sandy's square-tipped ears? Blackflies. They ate her ears. Until the people started putting pine tar on our ears, we were all getting eaten. She got it bad; the bugs squared them right off.*

Nancy: *Oh good, another group of people. How they can tell us apart I'll never know! Muddy, buggy, hungry. When is it going to snow?*

Kazan: *Finally, dinner! My favorite thing. So hungry, please more, please, please, please. Round and round!*

Buddy: *First frost! That's what we're howling about. Any day now we will move to the winter yard . . . away from these bug-infested woods, mud, roots. "Ahhwoooooo!"*

Kazan: *My favorite thing . . . the winter yard! Lots of new smells, fresh ground to make our own . . . close to the people. Not that many people here, though . . . but . . . there is the road cart. I hate that thing, I love that thing . . . daily pulling . . . my favorite.*

Sam: *Do you smell that? Coming from the dining hall? That smells gooood. Like, cooked-meat good.*

Buddy: *Snow! Now we're barking! Best! Thing! Ever! Rolling, sliding, peeing, freezing. We are into it now, boys and girls. Winter!*

Ten: *"Doggies"? Now why do they say that, like we are infants? In dog years, I'm twice their age, more trail miles than all of them. They think it's cute, "doggies." . . . Oh well, I'll put up with it. Getting visited by the humans is worth it.*

Sandy: *Oh Nancy, poor Nancy. Stupid porcupine. I thought lead dogs were smart? But really, you were the first one to get there. Full quill . . . maybe a hundred in your muzzle. Gonna be in you for a long time . . . poor Nancy!*

Buddy: *Here we go camping, group—skiers ahead! Out on the trail. Lotsa snow . . . but not too deep. Let's go! Big load to pull.*

Ten: *All right, my favorite thing, pulling out on a trip. Except . . . argh. We caught the skiers in five minutes. Waiting is not my favorite thing.*

Buddy: *Sandy, would you just stop barking!*

Nancy: *Why don't the dogs go ahead and let the skiers catch up for a change?*

Ten: *No trail. Deep snow. Love it!*

Sam: *Just a tussle. No one got hurt. Whew. People sure get worked up over a little scrap. It just looks bad, but it is not. And now it is over and done with. And Chimo had it coming. He's all pretty and no pull.*

Ten: *Ahhhhh. Paradise! Smoke from the fire, people talking nearby, big ole chunk of lard for dessert. Fresh snow to make our own. Many visits from the humans.*

Buddy: *Hear that? Wolves! Let's howl with them! Best they not visit us, though.*

Homeplace, Me, and Baffin Island

Paul Landry

There is a town in north Ontario
Dream comfort memory to spare
And in my mind I still need a place to go
All my changes were there.

—Neil Young

I took the night train to Toronto for my interview with Wendy Pieh. After an hour-long chat with Wendy, she offered me work for the summer—an intern program, assistant instructor—and given that I had some practical skills, asked if I was available in April to get Homeplace ready for the summer.

I hitchhiked across northern Ontario to Hurkett and the Black Sturgeon Road. After waiting for a couple of hours at the bottom of the road without one single car going north, I called Homeplace. Lorne Tippett answered. He was alone at Homeplace. I asked him if he could come pick me up. He told me he did not have a driver's license. I asked him if he knew how to drive, and when he answered yes, I suggested he come pick me up. Lorne and I spent the next two weeks alone at Homeplace, doing odd jobs to get the place ready for the summer, not knowing what a summer looked like there, as we had never experienced one. Wendy Talbot was next to arrive, then Greg Logan, and before long we were well into the 1979 summer staff training.

The next ten years at COBWS helped shape the person I became for the rest of my life.

* * *

V. WINTER

Winter came quickly to Black Sturgeon Lake. The dogs were curled up with their noses tucked in under their tails, as the temperature hovered around the minus-thirty-five-degree mark on a cold December night. We were standing around a blazing fire to keep warm, and I was captivated by Alistair McArthur's stories of driving dogs in Antarctica when he worked for the British Antarctic Survey. It was my first winter training at COBWS. For the next six days, Olivier LaRocque, Wendy Talbot, John Mordhorst, Alistair, and I traveled along the shores of Lake Nipigon and through the old trappers' trails on the east side of Black Sturgeon Lake, stopping at the abandoned trappers' cabins, Wahoo Lodge and Hole in the Wall.

Homeplace was busy in the summer, but in winter it relaxed and came close to hibernation. On average, six to eight staff worked the winter programs. In the early years there was one student group at a time, and as we grew we expanded to two groups. The first dog team was leased from Robert Common, and afterward we slowly built our own kennel, reaching well above twenty dogs, well cared for by devoted dog coordinators—I think that's what the position was called—John Mordhorst, Guy Lacelle, Geoff Murray, and Tim Morin, to name a few.

Skiing, snowshoeing, driving dog teams, simulated hypothermia rescues, blazing fires, smoky fires, sleeping under a nylon tarp at minus forty degrees, a hot sauna upon returning to Homeplace, hauling water from the lake to the kitchen, starting frozen vehicles to get students back to Thunder Bay, no electricity, kerosene lanterns, woodstoves . . . So many memories of a simple life with good folks on the frozen shore of Black Sturgeon Lake.

In the spring of 1986, my wife, Matty McNair, Geoff Murray, and other COBWS staff went north to Baffin Island for a dogsled expedition. They met Ken McCurry, Government of Northwest Territories regional director for the Baffin Region and a very experienced dog driver himself. He wanted to start an Outward Bound program in Baffin for Inuit youth. The following November, Geoff Murray and I flew to Iqaluit to meet with Ken and other community leaders. It was my first visit to the Canadian Arctic, and I fell in love with the place and its people. So much so that Matty and I decided to move to Iqaluit and made it our home for the years to come. Anyway, we did start an Outward Bound program in

Baffin; Geoff Murray oversaw the first year of operations. The program catered to 60 percent students from the Baffin Region and 40 percent from southern Canada. We built a cabin, found and opened a rock climbing site, and in the later years had Inuit staff work the courses. Very successful.

Matty went into labor early one spring evening in 1986. We packed up our VW van, strapped our one-year-old son, Eric, into his car seat, and headed toward the Thunder Bay hospital. Rob Linscott quietly followed us down Black Sturgeon Road until we reached the highway. I guess he did not fully trust the reliability of our VW van. We dropped off Eric with friends and checked into the hospital. Our daughter, Sarah, was born early on May 9. Eric and Sarah spent the next four years living with us adults at Homeplace. As I witnessed Eric and Sarah grow and mature into modern polar adventurers and guides, I've often thought of the impact Homeplace had on them. The formative years of their lives were spent in one of the most vibrant outdoor guiding communities that ever existed in North America.

Forty some years later, I've been asked to write about what made COBWS unique. As I write about my time with COBWS and at Homeplace, I reflect on all those special moments and memories—a few of which are noted above. But it is much more than special moments and memories. COBWS and Homeplace molded and shaped the person I am today. The interactions, debates, friendships, and work relationships with countless special people all contributed to my personal development. The leadership skills, the people skills, the technical skills, the love for the outdoors, the love for people, service to others, care for the environment, the importance of community, consensus decision-making—these are all gifts that COBWS and Homeplace bestowed on me.

But back to the question: What made this place so unique? I do think the answer is quite simple: *everyone*—staff, board members, and volunteers. We all made COBWS what we remember it to be.

So thank you COBWS and Homeplace, for giving me so much. Thank you to every one of you whom I met, worked with, and lived with while I was at COBWS and Homeplace. You have given me so much.

Sled Dogs Fly Free: Baffin Island 1987 Reconnaissance Expedition

Sara Harrison

I will never forget the spring I participated in a reconnaissance of Baffin Island as a potential course site. This shared journey remains one of the most memorable, remarkable, and personally fulfilling expeditions that I have been blessed to have been a part of. The goal of the expedition was to determine whether Baffin Island would be a good location, both geographically and culturally, for running future dogsledding programs during the months of April and May. This is the story of the staff expedition that led to the development of the first pilot Baffin Island dogsledding program the following year. This story has been supplemented with information that I gathered from Matty McNair's "Baffin 1987 Reconnaissance Report."

We departed on March 27, 1987, from Thunder Bay and flew to Iqaluit with our beloved team of five sled dogs and our outgoing, talented, fun, and experienced winter staff team members: Ruth Goldman, Matty McNair, Tim Morin, Ian Thomson, and me. We definitely had a guardian angel looking out for us from the very beginning, as we were not charged any additional fees for flying the dogs up to Baffin Island or for all the extra outdoor gear we brought along as well. When we arrived in Iqaluit, we immediately noticed how friendly and welcoming the community was; they provided us with some great government housing to stay in and an excellent nearby location for tying up our sled dogs. That evening, the northern lights were out in full force, brilliantly illuminating the night sky and making me feel that we had, indeed, truly arrived in the legendary High Arctic.

We spent one day in Iqaluit and then flew on to the village of Pangnirtung, which was the starting point for our seventeen-day, 180-mile journey to

Broughton Island. Once we arrived, we had many tasks to complete during our layover day, including cutting up seal meat to supplement the dogs' food supply. We had the opportunity to visit the village art cooperative and saw some beautifully woven wall hangings and other impressive traditional Inuit artwork. We also went to the community center to discuss and receive feedback on our intended route with community members, which was invaluable.

The first five and a half days of our trip involved traveling northeast up the Kingnait Fjord. When we departed from Pangnirtung, we initially made a fast downhill descent toward the fjord, which resulted in us needing to entirely repack our sled at the bottom of the hill due to shifting, uneven pack loads. Once out on the pack ice, we also had a close encounter with an Inuit dogsled team that was traveling in the traditional fan hitch formation, which required skillful dogsled maneuvering in order to avoid a collision. We were quickly learning new winter traveling skills! Not surprisingly, there were also a fair number of Inuit traveling back and forth along the fjord via snowmobiles. The temperature the first night was in the minus-five-degree range, but fortunately it was not too windy.

The weather was about to change dramatically the following day. Along with very cold conditions, the wind picked up considerably, resulting in complete whiteout conditions that forced us to stop early and dig in for the night in order to keep our tents from being blown away. This was one of the ongoing weather challenges we faced while traveling across the wide-open, frozen fjord terrain. On the other hand, when the wind was quiet and the sun was out, traveling along this beautiful fjord coastline with an enthusiastic team of dogs was a musher's dream come true.

One of the highlights of our travels up the Kingnait Fjord was the unexpected opportunity for Ruth and me to travel back to the base camp on Ski-Doos with Jacobee and Adam, two Inuit men who were working with us to provide food caches along sections of our route. They had set up their camp further down the fjord to be able to net arctic char at the base of a river inlet, and had already netted three hundred. They invited us into their canvas wall tent and shared tea and bannock with us.

It was a rare opportunity to have a longer conversation with Inuit men who were approximately similar in age to us and to learn about their life experiences growing up on Baffin Island. The topics we discussed were wide-ranging, and one of the most notable involved the personal and cultural trauma of being sent away to residential boarding schools at a young age, which is why Inuit communities have now insisted that there be local school options for their children. The widespread community movement for greater self-governance was a key topic that they shared with us as well. We invited them back to our camp for dinner, which included lentil chili, caribou, and arctic char. They also provided us with a generous supply of arctic char, which we happily lashed onto the top of our dogsled. The openhearted generosity of the Inuit people was once again on full display.

The most challenging and rigorous part of our expedition included the seven days spent traveling over the one-hundred-foot high barrier rise, through the Kingnait Pass, then the descent down the frozen Padle River and on to the Kangert Pass, eventually arriving at the Kangert Fjord. This involved sledding up and over very uneven terrain and frozen creek beds, then navigating down technically difficult frozen rivers, which was particularly challenging for the dogs. By this point in the trip we were about two miles away from the Arctic Circle, and it was beginning to get light by four in the morning.

To celebrate passing over the barrier milestone, we opened a gift package from Pamela Ramage that included Ovaltine, toffees, peppermint schnapps, and the *National Enquirer*. We were all very tired, but also very happy to have successfully tackled a difficult travel day. The weather we experienced continued to be extremely cold and windy, and there was little wind protection. En route to Kangert Fjord, we had to take a layover day due to high winds, blowing and drifting snow, and cold ambient temperatures that made it impossible to travel. We built snow blocks to protect our tents and keep them from collapsing. Unfortunately, the dogs kept getting completely covered by blowing snow during this blizzard. We also were experiencing the daily ongoing challenge of how to dry damp clothing caused by high physical exertion and sweating during the day. Sadly, we never did succeed in making any breakthroughs in tackling this particular problem.

The last four days of our trip involved traveling fifty miles down the Kangert Fjord, north along the Canso Channel (west of the Davis Strait), then northwest to Broughton Island. Happily, we had much better travel conditions during the last portion of our trip.

On the third-to-last day of our travels, April 14, we met up with Brent Boddy, who had been on Will Steger's dogsledding expedition to the North Pole in 1986. We hooked up our sled to his komatik, and we traveled with his friend Paul twelve miles to where they were camped at an emergency shelter. Ian Thomson and Tim Morin skijored behind us with our team of dogs. We had a great dinner together, all squeezed into the small emergency shelter.

The next day, Brent and Paul hooked up their two teams of twelve and fourteen sled dogs and gave us a lift out to a geographic point in alignment with our final destination of Broughton Island. It was amazing to see how Brent skillfully commanded his fourteen sled dogs as they effortlessly wove in and out from the fan hitch formation. This was our last full day of traveling on the ice, with good travel conditions and bright, sunny weather.

The next day, April 16, we arrived in the early afternoon at Broughton Island. There was an amazing sewing center there with incredibly finely made kamiks, traditional Inuit boots. There also was a little café with lovely soapstone carvings. We visited the community center, where there was an enthusiastic group of town girls playing volleyball.

The following day, April 17, we flew back to Iqaluit, where we were able to take our first shower after seventeen days of rigorous, sweaty travel. Now that was a heaven-on-earth experience! That evening, John and Nellie, friends we had previously made in Iqaluit, invited us over to enjoy one final caribou chili dinner before we left, and it was so delicious!

It was rewarding to see that our reconnaissance expedition successfully laid the necessary groundwork to be able to move ahead and develop two pilot cross-cultural dogsledding courses the following year in 1988. Mission accomplished! I think this trip was a wonderful reflection of the dedication, wholehearted teamwork, and adventuresome spirit that embodied COBWS culture.

One final interesting historic note: As far as anyone in Pangnirtung can remember, we were the first white people to complete this route from Pangnirtung to Broughton Island by way of Kingnait Pass since it was first surveyed back in 1930. That was pretty amazing to find out!

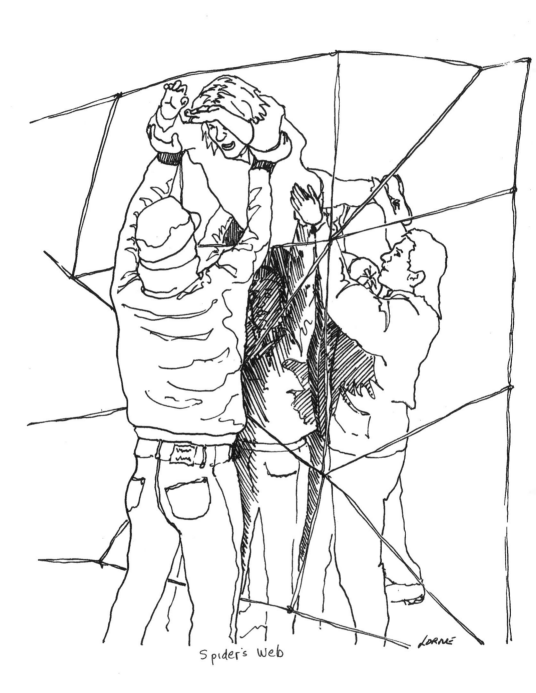

VI. STUDENT VOICES

Joseph Campbell described the mythic structure of the hero's journey. In narrative forms, the hero answers a call to adventure by departing from their home environs, meets a variety of challenges, and then returns home changed or transformed, with the power to share his or her learning with the broader community.

In physical and psychological terms, that same structure is embodied by an Outward Bound course. Just substitute the word *hero* with the word *student*. Homeplace is where the planning and preparation for the students' journeys take place. It represents the familiar and ordinary world from which the student is called to embark on an adventure into a special world. In this case, their step from the known into the unknown involves an extended canoe expedition through a remarkably pristine wilderness area not governed by our traditional time-bound world, a place where magic is possible.

In the hero's journey that Campbell described, the hero often meets a mentor who helps prepare them for the challenges that await them. In the context of Outward Bound, the student learns from their course instructors. Once inside this vast wilderness area, the student encounters a series of trials and tests—portages, long days, unpredictable weather, navigating, working as a member of a team—and meets them, successfully.

Prior to returning home, there is a time for reflection: Outward Bound's solo experience. Finally, the student returns from this special world, initially

OPPOSITE: *Team Challenge at the Ropes Course* by Lorne Tippett.

back to Homeplace, and ultimately their own home and community. Their adventure has enabled them to grow in spirit and strength, giving them the ability to share new knowledge only attainable from experiencing the journey.

Outward Bound is an educational experience of self-discovery that uses the challenges and risks found in wilderness environments as its teaching medium. Encountering a series of progressively difficult physical challenges, students must call upon individual reserves of strength and perseverance that they might not have thought existed. There are times when success requires the help of companions and reliance upon the overall strengths represented within a group of students. Through concrete mastery of seemingly overwhelming situations, they discover that they really are the masters of their own lives.

Outward Bound asks for complete efforts, in contrast to a regular school system that seldom calls upon the whole nature of the individual. Mastery in the Outward Bound process involves the fullest gestalt of the learner. The accompanying possibilities and sense of one's own capacity and self-confidence is a major step toward Hahn's ideal individual who possesses a "sense of responsibility towards humanity." The final power of an Outward Bound experience can be the strength students feel upon returning to their home environments, where they are often better able to relate to other people and take control of their lives.

In the series of essays that follow, you'll get a glimpse of the student experience. Patrick Gorry ("A Cold Paddle"), Ilona Hitchcock ("My Summer 1981 Outward Bound Course: Memories and Legacy"), Amanda Harris ("So, What Does COBWS Mean to Me?"), Susie Specter ("Student Remembrance of the 1980 Fire Evacuation Course in the Boundary Waters Canoe Area"), David Gouthro ("My Outward Bound Experience with Apple Canada"), and Bob Ramsay ("If I Live, You Give") all participated in COBWS courses originating from Homeplace during its early years. Some forty years later they put pen to paper and recalled vivid memories. —Ed.

A Cold Paddle

Patrick Gorry

In September 1980, I flew up to Thunder Bay for a two-week Outward Bound course. I knew just enough about Outward Bound from a fellow student in my MBA program (which I had finished the previous year) to be inspired to go. After nine long months working for a major Canadian bank, I was ready for a break and seriously overdue for some adventure.

On arrival at Thunder Bay's modest airport, several Outward Bound instructors held up signs and swiftly escorted me and other students willingly onto a former school bus. Off we went into the wild blue yonder—onto the highway heading east and then north into the bush. I recall one participant had come straight from her office to the Toronto airport, and she was wearing high heels. It seemed funny at the time.

Little did we anticipate what would happen next. I was deep in conversation with a young woman when the bus suddenly stopped in the middle of nowhere. The door opened, a fellow dressed for the great outdoors climbed aboard, and he announced that we had five minutes to grab whatever we needed for the next few days. A mad scramble resulted as people dug into their luggage, grabbing toothbrushes, clothing, snacks, you name it. I think I was relatively lucky, as I already had on wool trousers and a heavy sweater from army surplus. I believe the woman with the heels found more suitable footwear in the nick of time.

The bus then disappeared. We were left in a clearing by the side of the road in what became a steady rain. At some point I remember splitting into groups (my group was M-2; the *M* is for *management*), erecting a tent, and then getting ready for dinner. The instructors did the cooking that first evening. Whatever it was, we wolfed it down.

Darkness eventually crept in; it felt early, but it was mid-September, and we were not that far west of Lake Nipigon (in other words, way north of Toronto). Soon we hit the sack. It wasn't a sit-by-the-roaring-fire kind of evening—too wet for that. The five men had one tent, the two women another, and our two instructors, Chuck Luckmann and Teresa Legowski, shared a third.

The next day, or maybe it was two days, we learned to climb, also how to belay each other, and how to rappel back down a hundred-foot cliff (which looked two hundred feet high from below). Some of us were born climbers: Rob climbed a pitch called the Crack of Dawn blindfolded on his second attempt, and Dave Switzer seemed to be at the A+ level from the get-go. The rest of us were a more cautious bunch and needed encouragement, and some of us froze while climbing. I don't mean we were cold, although we were. Climbers freeze when they can't climb any higher and yet they can't descend, so they're stuck until they become unstuck.

After all the climbing fun and games, the Outward Bound bus returned and took us further north, up to Outward Bound's base camp on the shores of Black Sturgeon Lake. Homeplace was quite a hive of activity compared with our little climbing camp in the bush. We were reunited with our luggage, enjoyed hot showers and clean clothes, and then commenced to prepare for our expedition. I recall being led through the kitchen to see all the different types of beans. We were told that taking meat along for the ten-day canoe trip would be impractical, hence the beans would be our major source of protein. There were a few jokes about flatulence, of course, but Chuck assured us that if the beans were soaked long enough before being cooked, we would not be jet-propelled.

At Homeplace we were also allocated paddles and life jackets and sleeping bags—everything we could possibly need. Although only mid-September, it was a lot colder than usual, so hypothermia was a real concern. Normally the Outward Bound instructors stage a rescue out on the lake, where a volunteer falls from their canoe into the water. The wet victim is then plucked from the water, taken to dry land, and placed into a sleeping bag to be warmed up using body heat. I recall Chuck nixing the demonstration, a blessing in disguise, perhaps, given the temperature of the water.

Finally we were set to go. The next morning we hopped on the bus and drove further north. Soon we were left with our canoes and equipment by the side of a lake, the name of which I do not remember. During the next several days we paddled and portaged and camped by one beautiful wild lake after another. There were occasional snow showers to endure, but no rain. Nothing like long underwear, wool shirt and trousers, and a waterproof jacket to keep a paddler high and dry. Some of the nights, though, were truly cold, so it helped to claim the middle of the tent, not be next to an outside wall. We learned quickly to wear everything we owned into bed and take our boots too, so they wouldn't freeze.

Chuck surprised us by being a very accomplished fisherman. The whitefish that seemingly jumped right onto his fishing line were delicious. Some of the lakes we crossed had probably not been visited by humans in a year or more, so the fish were, shall we say, sitting ducks. And for the same reason it was not easy sometimes to find the portage trails. It sure made one realize what a vast landscape there is north of Lake Superior. I should mention some words of wisdom from all those years ago that have come in handy from time to time: Chuck encouraged everyone to not waste energy keeping a full bladder warm. Best to head to dry land when paddling in cold weather and go to the bathroom regularly.

One morning, Chuck and Teresa decided that we were ready for our solos. They dropped each of us off on our own solitary stretch of rocky beach with only a tarp and a sleeping bag, and several tea bags and some matches. We had to spend the rest of that day, the following day, and most of the day after that by ourselves. We had a little journal with a pencil in case something profound came to mind. In my case profundity eluded me, and so I paced up and down the shoreline for two whole days. I had a sneaking suspicion that some brown bear was watching, so I kept moving. For something to do, I made a fire and burned everything I could find while I brewed one cup of tea after another (if you come from England, you are necessarily a tea tank when stressed). Sleeping under the tarp was tolerable and I was warm enough, but a stiff wind blew up on the final morning before pickup. There was nothing to do but pace. No food, no tea bags; I was not very happy. Finally, Chuck and Teresa rounded the point only to announce that it was too windy to land, so they would return later. I was thrown a chunk of bannock from ten feet out, which was some consolation. After wolfing down said bread, I continued the patrol of my little beach until, many hungry hours later, I was rescued.

It was quite pleasant to be back with M-2 and eat some actual food. I was half-starving, and I had missed everyone. But what was astonishing was sitting around Chuck and Teresa's big fire and listening to the others read from their journals. Some folks in M-2 were downright philosophical. I recall Steve had written in his journal that, living with his wife and small children, he barely ever had time for himself. For the first time in a long while, the solo gave him an opportunity to collect his thoughts and think about his future. Twelve years later, I came to realize what he meant firsthand after my son was born.

The next day we started on our final expedition without Chuck and Teresa. As a group, we decided to put the pedal to the metal and try to leave our esteemed instructors far behind. So over the next couple of days we paddled and portaged like madmen. The weather remained cold but was a little sunnier and drier; not bad, considering it was now late September. Of course, after a week out in the bush we were toughening up. Somehow, Chuck and Teresa were not far behind when we decided we had reached our objective and stopped paddling. But I do remember Chuck saying something appreciative, as we had covered some thirty-five miles or more one of the days, which exceeded his expectations.

It was certainly a pleasure to be picked up by the Outward Bound bus after our final expedition. Somehow they found us. This was well before the age of the cell phone. On our way back to Black Sturgeon Lake, we stopped for a while in civilization—that is, the main street of Armstrong. It felt rather strange to be back.

Homeplace this last time around meant R&R, showers, and clean clothes. One final task, however, was the marathon race. I suppose we were all in about the best physical shape we'd been in years. The marathon would consist of a canoe race, then a run through the forest on gravel roads. I am pleased to remember that M-2 won the trophy, a testament perhaps to our goal-oriented approach to Outward Bound's challenges. I do not recall a celebratory dinner, but we did have a celebratory sauna together (everyone in M-2, including Chuck and Teresa).

On our last day, the Outward Bound bus dropped us off at the Thunder Bay Airport. We were just a few minutes late, but the Air Canada plane had already pulled away from the terminal. Luckily the gate agent called the pilot, and he brought the plane back to the apron. The ground crew wheeled the mobile steps in place, and we grabbed our seats. I vaguely recall that I sat in the back row where the galley was. The flight attendant asked me what I had been up to. I guess I looked like I'd been in the woods for a while.

Home again in Toronto, my office colleagues had little interest in my Outward Bound adventure. Hard to describe, I guess, and I had not taken many photographs . . . I was too busy paddling. Alice Feldman, another student who happened to live on the same street as me, took some very fine photos and gave me some several some weeks later. One thing I did notice on returning to the big city was that I could take subway stairs three at a time, but that unusual skill diminished all too quickly. I did manage to convince two friends to each do an Outward Bound course at Black Sturgeon Lake. One loved it, the other had a so-so experience. A lot depends on your instructors, and we were blessed to have had Chuck and Teresa.

Two years later, in 1982, I went on an Outward Bound alumni rafting trip through Canyonlands National Park in Utah and almost drowned. Our raft had seven paddlers, including our instructor. By the time we reached Satan's Gut, it was our second-to-last day on the river. We had gone hiking and done a solo as well as run three dozen rapids, so we felt we were getting pretty good. But not good enough. We were the first Outward Bound raft on the Colorado to flip in eight years. I happened to be right at the front next to a big hole, so I was thrown in first. I remember dropping to the bottom of the river and seeing huge boulders flash by, then I was spat out, fortunately. Somehow my sunglasses stayed on.

Evidently, Outward Bound courses are not entirely without risk, but what is? Carpe diem—take a course—that's what I would recommend with the benefit of forty-two years' hindsight. You only live once.

My Summer 1981 Outward Bound Course: Memories and Legacy

Ilona Hitchcock

The year 1980 was a challenging one for me. We had just moved to Hamilton, Ontario, from Vancouver, British Columbia. I had left behind my job, the mountains and the ocean, and a life I loved. In this new life, I had a new home and a lovely new baby daughter who cried day and night. At the same time, my husband, Adam, was starting his new job and was occupied 24/7. Everything that had defined my life seemed to have evaporated, to be replaced with a dull Ontario sky and the lonely exhaustion of a sleep-deprived first-time mother. When our friend Patrick Gorry came to visit, I listened hungrily as he recounted his recent Outward Bound adventures. It sounded wonderful.

So, inspired by Patrick, in the summer of 1981, I left one-and-a-half-year-old Julia and my husband to cope on their own as I flew off to Thunder Bay and Black Sturgeon Lake. It was wonderful. From our first stop at the Wall, Outward Bound reinforced the idea that what is almost impossible alone can easily be accomplished by working together. This beautiful wilderness setting and interesting people offered me nourishment, inner strength, and joy.

Some memorable highlights included:

Rock climbing with Christo Grayling was challenging, fun, and something I had never done before. Climbing on the wonderful play structure in the trees, we further learned to trust fellow brigade members.

The canoe expedition on stunningly beautiful lakes was the core of the experience... especially Smoothrock Lake. Like Patrick, who lured me to Outward

Bound, I had the good fortune to have Chuck Luckmann as one of the guides for our expedition. Every member of my brigade was a joy to get to know.

The night paddle under a full moon, everyone singing as we paddled, was haunting and perfect.

Then the solo on Smoothrock Lake. I chose an excellent rocky spot with a gorgeous view where I could enjoy both sunrise and sunset. My good luck held, and the weather was clear and sunny with starry nights.

An enriching detail was that, while on solo, we had to make something for another brigade member, whose name we drew beforehand. I received a piece of birch bark with a thoughtful, personal poem written just for me. I still have and cherish it.

What I took away:

First of all, I returned home stronger, happier, and more prepared for life as a new mom and for the challenges to come. I had been on canoe trips before, but now I had the knowledge and confidence to plan, outfit, and make it all work.

Once our children were in their teens, we started annual family canoe expeditions. Rotating among Algonquin, Killarney, and Temagami, our family has gone on five- to ten-day wilderness canoe trips every year for the last twenty-five years. Always inviting others, we have had guests from Germany, Australia, Switzerland, Brazil, Japan, and China. Now our children are in their forties, and we are in our seventies. The annual wilderness canoe expeditions continue to bring us together.

Inspired by my good memories, both my children attended Outward Bound in their late teens: my daughter, Julia, at Black Sturgeon Lake twice—once for the summer school and again for the winter. My son, Peter, attended Outward Bound in the Yukon with sunlit nights and a grizzly cub sauntering through camp one night (after which they promptly made a midnight exit and paddled through rapids, capsizing en route to a safer camp spot).

So Outward Bound has played a big role in our family. Only my husband, Adam, has not done an Outward Bound experience. He has had to put up with our stories ever since.

It was with great sadness that we learned of the closing of Homeplace at Black Sturgeon Lake some years ago. All things must end, and I am left with gratitude for having been part of something special.

So, What Does COBWS Mean to Me?

Amanda Harris

In the late 1970s, I was working in the outdoor education field in southern Ontario. I heard about an Outward Bound school in northwestern Ontario and requested information. I couldn't afford the course tuition, so I phoned the school, and they agreed to have me volunteer in the Toronto office to help pay for part of my course. There, I met the executive director, Alistair McArthur. He was very welcoming and assured me that my stuffing of envelopes would eventually lead me to some rock climbing, canoeing, and all kinds of adventures.

Later that summer I had the opportunity to take an Outward Bound Educators course. I was interested in working at COBWS; however, I thought it would be important to be a student first, to experience firsthand the twenty-eight-day standard course. I remember being picked up at the Thunder Bay Airport by an interesting looking guy named Baz Stevens, who remains a dear friend to this day. We rode in a van for a couple of hours up a bumpy and dusty road that led us to Homeplace. After the airport pickup, I had heard that one usually gets dropped off at the side of a river or at a rock climbing site, but Baz took us to meet our two instructors, Bill Templeman and Greg Logan, who were still prepping the course at Homeplace. That's the thing about Outward Bound courses: They are as unique as the people in them.

The course was magical! I think there were seven students along with our two instructors, Logan and Uncle Bill. I remember many things about that month: the expression *fair dinkum* (Australian slang for *unquestionably good*), Wendell Beckwith's Best Island home on Whitewater Lake, Kopka Falls, friendships, challenges, and an instant love of this community of people called Homeplace. I don't think I had a true student's experience, given that I was already dreaming of returning as a staff member.

VI. STUDENT VOICES

On our final expedition in July 1979, we were camped a couple of lakes away from the course where a young lad drowned. This sobering and tragic event brought us back to Homeplace, where we all shared in the grief of a young life lost too soon.

After the course I was able to speak with Wendy Pieh. She invited me to come back anytime. That's the thing about Wendy—incredibly trusting in people's goodness, strength, and wisdom. I learned early on that Wendy was not a normal leader. Neither were *most* of the people in leadership roles at COBWS.

I had come from a family that inspired me to do whatever I aspired to, and people like Chuck Luckmann, Wendy Pieh, Ian Yolles, Alistair McArthur, John Mordhorst, Greg Logan, Baz Stevens, and others were from the same cloth. There was a sense of trust and confidence that came with the leadership. It inspired me and others to be totally open to learning and to challenging ourselves to be the best we could be.

I have a distinct memory of Chuck Luckmann offering me a position that I wasn't sure I could do, but his confidence inspired me to challenge myself to do what was difficult, which is of course a major theme at Outward Bound.

My fellow COBWS staff were incredibly talented and unique—always learning, traveling, playful, and joyful. I learned early on that the staff were authentic—no airs, no pretentious folks, and no autocrats. The community was one you wanted to be a part of. The consensus decision-making format for the community meetings was remarkable: lengthy, frustrating, inspiring, and magical! One person of particular significance to me at Homeplace was Bertha Bumchuckles (Ginger Mason). She brought remarkable, nutritious food to the community, and she hugely inspired my lifelong passion for home-cooked, love-filled vegetarian food.

Thinking back, I realize I felt some grief leaving the Outward Bound and Enviros worlds and transitioning to the real world. The intensely close relationships peppered with heartfelt feedback were hard acts to follow. It took me some years to find a new tribe of like-minded friends to ride along with on my journey.

My time at COBWS was such a special part of my life. I learned and grew so much. I met an extraordinary crew of characters, and it launched me on a journey of discovery, joy, learning, and love. Bob Pieh wrote, "Be tough yet gentle / Humble yet bold / Swayed always by beauty and truth." This has been a silent motto in my life. Although I never had the good fortune to meet Bob, I so appreciate his dream of making COBWS a progressive and passionate community of outdoor educators with a heart.

Student Remembrance of the 1980 Fire Evacuation Course in the Boundary Waters Canoe Area

Susie Specter

Instructors: Ian Yolles and Rob Linscott. Brigade of seven students from Canada, the United States, and one from Singapore. All of us in our twenties.

Most of northwestern Ontario closed because of fires. We came anyway. Crossed the border into Minnesota with Singaporean hidden under seat (no US visa).

Expedition: Two-week paddle in frequent rain. Portages muddy, funny disasters, slipping and sliding with heavy packs and canoes. Cheerfully singing many miles a day to keep our spirits high.

Circle time. Ian reads out loud Mircea Eliade philosophy.

Three-day solo. Fasting. Singing. Writing. Communing with Mother Earth. Not afraid or anxious. Rob cooks delicious off-solo meal. Smiles beam from mosquito-eaten faces.

Being a badass jock. Rock climbing. Marathon running. Feeling tall as a mountain completing a course. Celebrating with a banquet at Homeplace.

* * *

Staying on to assist Bertha Bumchuckles with trips food for the rest of the summer.

Awesome friendships. Great talks on the beach. Many friendships to this day remain.

My Outward Bound Experience with Apple Canada

David Gouthro

At the time of my introduction to Outward Bound, I was the national training manager for Apple Canada, based in Markham, Ontario. I first heard about Outward Bound through Ian Yolles, a friend of a friend of mine (gotta appreciate random connections). I loved what Outward Bound stood for and began wondering about whether it would be a good professional development opportunity for Apple Canada employees across the country.

To check it out, I registered for an abbreviated nine-day Managers course, which was led by Peter Morgan and Rod Taylor. This was in the mid-1980s. Needless to say, I found the program to be valuable in a number of ways. The most important was that I felt it would be a fabulous program for the Apple employees across Canada.

We ran a pilot program with a diverse group of nine Apple Canada employees and one from Apple UK (it was a reward trip for him). Turns out, he was a strong fellow whom everyone wanted in their canoe. The pilot program was a tremendous success.

The Outward Bound team went to work customizing a five-day program that would be run out of Homeplace near Black Sturgeon Lake in northern Ontario. The program was designed as a volunteer offering to all Apple Canada employees—over 100 of our 140 employees (at the time) signed up immediately.

Each course included the same components, although they weren't always experienced in the same order:

- A precourse introductory meeting on Sunday evening to get everyone up to speed on what was going to happen during the upcoming week

- A flight to Thunder Bay followed by the drive to Homeplace
- Half a day negotiating a high ropes course
- Bouldering, otherwise known as rock climbing, but low to the ground so that no ropes or technical gear is required
- A full day of rock climbing
- A canoe expedition that required planning, route finding, portaging, camping, decision-making, teamwork, and leadership
- A four-hour solo experience, which was a long time for some folks who had never spent that much time alone before
- A group sauna following the completion of the course prior to boarding the plane home in Thunder Bay
- The return home

There were nine regular courses and one in the winter for a brave group of souls. The overall program was a success, in many ways:

- Most participants would say they accomplished things they never would have imagined.
- Employees had the opportunity to get to know each other, really well. In many cases they were meeting their fellow Outward Bound peers for the first time.
- Participants were inspired by the willingness of some of their colleagues to demonstrate great courage in activities that were far beyond their comfort levels.
- New friendships were formed based on a shared Outward Bound experience, many of which continue to this day.
- There was also a great sense of appreciation for Apple Canada's willingness to make such a program available to any employee who wished to attend, regardless of their job title, role, or location.

Months after all the courses had been completed, I continued to hear stories of how the members of Outward Bound groups stuck up for each other, especially when someone in a regional office would make a harsh comment about one of the head office employees. Comments such as the following were common: "Don't be so critical. I got to know person X on Outward Bound, and they are a great person." This was a fabulous and totally unanticipated outcome. Of course it's hard to put a specific dollar value on it, but it was worth a lot as a contributor to the wonderful Apple Canada culture.

Some of my specific memories included:

- Waking up to snow when it was the wrong time of year for it—on our pilot course, no less!
- Having one of my boots sucked off in the mud when we were dragging our canoes through a swampy bog. I kept those boots for years as a memento!
- Observing one of our more timid members with a severe fear of heights attempt a rappel and overhearing a senior manager comment that her screams reminded him of the sounds his wife made when giving birth. Her courage and willingness to try something new despite her fear inspired others way more than the individuals who made every activity seem easy.
- Heading back up to Homeplace with a television crew that wanted to do a short feature on Apple. At one point in the filming, the canoes had to be walked through shallow water in a culvert before entering Black Sturgeon Lake. One senior manager decided to play it cool and leap into the back of the canoe as it entered the lake. Unfortunately his balance wasn't quite as good as it needed to be, resulting in the canoe tipping over and spilling everything into the lake—including the person in the bow who happened to be one of his supervisors. Funny how I remember some scenes so much more vividly than others.
- Experiencing a group sauna before we headed back home on the last day. That was a highlight of a different sort.

In the spring of 2019, three of us decided to attempt to have an Apple Canada reunion in Toronto. The only criterion for attending was being employed sometime in the 1980s. Over one hundred former Apple employees attended. In many cases, we had not seen each other for over thirty-five years. Many of us had been on Outward Bound together, and a lot of the memories we shared were of our adventures together.

All in all, the Apple Canada Outward Bound adventure was a wonderful time of personal growth, insight, and camaraderie that many of us feel so fortunate to have experienced.

If I Live, You Give

Bob Ramsay

Until the mid-1980s, I was a city boy. I never went to summer camp, never learned to fish or paddle a canoe. I couldn't build a fire, let alone a cabin.

But my friend Cathy Yolles called one day to ask if I'd speak with her brother, Ian, who ran the Outward Bound school in northern Ontario. He was looking for volunteers for a guest expedition, what we today would call influencers who could either spread the word or donate money. So I spoke with Ian and told him I'd love to go on their weeklong trip with eight other corporate types. I said I'd be happy to tell the world about my experience, which would all be new to me, and while I wasn't able to give them much money, I loved raising it for good causes and would be happy to do that for Outward Bound.

One night I sat down to write my fundraising piece, which I'd send to one hundred or so friends in the mail. On the cover was a photo of me in a suit and tie, wearing a climbing helmet with cliff-climbing gear on my shoulder. The headline read, "If I Live, You Give." My pitch was that I was doing this dangerous thing, and if I made it back alive people should send $50.

As a courtesy, I sent my text to Ian Yolles and waited for his enthusiastic reply. I just knew it would raise a ton of money. Ian didn't reply—at least then. But eventually he did call. He seemed hesitant, hedging his words, unlike in our first call when he was all enthusiasm. He asked if I might want to change the headline.

Change the headline? Why would I do that?

"Well, Bob, because it implies there's a good chance you won't make it back, and that's just not true." He then went on about Outward Bound's safety record and how its courses are all about facing perceived risk to reduce your real fears.

I couldn't easily dismiss Ian's points, given that I'd never spent even one night sleeping in the wild.

Ian went on to suggest a replacement headline. How about, "If I Meet the Challenge, You Make the Donation"?

"What? No . . . no, that doesn't work at all. No one will give a cent to that!"

Ian went silent. Clearly he was torn. Here was this guy, a good friend of his sister's, who'd agreed to come on the trip and had offered to raise funds from his network of friends.

So he backed down. I'm sure this violated every value in his body and soul. But he agreed to stick with the headline and the copy I wrote. He was in the truth business; I was in the truth-in-the-service-of-cash business.

The final lines of my pitch said that if I did make it back alive, I'd let them know and they could send their checks. This prompted some friends to send their donations before I went, including some big checks with notes that said, "I'll give them more if you don't come back alive!"

Out went the fundraiser bearing my words, and back came many thousands of dollars.

The actual guest expedition was life-changing for me. I learned I was tougher than I thought I was, physically and emotionally, and oh wow was it ever fun. It led to three more Outward Bound trips, including one mushing dogs on the ice floes outside Iqaluit.

But there were two more enduring benefits.

One, I became a lifelong friend of Outward Bound and a later-in-life outdoorsman. In 1992, my wife-to-be, Jean Marmoreo, persuaded me to take three months off work and hike one thousand miles of the Appalachian Trail, and in 2019 we circumnavigated Manhattan by kayak.

Two, I became a lifelong friend of Ian Yolles. Not only did I introduce him, albeit unintentionally, to the woman who would become his wife, but he also was an usher at my marriage to Jean twenty-nine years ago.

All because of a crazy headline.

VII. HARMONY OF TENSIONS

We considered "Harmony of Tensions" as a title for this book. It comes from the *Fragments* of Heraclitus, the ancient Greek philosopher whom Bob Pieh liked so much. Fragment #56 translates as follows: "The cosmos works / by harmony of tensions / like the lyre and bow."

Both Heraclitus and Bob Pieh believed that a metaphor captures the mystery of how the universe works as well as math and physics. With proper judgment, balancing the tensions of the present moment might lead to a harmonious life.

Another primary title we considered was "Remote Utopia." Homeplace on Black Sturgeon Lake was remote, isolated within the vastness of northern Ontario. We were idealists striving imperfectly for harmony with each other, the surrounding wilderness, and the competing tensions within the community and each individual. Through awareness of these tensions, learning from the obstacles—which is living Outward Bound—we truly felt on a path toward happiness and harmony.

"The Story of the Bear" by Charlie Orsak can be read both as literal truth and as metaphor. How do you corral a bear? How do you corral truth and beauty without experiencing danger?

In Mary Morgan's "A Summer Adventure," she describes the freedom and bliss of personal discovery. The obstacles became the way.

In "On Patterns: Finding New Leaders," Susan Fenton Gibson speaks to finding her identity as a woman and as an effective leader. She talks about the

OPPOSITE: *Whitewater Canoeing on Black Sturgeon River* by Lorne Tippett.

gifts the Canadian landscape and people at COBWS gave her as she pursued her journey of earth steward and mentor.

Rod Taylor contributes "The Impact of COBWS on My Life," likening his experience at COBWS to a utopian love he never experienced again. That might sound corny, but it wasn't for him.

In "Remembering Bob Pieh, My Mentor," John Huie describes Pieh as an educational philosopher and practitioner whose goal was to change lives by giving them an Outward Bound course full of tension and harmony, like focusing on your breath, in and out: "Dunk 'em and dry 'em. Dunk 'em and dry 'em."

In "Granola Spirit," Charles Luckmann muses on what it means to be an idealist today facing existential threats at every turn. Surely Bob Pieh would meet the challenge. Surely many people drawn to Outward Bound would too. Can COBWS be a model for the twenty-first century? How memorable would that be? —Ed.

The Story of the Bear

Charlie Orsak

I believe this story captures the essence of COBWS. First a few caveats. Research has shown that eyewitness testimony is often unreliable. Moreover, I must admit that my recollection is likely influenced by my love of a good story, especially a funny story. In other words, this tale is best seen as *truth-y*.

In 1981 or thereabouts, a bear began visiting the back porch of the kitchen. At first the bear was responsive to the usual measures—banging on pots and stern language. Unfortunately, over the course of several days the bear began to frequent the student campsite, on one occasion being chased by a junior brigade, as we referred to them at the time. This made for a situation in which, in Alistair McArthur's words, all the "risk ducks were in a row." A call was then made to Peter Mitchell at the Ministry of Natural Resources.

Although Peter was a friend of the school, he was unwilling to invest his time in relocating a bear "from the middle of bloody nowhere." Go figure. However, he did offer a DIYBT (do-it-yourself bear trap).

"We'll take it! What could possibly go wrong?" True to his word, said apparatus was delivered a few days later. The contraption consisted of two barrels welded end to end, with a trigger at the back end wired to a spring-loaded door in the front end. Simple procedure, Peter explained. Put some bear cuisine on the trigger, set the door, wait for the bear to crawl in, and voilà, problem solved. The trap was situated behind the trips food house and the trigger baited with leftover lasagna.

The next morning the bear was spied ambling behind the trips food house in the early light, followed shortly thereafter by the sound of the trapdoor slamming shut. The trap was cautiously approached but . . . no bear, no lasagna.

Deflated but not defeated, a bratwurst was then duct-taped to the trigger. (Every good adventure story should include duct tape.) The next morning, being a creature of habit, the bear reappeared, and again the trapdoor slammed shut. Chastened by previously being outwitted by an animal not known for higher-level thought, we were prepared to find an empty trap.

Au contraire. Before rounding the corner, the sounds of success were evident. It is difficult to describe the sound of a member of the genus *Ursus* suddenly finding itself involuntarily confined. Suffice it to say it sounded like a very pissed-off bear in a large tin can. Nothing draws a crowd like a canned bear. At that point a weakness in our planning was revealed.

"What the hell do we do now?"

As the saying goes, we were the dog that finally caught the car. A quick check of the instructor's handbook yielded no answers. (Of course, the handbook was later updated to cover this scenario. See Section 3, Subparagraph 2a.) In any case, after a few minutes a consensus was reached that the bear would be relocated far enough down the road to discourage its return. Seats were removed from a van, climbing slings snaked under the trap, and the trap loaded. All the while the bear continued to express displeasure. But who would do the transporting? To their eternal credit, representatives of French-speaking Canada stepped forward in the persons of Guy Lacelle and Robert Sauvignon.

Now the thinking was that because the bear had entered the trap headfirst and its diameter was only slightly less than the barrel's, there would be adequate time to reach safety between the time when the door was opened and the bear backed out. Funny thing about bears: When motivated, they can do amazing things, including turning around in a barrel.

Rather than being greeted by a relatively benign rear end, the relocation crew was greeted by an angry front end. How do you say in Quebecois, "Suddenly learning to fly to the roof of a van"? In any case, all's well that ends well. The bear reportedly circled the van a few times, and after declining to be debriefed, scrambled into the bush, never to darken the kitchen door again.

A Summer Adventure

Mary Morgan

In the summer of 1981, I was back at COBWS, at Homeplace on Black Sturgeon Lake. It had already been a full year; I had paddled in a dugout canoe with Juliet Westgate (Duff), my Outward Bound buddy, from the Colombian border into Panama, living with the Kuna Indians; and I also had worked in Alberta for a couple of months in a group home on a farm, where I was beaten up by one of the boys and the company provided no support to me or to the young man who had hurt me, so I left. I hitchhiked to Yellowknife to see (Victoria) Moon Joyce, another Outward Bound buddy, and fell in love with Bonnie Dickie.

    COBWS was a paradise for all of us who landed there. It was the first Outward Bound school that was led by a woman, and Outward Bound was operating in thirty-two countries. Wendy Pieh hired us based on our spirit and curiosity. She knew we could learn hard skills; it was the soft skills that were innate, which could be nurtured and developed. Outward Bound was for sure a man's world at that point in time—the senior staff and the most experienced at the school were men. Having a woman program director, though, whom the men respected and most were in love with, created a space for women to occupy. In another ten years, all the senior staff at COBWS were women. Interestingly enough, when there was an Outward Bound International review in 1995 by senior Outward Bound officials—all men, who were visiting the school to assess whether it was meeting the Outward Bound standards—their report stated that the school had a "gender problem," the gender problem being that senior staff at COBWS were women. Sexism is everywhere, it seems, even in paradise.

* * *

After my three-week course in July, when I assisted in the instructing with Rob Linscott, Bonnie arrived at the school. There were many feminists and a few lesbians (five) working at the school. The men were our brothers, and no one seemed to care about sexual orientation or strong women. But of course there was homophobia! At that time it was expressed through a tolerance of homosexuality; just don't show you are a homosexual. I remember one lesbian was told not to let her partner come because "it would be hard for the students." And as women loving women at the time, our own internalized homophobia was stronger than the homophobia in our community. Internalized homophobia is when you don't want people to know you are homosexual, so you operate on fitting in and not coming out, even in safe communities like COBWS.

The women were the spirit at the school. Bertha Bumchuckles ran the kitchen with great enthusiasm and rigor. There was a boom box playing feminist women's music all the time, and the men and women all sang along to Cris Williamson, Ferron, Holly Near, Sweet Honey in the Rock, Heather Bishop, and many others. Women's music was the way that lesbians connected with each other. If I went into someone's living space, I'd check out their albums, which transitioned to cassette tapes over time. If there were any women's music artists, then you had a good idea you were in a sista's home.

We were living communally, in old cabins with two or three in a room. The more senior staff got their own rooms, and some even had their own shacks, which would be big enough for a single bed and had pegs or nails on the wall to hang clothes on. The school was in an old MNR research station on the shores of Black Sturgeon Lake that we leased for $1 per year. The lapping of the water was heard from all buildings.

Part of living communally required that we all do chores; working in the kitchen was one of them. Bonnie loved working in the kitchen—chopping and cooking for one hundred people at a time. We'd hear the gong that sounded fifteen minutes before the meal, and that meant finish what you were doing, wash up, and get to the dining hall. At the hall we'd stand outside, waiting for everyone to come. We'd hold hands and have a moment of quiet, or someone would lead in a short song that would center our spirits before nourishing our bodies, or they'd read a poem or quote that we'd reflect on for a minute or two. Then we'd head into the dining hall and eat great vegetarian food. I learned how to be a vegetarian at Homeplace—it was economical and healthy for all of us.

VII. HARMONY OF TENSIONS

We had community meetings that occurred at the end of each month, where we'd deal with logistics, what was needed, what we learned, and what needed to improve. Juliet, and a few men, would knit the most amazing socks during these meetings. We'd have a party in the evening. Not much drinking, a bit of toking, lots of dancing, and just plain fun. Sometimes six of us women would go out in canoes on the lake and sing to the moon or whatever. It was like adult summer camp!

Bonnie, Moon, and I decided to travel to Toronto for a week before the August courses began. We decided to hop freight trains out of Marathon, which meant we had to hitchhike there. We were heading out on an adventure. Moon and I had hopped freights before; Juliet had taught me back in 1978. I then taught Moon. Bonnie had never done such a thing, but she was up for it. We took small backpacks when we left Homeplace. There was a town run, so we got a ride to the end of the gravel road that took us to the Trans-Canada Highway. We got a lift to Marathon in no time.

The thing about hopping freights is that it is illegal! Hence you have to be careful whom you ask about when the freight train is arriving and leaving. There are workers in the yards who put the train together, and they are usually pretty easygoing—at least with young white women in their late twenties and early thirties. We dumped our packs near the tracks, so it wasn't too obvious that we were there to hop freights, and started to check out the freight yard. We needed to find someone who could let us know which train would be leaving for southern Ontario. I remember leaving the packs, but Bonnie was a bit worried they'd be stolen. I told Bonnie we didn't have to worry; just leave white light around them and they'll be protected. "Protect our bags," I said out loud to the white light I could imagine settling over our small mound of backpacks.

We were in luck. Magic was in the air! One of the yardmen let us know that the train was arriving in an hour, and he showed us the track that the train would be stopping on. This was critical information, because in a freight yard there are many train tracks. We went to a store and got something to take with us—Moon picked up a bottle of brandy—and we headed back to our packs and settled near the line that the train would be stopping on.

The train came, we found a boxcar that was open, we hoisted our packs up, and then scrambled up and inside, helping each other. Juliet had taught me that it is important to put a block of wood in the track that the door slides on to open and close. That way, if the door does move to shut, there is something that will ensure that it does not close. Juliet had heard of a case when someone had *not* done that. Months later, when a worker opened up the door he found a skeleton. We didn't want that to be our story.

The train hugged the shores of Lake Superior. We had pulled out sleeping bags to sprawl out on, and we leaned on our packs. I pulled out my harmonica and played some tunes. Moon passed the bottle to each of us. The sun was going down over Lake Superior, and the sound of the train lulled us all into our own thoughts. It was glorious! We were the queens of the road, with our hearts wide open and the sense of freedom so strong in our beings. This was how I wanted my life to be.

On Patterns: Finding New Leaders

Susan Fenton Gibson

We have all seen the videos of flocks of starlings patterning and repatterning in the sky, known as a murmuration. Well, the early 1980s COBWS board members embodied a murmuration of minds.

We were all raised on stories about Canada's wild north. Some had heard Glenn Gould's "The Idea of North" on CBC Radio as he toured northern Ontario's truck stops. Many had camped, cottaged, and canoed. My mother and her sisters had paddled to school on the Pickerel River south of Sudbury from my grandfather Fenton's fishing camp, Wanikewan, past the pink granite cliffs of the Canadian Shield. We had steeped ourselves in the Kurt Hahn philosophy then operating in the northern Ontario Outward Bound wilderness camp, Homeplace, on Black Sturgeon Lake near Lake Nipigon. Led by chair Joanne Raynes, the board was the glue that provided the vision and funds to operate the summer and winter programs at Homeplace.

As an early member of the 1970s founding board of the Sierra Club of Ontario, I had pledged my life's energies to protecting Canada's wilderness. John Muir and Aldo Leopold led me. Kurt Hahn anchored my experiential actions. As an autodidact, I understood that the depth of leadership Canada needed could be taught in our vast northern spaces. I knew that there, in the calm and green comfort of the pine-scented northern lands, we could build the skills we needed for Canada to thrive. It would be a decade before I got the opportunity to learn the art of compassionate leadership.

In February 1982, several board members knew they needed real-time Outward Bound experience. So I, Joanne Raynes, Rob Noyes-Smith, and several other people emerged from a flight to Thunder Bay, and in unparalleled Outward Bound mode, settled into Homeplace two days later. After igloo building and sleeping out at minus eighteen degrees (yes!), we knew we were in for the full experience.

Our leaders, Paul Landry and Guy Lacelle (gone too soon), quietly—sometimes with actions, sometimes with words—taught us to survive brutal winter temperatures. I watched. I learned. They were direct, experienced, calm, and compassionate. Not militaristic! Not formulaic! Not old-school pale-male leadership. Patterns were forming for me.

Homeplace was so welcoming. So comfy, so endearing. Other COBWS staff quietly showed us by example how to clean and cook wholesome, pulse-centered, deeply satisfying meals. I learned what community was—a gentle lesson in a loving environment, sequestered from exterior storms and threats. A holding of hands. A pattern for my future. Leading me to adopt a vegetarian diet after breast cancer in 1985 (now healthy and fit at eighty-one!). What a pulsating gift from Homeplace!

After the initial adjustment period we were well prepared for our twenty-four-hour winter solo outing. My most profound lifetime experience awaited. Alone, mostly confident, I carved a deep space in the snow to build my fire and cook my macaroni. After that exertion I fell asleep in my plastic shelter secured to a pine tree with string. In the morning I was joined by a Canada jay, happily feasting on the remains of my earlier meal. We exchanged views on wilderness—essential to the jay's survival and essential to humans' spiritual and physical thriving, and as we have now learned, essential to human survival as a species beset by runaway climate change.

A deeper confidence and knowing were gifted to me in that unique solo time. I began to understand my leadership gift. I recommitted to my earlier vows to protect and increase Canada's wilderness lands. And I linked my Ontario provincial cabinet office skills to know when and how to implement new policies. In public policy change, timing is queen.

After the solo survival outing, preparation began for our seven-day dog-team adventure on frozen Black Sturgeon Lake. The full winter course was ten days. We left for expedition on day three.

Safety first: Pam Bresnahan, Homeplace support staff, jumped into a circle in the icy water carved out by Paul and Guy. We pulled her out, stripped her, and Joanne and I began warming her with the heat of our naked bodies. Men stood and stared. Paul inquired, "Haven't you guys seen a naked woman before?" We howled. The men faded away.

Now the Kurt Hahn concept of leading from behind began. Gradually Paul and Guy moved to the rear of the group and were deliberately silent when questioned. This sparked the final step in the coming together of the group on day six of the expedition. We had now become the leaders.

Most keeners had learned the hard way that the group to which they newly belonged could only proceed at the pace of the slowest. We learned this at our own speeds. The faster, fitter folks learned, if slowly. The rest of us, with knowing, collaborative smiles, got it sooner and became less fearful of failure. A relief for me! Our first of several leadership lessons. The natural leader of the group emerged. Others assisted. The northern wilderness had taught us to work together—with no written exams. For all to survive, we had to glue, each separately joined. Patterns learned.

All winter trips end with snow angels, celebrations, and a sauna at Kangas in Thunder Bay, still the best sauna in Ontario. Then home to embrace all that we had learned.

As members of COBWS board of directors, we were proud that future COBWS leaders would use their Outward Bound skills to be a force for change and good at any level of Canadian society. We knew that we were creating leaders with deep respect for Canada's natural history, people who understood that nature is a conduit to our mental health. (Forest bathing is beginning to be prescribed.) We were slow to include First Nations in our quest. Now we are smarter. This century, First Nations are sharing their vast knowledge and leading the way forward.

It took some years and several huge life experiences to understand my unique leadership gifts. I am a servant leader, a twenty-first-century construct, a sister of leading from behind. Mostly I could recognize servant leaders. Matched with my success as an effective change agent for women, I was ready to roll as a mentor for Canada's wilderness and to find future leaders to save it.

In 1985, the COBWS board of directors, led by Robert Couchman, promoted senior staffer Ian Yolles to be the fourth executive director, following Bob Pieh, Alistair McArthur, and Peter Turner. Robert understood that Ian's unique union of professional training in adult education at Antioch College, his wilderness experiences, and his long tenure at COBWS would amplify the school's founding vision.

Timing is all. In 1987, the *Our Common Future* report, prepared by the World Commission on Environment and Development, declared that in order to survive humans needed to save at least 12 percent of our natural heritage. World Wildlife Fund (WWF) Canada, led by president Monte Hummel and chief conservation officer Arlin Hackman, initiated WWF's amazing decade-long Endangered Spaces Campaign to protect 12 percent of Canada's wilderness. Then chance allowed me to help fund this program.

Our tiny, two-person, anonymous foundation wrote a first check to WWF for $100,000 in 1989, followed by similar yearly donations until 2000. Megafunder Glen Davis (tragically deceased) weighed in with others to make it happen. The Endangered Spaces Campaign protected an additional 96 million acres of wilderness from 1989 to 2000, an increase of 100 percent.

As of December 2022, foundation colleagues Alan Young and Cathy Wilkinson are leading, with others, Canada's largest-ever wilderness and social projects. With over $1 billion from the federal government and environmental foundations funded through the Project Finance for Permanence (PFP) model, projects for four immense protected areas totaling over 600,000 square miles are up and running. Modeled on the 40,000-square-mile Great Bear Rainforest in British Columbia and in partnership with First Nations, these four massive projects encompass all the Northwest Territories, a British Columbia marine area called the Great Bear Sea, a proposed marine area in Nunavut, and the Omushkego area in northern Ontario.

Patterns evolving, all thanks to my COBWS experience!

The Impact of COBWS on My Life

Rod Taylor

After my marriage and the birth of our daughter, the time I spent working at COBWS was the greatest and most impactful experience of my life.

It has been forty years of business, politics, and philanthropy since I was first introduced to the group of young leaders that made COBWS what it was. Yet that cohort continues to be the most impressive group of people I have ever had the privilege to work with. Leadership just came so naturally to all of those people. They absolutely embodied that old adage that the best leaders are those who follow well. It was the first place I had ever been where no one ever had to be asked to do something, and more likely than not, many had to be told to take a break. Those in positions of authority never needed to remind others of their position. In fact, to a casual observer it would have been difficult to discern what, exactly, the hierarchy was. People actually fought to do the dishes, and once I had the chance to scrub away to the tunes on the old kitchen boom box, I understood why.

It honestly was as if I had stepped through a portal into a new world. Community meetings were amazing. Everyone, regardless of their position, had a right—if not an obligation—to speak their mind. To a young, silver-spooned male from Toronto who loved the Stones but had never even heard of the Canadian folk singer Stan Rogers, it all seemed unimaginable. If there truly were something called free love, then I had found it. And I don't mean that in a sexual sense. I mean that I'd never had a brother, and now I felt like I had a dozen brothers.

Everyone was just so talented. I remember meeting the other people in my intern group and thinking to myself that I was way out of my league. Music, art, juggling, making a Grumman actually dance, making an eggplant moussaka that I actually loved . . . many times I wondered how it was that I had been allowed to join this troupe of magicians.

I also absolutely loved my students. It was just such a privilege and a responsibility to be an instructor. I remember listening to my first course director talk at the start of a course. She said it was an honor to share the circle with the students because each of them had already done something remarkable and courageous simply by showing up. That sentiment was probably just an accepted reality for those who worked at the school at the time. It affected me profoundly.

I learned so much in those years, not just about others but about myself:

- I learned that a fifty-six-year-old student who described herself as "just a mother and a housewife" would show me the true meaning of the words *grit, courage,* and *compassion.*
- I learned that those who speak the softest are often the ones who should be heard the most.
- I learned to never judge a book by its cover, and that I should reconsider how and why I judged the book in the first place.
- I learned that the world needs way more women in positions where they can truly make a difference.
- And I learned that one of the greatest things you can ever give or receive is trust.

I wish I could say that in the ensuing years I have always lived up to the example provided me through my exposure to COBWS. But I suppose one of the most important things I learned was not to stop trying just because you made a mistake. In retrospect, the tolerance and patience afforded me—an exuberant, testosterone-driven, and at times inappropriate kid—affected me the most and were just such incredible gifts. It feels wrong not to take the time to list the names of all the people who were so kind, who inspired me, but it would fill this entire book, and I would be sure to miss someone.

VII. HARMONY OF TENSIONS

Despite the miserable job I have done at keeping in touch, I miss those days and those friends terribly, and I have one real regret. I know that all those remarkable people eventually went their own ways and did remarkable things out in the world. Still, it seems to me that an enormous opportunity was somehow lost. I think of all that extraordinary passion, wisdom, judgment, leadership, and compassion—all in one room—and I can't help but wonder whether there could or should have been a way to keep that nucleus of good together somehow, and to collectively apply it to today's more pressing issues.

Perhaps it is still not too late.

Remembering Bob Pieh, My Mentor

John Huie

After my first quarter in graduate school at Emory University in Atlanta in 1964, I ran out of money and went looking for a job. A bulletin-board notice announced that Bob Pieh, headmaster of the Anniston Academy in Alabama, was inviting applicants for a teaching and coaching position. I sent him my rather skimpy résumé: one year teaching and two years as a US Army artillery lieutenant. Later I accepted his invitation for an interview. That interview led to a lifelong connection and friendship with one of the most unforgettable characters I've known.

Ruggedly handsome and not at all like other headmasters in my memory, Bob walked me around the campus and showed me the modest facilities while asking probing questions: What draws you to teaching and coaching? Tell me about your limitations and disappointments. And what goals are you working on now?

Welcoming his friendly directness and drawn to his personal warmth, I noted that he moved like an athlete and talked like a philosopher. *Nothing superficial about this man*, I thought. *I'd be lucky to have a mentor like him. Hope he offers me the job.*

After about an hour chatting in his office, Bob leaned forward with intense eye contact and said, "John, it would be good to have you here at this school, and I'm going to offer you a job teaching and coaching, starting in the fall. I need to tell you, though, if you accept the job, you'll be working for a new headmaster. I won't be here next year."

"I'm sorry to hear that," I said. "Where're you going?"

"I'm going to northern Minnesota to start an Outward Bound school in the Boundary Waters Canoe Area. We'll be the second Outward Bound school in the United States."

VII. HARMONY OF TENSIONS

Having never heard the two words *outward* and *bound* rubbed together, I asked, "What's an Outward Bound school?"

Bob launched into a fifteen-minute dissertation on the history and philosophy of Outward Bound, and I heard for the first time the story of the program inspired and developed in Great Britain by German Jewish educator Kurt Hahn, who had fled from Nazi Germany just before World War II. I listened carefully to Bob's words:

> . . . unique wilderness rite-of-passage experience for young men . . . thriving now all over Great Britain . . . came to this country in 1962 . . . connecting students with the natural world . . . fostering self-discovery, building character, teamwork, and the service ethic . . . going beyond self-imposed limits . . . learning on the knife edge of existence . . . Outward Bound schools on several continents wherever the British flag has flown . . . creating a culture of aspiration . . . motto from Tennyson: "To serve, to strive, and not to yield . . ."

He amplified and expanded as I took it all in. Finally he paused to summarize: "Ultimately, Outward Bound is about offering young men[1] the chance to find a sense of harmony within themselves, with each other, with the natural world . . . and with the cosmos."

"That's the best thing I ever heard of," I blurted.

Allowing a smile, leaning forward, looking deeper into my eyes, he said, "Well, if you really feel that way, why don't you come with me?"

Extending my hand to shake his, I said, "Let's go!"

That was the beginning of a sustained bond over the decades.

As a new assistant instructor at the Minnesota Outward Bound School (MOBS) glad for a break from the heady intellectualism of graduate school, I relished at age twenty-seven the physical challenges, soaked up the philosophy and spirit of Kurt Hahn, and watched Bob with admiration as he inspired and

---

1. Bob Pieh ran the first two Outward Bound courses for young women at MOBS in 1965. Other Outward Bound schools followed Bob's lead. Bob also hired the first women instructors. —Ed.

trained the wild and wonderful staff mavericks and idealists assembled in the summer of 1965: teachers, dropouts, medical students, Eagle Scouts, British chaps, and miscellaneous vagabonds of the 1960s.

Bob, his wife, Vi, his daughter, Wendy, his son, Jerry, the program director, and Jerry's wife, Lucy, all gave us the feeling we were part of one dedicated, extended family, building community together and striving for our highest and best.

As wide-eyed students peeled themselves out of the buses after the long, hot ride from Duluth to Ely, Minnesota, we formed them into groups of ten, then gave them a warm welcome and time to switch from street clothes to long pants, tennis shoes, and T-shirts. Eager for any inkling of information and still not sure what they were getting into, students circled around Bob to listen.

"We want you men to get a feeling for the wilderness environment right now so you can learn to appreciate its wild beauty and some of its variety and unpredictability," he said. "This will be your home for the next twenty-eight days. Follow me now on a quiet walk through the wilderness. Stick together with your instructors, follow each other in single file, stay loose and nimble, and soak up the wild beauty. Let's go!"

In one long line, about a hundred young men and instructors followed Bob off the road into the unknown, first very slowly and then gradually picking up speed. Eventually we were running, and the run lasted for about an hour as Bob circled, weaved, and bobbed through thick underbrush, jumping over rotted logs, ducking under branches, rambling and roaming faster and faster through the wilderness. Lots of hooting and hollering was heard as wild energy exploded.

At last, Bob led us into a watery mud bog at the swampy end of Spruce Lake, too thick to swim in. Waist-deep in muck, we swatted mosquitoes and wallowed and groaned our way two hundred yards until we reached clear water and made our way to the dock ahead. We clambered up and assembled with our respective brigades before jogging off to hot showers. Later we unpacked our gear inside platform tents, home for the next two weeks of base camp training, which was followed by a two-week canoe expedition.

That "quiet walk" initiation—repeated at the beginning of every course—made a statement to each of the young men from cities, farms, and suburbs, some away from the comforts of home for the first time: *We're in for something wild and crazy; going to be tough, just like they told us. Not a cakewalk. No way to escape or avoid it now. Gotta dig deep. This is for real, and I love it!*

And that's exactly how I myself felt. *This feels like my kind of tribe, nothing predictable about it. Wild and crazy with serious purpose, a deep dive into the unknown. Shed the shackles of civilization for a while. Let the inner wild man loose! After the quiet walk, what's ahead? A chance for personal growth; connection and community; stretching body, mind, and spirit. Am I coming alive or what?*

Rolling out of our tents and cabins for a run and dip at six in the morning, we jogged out the dirt road at least a mile or so and then back to the dock to jump into Spruce Lake. I was told this was the tradition at Outward Bound schools all over the world: "Dunk 'em and dry 'em."

I had been tromping around in the swamps and jumping in the cold-water springs of southern Georgia all my young life. I loved doing it.

Along the curvy dirt road, Bob had placed Burma-Shave–type messages on wooden signs about five hundred yards apart:

> Be Tough
> Yet Gentle
> Humble
> Yet Bold
> Swayed Always
> By Beauty
> And Truth

We bantered with students after our runs: "Did you make it to *Humble* today?" And some would brag: "I got all the way to *Bold*, and tomorrow I'm going to *Beauty*," or "Tomorrow I'm going to get to *Truth*."

I still have the faded gray *And Truth* sign in my garage today, and I still use Bob's mantra on my signature block—one more example of his abiding influence and not a bad reminder of how to live.

* * *

When I learned that Bob usually took his morning run much earlier than most of us, I started getting up earlier to see if I could run alongside him. I had to go way beyond *Truth* to find him and then try to keep up with him on the return. This gave me the chance to chat personally and to ask him questions about his life and philosophy.

On runs with Bob in the waning weeks of August 1965, my first summer, I learned bits and pieces about his early years in Madison, Wisconsin, where, after his father died, he caddied at the local golf course, cut lawns, and shoveled snow for tips. He talked modestly about his high school athletic achievements and his academic successes. He shared stories about growing up among the Irish and the Italians, and how he came to accept people from all parts of town and to understand the importance of community. Having lived and worked in many different settings from Wisconsin to Alabama to Minnesota, Bob told me that he was never long-term career-oriented.

When students came down the last leg of their morning run, they often would find Bob (in his early sixties) and his close friend and waterfront director Art Thomsen (in his seventies) walking on their hands for minutes at a time. These two passionate and highly developed men had worked together in the Physical Education Department at the University of Wisconsin. They delighted in showing students what the human body could do with discipline and practice.

One night early in the first week of each twenty-eight-day course, we gathered around tables in the dining hall. Bob walked around the tables like a football coach, talking to every young man in the room.

"You have the chance of a lifetime now. You are here for four weeks. You'll be challenged to give your best, to discover both your strengths and your needs for growth. This is the time to be honest with yourself, see what you've got inside. What do you want to do; who do you want to be? On the long expedition coming up, you'll have the chance to keep on going when it would be easy to quit. American philosopher William James says most of us only use about 10 percent of our potential. This is the chance for each of you to dig deep and give 100 percent. You have more in you than you know—both guts and kindness.

"I want you now, at each table, one at a time, to light your candle from the main candle and place it in the holder. As you do this, make a pledge to

VII. HARMONY OF TENSIONS

yourself to give your very best effort and to strive for your goals and to be a helpful team member in the days ahead."

This was hard to pull off, yet Bob connected. Not a snicker or sneer in the room. It felt like an open invitation and not an imposition. He knew how to reach these young men; he had the charisma and the touch. It was mesmerizing.

Bob often closed these candle-lighting and goal-setting talks with a quote from Rabbi Hillel: "If I am not for myself, who then is for me? But if I am for myself alone, what am I? And if not now, when?"

That quote struck me deeply, and I have used it often over the years. I think it struck everyone deeply, largely because of the way Bob set the tone and framework. I think he had honed this kind of ritual with teenage boys in his Shining Trails program of previous years, which featured canoe expeditions into the Boundary Waters Canoe Area from a small resort near Ely, Minnesota. Movies were shown several times during the two-week training phase. Two that stick in my memory are *Twelve Angry Men* with Henry Fonda and *High Noon* with Gary Cooper, each dramatizing an individual hero standing up for justice even when all the odds are against him. These movies gave us plenty to talk about with our brigades. Fonda and Cooper became metaphors for individual courage.

Above all, Bob was an inspirational educator, and clearly the purpose of Outward Bound was to inspire, to light the flame.

Bob's sense of humor was subtle, most often based on simple human behaviors, though he never laughed *at* people, only *with* them. He most often laughed through a glint in his eyes accompanied by a smile. On one occasion, however, at the dinner table with Bob and other staff, I asked, "Does anyone know how you can identify a true intellectual?" All conversation stopped. Poker-faced, I said, "A true intellectual is someone who can listen to the 'William Tell Overture' without ever thinking of *The Lone Ranger*." Bob split his sides laughing at that one, and the whole table joined in. It was good to see him relax and cut loose.

Over my three summers working with Bob at MOBS, I occasionally slipped a written note under his door, sometimes a recommendation, sometimes a critique of an aspect of the program. I remember once writing several pages, comparing the long canoe expedition in the Boundary Waters Canoe Area (BWCA) with the long climbing expedition in the Colorado Outward Bound program. The last paragraph said something like this: "Both kinds of expedition involve struggle, sustained effort, dealing with unexpected events, pacing, group communication, and shared decision-making. One obvious difference is that the long canoe expedition takes you on a horizontal journey, while the mountain expedition is a vertical trek, often with an unmatched peak experience as the ultimate reward."

Bob responded with noticeable irritation, reminding me firmly that canoe portages often offer a peak experience as the canoeist finally reaches the end of an arduous portage trail and sees the blue water. I came away impressed with how sensitive Bob could be if he felt you were missing the mystique of the paddling and portaging experience in the BWCA and Quetico Provincial Park. I had never done much mountain climbing in the first place, but I had experienced vividly the exhilaration of seeing blue water at the end of a long, rugged portage. Bob had that right.

The psychology of the solo became a special interest. I felt, prior to the long expedition, we could better prepare our students for the solo, and I asked Bob if I could add a solo prep workshop to the training schedule. With his approval, I met with each brigade to solicit thoughts and feelings about being alone for three days and nights in the wilderness. What will it feel like to be without food? Have you ever been alone before for seventy-two hours? What do we really need to live, to survive, and to thrive? Bob occasionally sat with us for these sessions and took us deep into Abraham Maslow's hierarchy of needs. We worked well together.

Feeling more and more at home with the Outward Bound life, I followed up on any authors Bob quoted or recommended, especially the writings of his good friend Sigurd Olson, who wrote in *The Singing Wilderness*:

> There is magic in the feel of a paddle and the movement of a canoe, a magic compounded of distance, adventure, solitude, and peace. The way of a canoe is the way of the wilderness and

VII. HARMONY OF TENSIONS

of a freedom almost forgotten. It is an antidote to insecurity, the open door to waterways of ages past and a way of life with profound and abiding satisfactions. When a man is part of his canoe, he is part of all that canoes have ever known.

Sitting on the dock with Bob between courses in early August, I welcomed his strong, positive performance evaluation: "John Errkilla says you really connect well with the kids. And you've come a long way with your hard skills these first two courses as his assistant instructor. He's a hard-driving wilderness veteran and tells me you hold your own very well. The course write-ups you've been turning in are excellent and show you really grasp what we're doing here. What's your self-assessment?"

"I think I'm ready to lead a crew, to tell you the truth," I said.

"I agree. So I'm assigning you to lead the Hennepin Crew next course. Dean Rau will be your assistant."

Dean Rau, steady and mature, was great to work with; we chose, with Bob and Jerry's guidance, an unusually demanding route for our long expedition, yet one that ensured exposure to the beauty of remote waterfalls and Indigenous rock paintings. I was thrilled to see the impact of wild beauty on students, and having earned Bob's confidence, I felt great.

Toward the end of my second summer at MOBS, Jerry Pieh departed to enroll in the Harvard Graduate School of Education. While there, he dreamed up and launched Project Adventure as the culminating activity for his doctorate. Jerry enjoyed a long and fruitful career as headmaster, trainer of teachers, and school reform consultant; he played an instrumental role in the unfolding of expeditionary learning, taking the Outward Bound ethos into hundreds of school systems across the United States. And one summer in the 1980s, Jerry and Lucy's son, Tim, came to work with the North Carolina Outward Bound School (NCOBS), bringing the joie de vivre and the Pieh brand of leadership to our community at Table Rock base camp.

After Jerry departed, Bob asked me to step in as program director. Challenged and excited to have this opportunity, I knew I had big shoes to fill. Jerry's creative leadership and strong communication skills impressed me, especially on the waterfront, where he taught drownproofing to every student brigade. Nearly all the instructional staff had more paddling and wilderness experience than I, but I felt buttressed by Bob's confidence and in tune with his philosophy and belief that Outward Bound was essentially an inner journey of personal growth. If there is tension between Outward Bound Athenians and the bust-ass Spartans, I felt Bob leaned to the Athenian side. Under his influence, I came to see Outward Bound as poetry in action.

Bob set the tone in his inimitable way and gave creative leadership to the highly skilled paddlers and BWCA veterans. He trained us in small-group facilitation skills, giving and receiving feedback, and situational leadership. I put myself on the training schedule to conduct what some considered the onerous task of demonstrating how to recover from swamping the canoe, whether in rapids or flat water. It required me and a partner to be in the water for long periods of time. I got a genuine kick out of doing this.

Bob engaged directly in the training program as often as he could escape from the loads of administrative work on his desk, which looked out over the first rapids of the Kawishiwi River, similar to a ship's captain on the high seas. He seemed to love leading calisthenics and introduced us to all kinds of skipping, jumping, balancing, and stretching. He also took time to explain the various initiative exercises: the ropes course, the wall, the balance wire, and more. He wanted us to learn how to set these activities up creatively and to facilitate them sensitively.

One day John Errkilla and I were having our crew practice on the climbing wall, teaching the best and fastest method for getting the crew over—a competitive approach. Bob got wind of this and called us in for a reprimand and reindoctrination. "The climbing wall is not a competition. Don't show your crew how to do it. Let them struggle. That's the learning we want." I could sense the influence of Heraclitus, one of Bob's favorite philosophers, who said, "It is in changing that we find purpose."

In our various conversations, I shared my feelings about racism and segregation and all the other horrors we white people have inflicted upon people of color. I described the work I was doing at Emory University, interviewing and writing about the crude, racist politician Lester Maddox, who ran for and subsequently won the governorship of Georgia.

I shared my admiration for the courage of Martin Luther King, whose church I had attended occasionally in Atlanta. Bob volunteered, "You'd be

VII. HARMONY OF TENSIONS

interested to know, John, that Coretta Scott, Martin Luther King's wife, was one of my students at Antioch College years ago. She was a lively participant in our outdoor program; she's a strong and beautiful person."

"Is Outward Bound mostly about the individual? Or is it mostly about the team, the group, the community?" I pondered aloud. Bob and I kicked this conundrum around.

"Care for oneself is the stepping stone to community. Hahn was very clear about this," Bob said. In a memo to staff, Bob wrote, "Social abstractions do not solve the problems of human existence," and "Being a Good Samaritan requires skill and composure under stress."

On expeditions I saw how small-group dynamics in the wilderness opened the doors for teamwork and gave many, especially nonwhite students, their first real taste of teamwork and inclusion. I became aware, in the 1960s and beyond, that the tension between Outward Bound as a cultivator of *individualism* versus Outward Bound as a cultivator of *community* would be with us for the long haul—just as it has been and is in all corners of North American culture today.

While I understood that Outward Bound was never intended to be an advocacy organization, I identified strongly with the way the experience raised student aspirations for a better, more humane, and more just society. We were planting seeds for the "culture of aspiration" that Kurt Hahn espoused.

Bob seemed genuinely interested in my yearning for a way to transcend racism. Once he told me, "The thing about Outward Bound is that students learn what matters: pulling your own weight and helping others when needed. On the climbing wall or in the rapids, they can learn both to give and to receive help. I like to think of it as discovering the common human denominator."

"I couldn't agree more," I offered. "We really need an Outward Bound school in the South, where we could bring Black and white students into that kind of relationship."

In late summer 1966, Bob shared with the staff that he wanted to send two outpost brigades on a three-week expedition well up into northern Ontario, establishing, in effect, a new course model. He assigned me as instructor for one of the two brigades.

"We'll caravan two student groups and equipment way up north of the border and drop you off in the small trading village of Armstrong, Ontario. From there you'll be paddling on a small river many miles to reach Whitewater Lake, a large body of water where you'll likely encounter Ojibwe fishermen as well as Wendell Beckwith, an interesting, friendly professor who lives a hermit-like existence. Don't miss the chance to meet Beckwith," Bob advised.

He also told us about German settler Wilfred Wingenroth, who lived with his wife and child beyond Whitewater Lake. "You'll be resupplied by airdrop at midday on your second day on Whitewater Lake. Make sure we can spot your canoes. Be on the lookout for us."

I was thrilled to be given the opportunity to lead one of the two outpost brigades. I had the best adventure of my life: three weeks with one assistant instructor and ten rough-and-ready sixteen-year-olds, including one Black student, Ron Stone, by far the best natural leader of the bunch, who later became a youth counselor in Trenton, New Jersey. Ron showed up during my time at NCOBS for an adult leadership course at Table Rock, where we reconnected and shared Whitewater memories late into the night.

We navigated our route for seven days or so on a narrow river until we finally broke into Whitewater Lake. There, we put our students out on solo, spent time with the friendly, long-red-bearded recluse Wendell Beckwith, survived horrible hordes of mosquitoes at night, and welcomed the resupply by airdrop on the appointed day. Bob himself flew in with one bush pilot and a load of food supplies.

"Everyone okay, John?" he shouted from the door of the plane floating near our campsite, as we waded in waist-deep to accept bags of flapjacks, oranges, dehydrated apples, rice, Bisquick, powdered milk, two rectangular chunks of cheese, and matches and punk wrapped in plastic.

"All's well, Bob. It's been great spending time with Beckwith," I shouted in return. "Wendell introduced us to several Ojibwe Indians at his hideaway. I hope to find Wingenroth when we leave Whitewater Lake. Morale is high. We're ready for the next leg. Best trip ever," I said.

"Good. See you in Armstrong on pickup day," Bob shouted. He waved and ducked back inside the plane. We watched as the pilot took off from the water, gained altitude, circled once above us, and tipped his wings.

* * *

Later that summer I met the adventurous twenty-four-year-old Marjorie Buckley, who came to MOBS for a week to observe and to gather information as she strategized how to plan an Outward Bound school in her native North Carolina. She had made an in-depth study of Kurt Hahn and the history of Outward Bound. Impressed with her passion and intelligence, I thought to myself, *Maybe I can play a part in Marjorie's vision, bringing Outward Bound to the South.*

In addition to Marjorie, Bob hosted educational mavericks, including Bill Peruniak, a wilderness-minded school principal in Ontario; Euell Gibbons, naturalist and author of *Stalking the Healthful Herbs*; Sigurd Olson, author of *The Singing Wilderness*; and a stream of open-minded judges, ministers, and social workers who came to MOBS to see our methodology in action. Bob's most important legacy was his mentoring of many people who became influential leaders in the arena of social-emotional growth. He became an important catalyst in the development of Outward Bound as a uniquely effective social-emotional educational vehicle.

In 1970, I accepted Bob's invitation to become an assistant professor, working side by side with him in the newly designed McArthur College of Education at Queen's University in Kingston, Ontario. Our department was called Clinical and Field Studies, and all the students in the program were required to earn fifteen credits in our offerings: open country, community service, and group dynamics. I arrived at Bob and Vi's farm on the night of the first landing on the moon (July 20, 1969). We sat transfixed, watching the black-and-white television as Neil Armstrong stepped onto the surface of the moon and said for the world to hear, "That's one small step for a man, one giant leap for mankind."

Putting those words into perspective, Bob added, "All the space exploration to come won't change our need to stay close to the earth, which sustains us in life. Makes it more important than ever that we immerse students in the natural world."

Over the years, Bob sent me copies of various proposals he had written. One he shared was for a "Contrariety House" at St. John's College in New Mexico, where the great books focus in the curriculum and heady intellectualism had, over the decades, sometimes ignored the needs of body and spirit. I still have a copy of the St. John's proposal in my Bob Pieh file. The following is an excerpt:

> The College's building plan now includes what is termed a "physical education center." The proposed activities evolution described in this proposal departs from tradition. It requires more varied but less expensive facilities than those usually incorporated in a physical education building. Planning a suitable building will stimulate creativity.
>
> Perhaps the activity center could be called "Contrast House" or "Contrariety House." The evolutionary activities program would function in dynamic equilibrium with the academic program and express that "hidden harmony" which, according to Heraclitus, "is better than that which is obvious." Heraclitus also stated: "Men do not understand how that which is torn in different directions comes into accord with itself—harmony in contrariety, as in the case of the bow and the lyre."

One can imagine how seductive and appealing such a proposal would be for the decision-makers at a college focused on the great thinkers of Western civilization.

I remember Bob often emphasizing the "underlying connection between opposites," quoting, paraphrasing, or referencing Heraclitus: "Change is the only constant," and "You can't step in the same river twice." It seems obvious that Bob's aphorism—"Be tough yet gentle / Humble yet bold / Swayed always by beauty and truth"—reflects and captures the spirit of Heraclitus, expressing harmony and contrariety in the same sentence. And there's this Heraclitus quotation he often paraphrased: "Man is most nearly himself when he achieves the seriousness of a child at play." Bob understood paradox; he took play seriously.

Bob participated in programs at various growth centers that emerged in the 1960s and 1970s, especially Esalen Institute in Big Sur, California, where he sampled a range of modalities aiming at heightened awareness, drawing on sensory training, Zen, Gestalt therapy, and more. These modalities influenced him in significant ways and put him on the cutting edge of institutions he served, especially McArthur College at Queen's University. Bob had joined Bill Peruniak and Vern Ready, both Canadian educators, in designing McArthur College to be radically holistic and experiential in preparing teachers at the graduate level for teaching in Ontario schools.

Bob accepted my invitations to deliver staff workshops over the years at schools where I worked, such as Saint Mark's School of Texas, Verde Valley School in Arizona, and NCOBS.

Our last time together was at the Outward Bound International Conference in Cooperstown, New York, in 1988, where Bob was celebrated for his lifetime of Outward Bound leadership. At the conference I gave a personal tribute to Bob for his example and influence, "especially his focus on living in deep harmony with the natural world, the realm of the sacred, from which we derive values and meaning, no matter where we run our programs."

His handwritten note came into my mailbox a few weeks later: "Thank you for your Cooperstown speech. You made us laugh and you made us think—it was contagious!" He signed by quoting himself:

> Thinking about something and being unable to experience the truth of it is like carrying an unlit lantern in a dark room. One can experience the reality of who they are and who they can be by putting themselves to the test. Nothing will light the flame in one's lantern but the wind of one's going. Keep your flame lit, John.

Jerry Pieh shared with me the eulogy he delivered in 1993 on the death of his father:

> A brother of the silent places, Bob devoted his life to building community. He touched many lives and made a significant difference in the field of education with his intense commitment to and expectation of quality in human growth, community, and service.

Preparing this remembrance, I called my good friend Ted Moores, who knew Bob well over many years as a colleague and friend. Ted is the former executive director and chair of the MOBS board of trustees. I asked Ted to help me describe Bob's distinctive characteristics. Here is our profile of Bob:

> Compassionate, intuitive, gentle, inspiring, observant, insightful, creative groundbreaker (founder of MOBS and COBWS, key pioneer in design of McArthur College), driven, reflective, integrating thought and feeling, strong masculine presence combined with authentic sensitivity, open personality, love of simple things (especially in nature), trusting in people, ability to connect with others, total presence in any interaction, ability to instill confidence, prophetic insight into social-emotional education, ability to lead by supporting those around him to shine, ability to use ritual to cement important learning, unconcerned with issues of tenure or permanence, willing to morph in new directions, and committed to serve, to strive, and to gather no moss.

About a hundred of us aging mavericks gathered at MOBS for the fiftieth anniversary of the school, now called Voyageur Outward Bound School. We slow-walked out and back on the same curvy dirt road where, in the 1960s, we used to run every morning like gazelles, trying to stay well ahead of our student crews. At the end of our walk, some of us even charged off the dock and jumped into Spruce Lake, hollering a full-throated "Ooh-ahh," reenacting our old ritual.

We watched an old video of Bob in his prime as he articulated in his inimitable way the philosophical and psychological rationale for a wilderness-based rite-of-passage experience for adolescents. We honored his pioneering of the first Outward Bound courses for young women, directed by Jean Sanford. Wendy Pieh spoke eloquently about the way her Outward Bound years fueled her passion for building community, a passion she had applied as director of Outward Bound Lesotho in southern Africa, as well as her work as an elected legislative representative for the state of Maine. And all of us shared memories, tall tales, wild laughter, and tears as we allowed ourselves to go back to those times when Bob Pieh and MOBS had made such indelible impacts on our lives.

VII. HARMONY OF TENSIONS

A dozen or so of us old-timers gathered one morning close to the first rapids on the Kawishiwi River, near the spot where Bob and Vi Pieh once lived year-round in their rustic, quaint cabin nestled among small boulders and birch trees. Jerry Pieh offered reflections on his father's life and work, and then encouraged any of us who wanted to follow him in placing Bob's ashes into the rapids. Bob's children Jerry and Wendy went first, then Ted Moores, then me, moving precariously out on the rocks with a small container of Bob's ashes in our hands.

Across my mind came the memory of Bob, years ago on Whitewater Lake, ducking back inside the bush plane before my crew and I watched the pilot take off on the rippling surface, gaining altitude, circling once above us, and tipping his wing.

I bent down, pausing, remembering, and giving thanks for my lifelong friend and mentor, letting his ashes pour into the churning and shifting waves of the Kawishiwi River rapids that Bob, "swayed always by beauty and truth," loved so well.

Granola Spirit

Charles Luckmann

That was a memorable day to me, for it made great changes in me. But it's the same with any life. Imagine one selected day struck out of it and think how different its course would have been. Pause, you who read this, and think for a moment of the long chain . . . that would never have bound you but for the formation of the first link of one memorable day.

—Charles Dickens, *Great Expectations*

Four decades ago I spent many memorable days in northern Ontario at Homeplace with the COBWS community on Black Sturgeon Lake. Those days contributed to my idealism, believing that through education we could protect the environment and create healthy communities. I keep returning to COBWS as the closest I came to an educational utopia.

Looking back over the decades, having taught at nine schools in four countries, I now view Bob Pieh, the philosopher and educator who created COBWS, as one of the prophets of experiential education, alongside Kurt Hahn. After establishing MOBS in 1963, Bob went to Canada in 1976 and laid the groundwork for an ideal community for students and staff, incorporating concepts of self-improvement and renewal by immersion in nature, affectionately referred to as the Canadian bush.

It is my belief that Kurt Hahn borrowed these transcendentalist ideas, initially developed by Ralph Waldo Emerson and Henry David Thoreau in the mid-nineteenth century, to create pedagogy for the twentieth century that Hahn called Outward Bound. As described by Thomas James, Hahn was influenced by many thinkers, such as the Socratic dialogues found in Plato's

VII. HARMONY OF TENSIONS

The Republic; the philosophy of William James, a New England contemporary of Emerson, especially James's lecture to teachers and students on the educational "moral equivalent to war"; and the enlightenment ideas of Jean-Jacques Rousseau.[1] My premise is that on Black Sturgeon Lake, in the community at Homeplace, Bob and Wendy Pieh implemented these concepts, realizing as perfectly as humanly possible Kurt Hahn's goals for humanity.

As initially developed by Kurt Hahn, a small group would be placed apart from society, in a "healthy pasture," to begin an aspirational journey with nature as teacher. This Platonic quest, or hero's journey, would strengthen and transform the individual through self-discovery and sacrifice and through making meaningful choices as part of a small group (brigade) meeting challenges with the simplest technology (canoes, tents, a map, a compass, fire, and each other). They would journey together as a self-sufficient community, practice self-governance among equals (consensual and democratic), create new meanings to live by, and rewrite their personal histories and obligations to each other and society.

At the time I didn't think, nor was it stated, that we were striving to create a utopia for our students. But now, decades later, I think that is the ideal that Bob and Wendy Pieh were seeking.

As the editor of *The Journal of Experiential Education* (1992–1997), I searched for articles Bob Pieh wrote or books he published, but Bob didn't commit much to paper. Rather than talk about education and philosophy, Bob taught through example. In 1965, Bob implemented the first Outward Bound courses for young women with women instructors; other Outward Bound schools followed his lead. And many of the staff that Bob hired were inspired by his vision, as I was years later.

When I joined COBWS in 1979, it was the third Outward Bound school I had worked for. I had spent a summer with MOBS (1973); done an adaptive Outward Bound program at Southern Illinois University called Project Underway (1972, 1974); and completed three years with the North Carolina Outward Bound School (1975–1977). The educational concepts I embraced gave me the moorings I needed as I began my life as a white adult male—a

---

1. Thomas James, "Sketch of a Moving Spirit: Kurt Hahn," in *The Theory of Experiential Education*, ed. Richard J. Kraft and Mitchell S. Sakofs, 39–44 (Boulder, CO: Association for Experiential Education, 1985).

young man alienated by the Vietnam War, corporate capitalism, land-stealing settler colonialism, mindless consumerism, and racism against people of color. I now acknowledge that what I found at Homeplace allowed me to escape from the sins or dust of the world. COBWS created for me an ideal world that doesn't exist. Of course it wasn't all perfect, but each Outward Bound course I taught was a joyful and wondrous experience. I was also reading a lot of poetry, such as that of Gary Snyder, whose poems were filled with Zen: "Tasting the berries / greeting the blueberries / learning and loving the whole terrain."

Now I'm asking myself, *Could what I experienced at COBWS be an antidote to current existential threats, such as climate change and a decline in biodiversity?* The Canadian writer, anthropologist, and scholar Wade Davis believes that young people want to commune with nature and serve others through meaningful engagement with both. Davis believes young people want to touch what's real, natural, and mythical. One vehicle Davis mentions to achieve this is through a national service program; many others also have suggested this as a means for young people to successfully meet the challenges facing us all.

After graduating from high school, every teenager would be required to spend a minimum of one year serving their country. Those choosing the military would serve longer, but others would choose from among such service programs as AmeriCorps, Canada Service Corps, the Peace Corps, and the Civilian Conservation Corps (1933–1942), which was a volunteer program in the United States for the unemployed during the Great Depression.

I've read that there is widespread support for national service programs. President Joe Biden has proposed creating two new public service programs in the United States: the Public Health AmeriCorps and American Climate Corps. Polls that I've seen surveying young people ages eighteen to twenty-four indicate that a majority are in support of service programs. Young people want to improve themselves and protect our environment. They want to serve their countries in multiple ways, not just militarily. A ten- to fourteen-day Outward Bound course, modeled on the educational pedagogies of Kurt Hahn and Bob Pieh, would be a profound initiation for young people beginning these service programs. They might even save us and planet earth.

* * *

VII. HARMONY OF TENSIONS

It was at Homeplace that I first heard the phrase *granola spirit*. It embodied freedom and adventure and eating simply, mostly vegetarian food you cooked yourself. Granola spirit was earth-centered. You aspired to live lightly and sustainably. You were in touch with the sacred. You wrote letters; you helped others; you aspired to live in healthy communities. At COBWS we traveled intricate water highways by canoe, leaving no trace of our passing. Now, forty-five years later, facing existential threats on many fronts, this book is regenerating my granola spirit for the road ahead.

VIII. PREVIOUSLY PUBLISHED

In 1985, COBWS staff launched *The Journal of COBWS Education*. It published eleven issues discussing the pedagogy of Outward Bound and outdoor experiential education between 1985 and 2007. From the 1986 issue, Robert Couchman's essay "Internal and External Rhythms: The Canadian Wilderness as a Learning Environment" posits that COBWS is unique due to its isolation in the vastness of the Canadian landscape

In "The Last Time I Saw Bob," published in 1997, Charles Luckmann reflects on his personal relationship with Bob Pieh, who died in 1993, and during a wild, nighttime canoe paddle, Luckmann sheds light on Bob the risk-taker.

Because our book is memoir, we shied away from including academic essays. However, we did include one: Philip Blackford and Stephen Couchman's essay "Learning to See New Landscapes: The Canadian Outward Bound Wilderness School," published in 1996 by Sage Publications in its book *The Ecology of Health*. Thoroughly researched and referenced, Blackford and Couchman's essay offers context to how COBWS fits into the matrix of Outward Bound schools worldwide. The authors discuss the remote program site and lack of financial resources as unique factors in the success of the school. They also provide specific insights into the curriculum. They explain why adventure-based, experiential learning is vitally important for youth today. —Ed.

OPPOSITE: Artwork by (Victoria) Moon Joyce captures the ethos of Homeplace on Black Sturgeon Lake.

Internal and External Rhythms: The Canadian Wilderness as a Learning Environment

Robert Couchman

It is with considerable appreciation that I take up my pen to respond to the kind invitation of the editor of *The Journal of COBWS Education* to write a few cogent thoughts on the Outward Bound experience. As a volunteer who has never participated in leading a brigade nor done more than hover on the perimeter of the Outward Bound community, I do not have the practical experience or knowledge to write in any real depth about the skills, both physical and emotional, that go into running a good program or teaching a student some vital skill.[1]

Given the fact, however, that I have been a respectful observer of the Canadian wilderness for many years, an appreciative recipient of the COBWS experience, and a student of human behavior and social change, perhaps I can offer a few personal thoughts on the unique experiential educational environment that has been developed at COBWS and why it so readily fosters growth and development in students and staff alike. In addressing this issue, which should be seen as the central issue of every major educational endeavor, I will place my attention on the adjective *unique*.

In most ways, COBWS is not unique as an Outward Bound school or as an experiential education program. We adhere to the basic tenets of Kurt Hahn and the North American evolution of the same. We use the wilderness environment as a classroom and believe in the power of successfully achieved progressive challenges. We even commonly accept the somewhat mystical concept of metaphor as a learning tool. In so many ways, COBWS is exactly the same as most other Outward Bound programs throughout North America.

---

1. This essay originally appeared in *The Journal of COBWS Education* (February 1986).

The factors that do make COBWS unique are its Canadian identity, its isolation within a vast wilderness area, and its strong tradition of community. Since 1976, these special factors have effectively interacted to give COBWS a unique and powerful quality among Outward Bound programs.

In rereading Roderick Nash's classic work *Wilderness and the American Mind*, I am struck by the amazing distinctions between the American treatment of the wilderness and the Canadian attitude, as described by Margaret Atwood in *Survival*, an analysis of Canadian literature. Nash describes a heroic people spurred on by unquestionable belief in Manifest Destiny. Wilderness is something to be "pushed back" or "conquered." Frontier heroes climb to the summits of the barrier mountains of Appalachia and see the rich plains stretched out before them. They clear the land of both trees and Native people and then push ever westward. While Nash's American wilderness is rugged, even dangerous at times, it is no match for the Daniel Boones, Davy Crocketts, and the Lewis and Clarks that confront the expanding borders of the new territories of the United States.

Despite its breadth and majesty, the American wilderness is also amazingly forgiving and, at times, downright friendly to its highly individualistic and determined inhabitants. In American folk tales and literature, the wilderness can be confronted and beaten back. Not so in Canada. Margaret Atwood describes a wilderness which is vast, dark, and unforgiving. The Canadian hero, unlike his American counterpart, travels into the forests and tundra regions and survives only if he learns to understand the elements and move with them rather than against them. The Canadian hero has enormous respect for the hostility and rawness of an environment that is only too able to crush his frail ship or cause him to freeze to death. For every successful Fraser and Mackenzie in Canadian exploration there is a Franklin or a Hornby who was overcome by the power of the continent's northern wilderness.

In addition to respect for the wilderness, the characters of Canadian wilderness novels generally pull themselves together in tight little communities against the immense hostility of the land. In particular, early French Canadian novels describe the essential human communion that exists in tiny villages tucked up against the winter hills of the Laurentians. From the closely knit voyageur brigades of the North West Company to the rural communities described by Margaret Laurence and Canada's Icelandic author

William Dempsey Valgardson, Canadians are portrayed as being highly interdependent people concerned, above all, for the welfare of the family and their communities. Rugged individualism, the hallmark of the American hero, is a trait that does not stand up well against the prolonged and isolated cold of the Canadian winter, nor against the blackfly-infested boreal forests of midspring.

In many ways, COBWS is a reflection of the classic village set on the edge of the immense Canadian wilderness. Through its short evolution, Homeplace has become a true community where respect for the welfare of its inhabitants, whether they be staff or students, has overshadowed the macho individualism that pits physical strengths and the mind against the storms of the region's larger lakes or the whitewater of the many wild rivers of the area. While many opportunities exist for personal challenge, equal emphasis is given to interpersonal relationships and the vital interdependence of brigade members as they negotiate terrain that constantly harbors potentially destructive forces just below the surface. In traveling through the area, one quickly develops a humble respect for the Albany/Ogoki watershed, or you soon encounter its dangers. Being the most remote wilderness Outward Bound school in the world, COBWS cannot afford to pay lip service to the importance of individuals looking after the collective well-being of the whole community. Unlike most other Outward Bound schools, the region inhabited by COBWS is not forgiving, and help is usually many remote hours away.

Those who visit COBWS from the US or Britain are quick to sense the cohesiveness of this community and the sensitivity that staff have for the wilderness that surrounds them. In this regard, COBWS is very much a part of the cultural tradition of Canada. Bravado and competition have little part to play in the lives of those who live at COBWS, nor do such elements manifest themselves in the program. Thus you do not find an instructor giving a student that "final nudge." The student must choose to challenge his environment; it is never something to be conquered. The Canadian wilderness demands respect from those who wish to move with the flow of its seasons and the mood of its stark isolation. Those who fail to learn this lesson are soon defeated.

Such imagery creates a very powerful environment for individuals to learn about themselves, and the need they have for the close support of other good folk. COBWS is indeed a special community and thereby a most unique Outward Bound program. Its close identity with Canadian spirit is intrinsic to its unique dynamic as an educational experience. One walks quietly across its portages and paddles humbly along its waterways, learning constantly to sense and move with the rhythms of the land. The exhilaration of achievement as one successfully navigates a difficult set of rapids is constantly balanced by the knowledge of the two-mile portage through a muddy swamp that lies just around the next bend. While the personal rewards of achieving the first task are only too evident, the will to undertake the latter task with equanimity is a lesson about life itself.

COBWS students gradually learn that you can only conquer your fears and misgivings. The wilderness can never be conquered, only respected.

The Last Time I Saw Bob

Charles Luckmann

I met Bob Pieh in 1973 when he was the director of MOBS. It was my first summer with Outward Bound. At twenty-two years old, I was hired as an assistant instructor. I don't recollect ever having a conversation that summer with Bob (nobody called him Dr. Pieh).[1]

The image that remains from that time was his unusual gesture, when talking to a group, of slightly turning his head, touching his eye with an index finger, and giving the impression he was on the verge of unveiling the wisdom of Ulysses.

To say that I put him on a pedestal is an understatement. I worshipped him from afar. *Someday*, I told myself, *I'm going to follow in the footsteps of Bob Pieh.* However, as far as I could tell, Bob didn't know I existed.

After that summer, I went on to teach for NCOBS. I also spent a couple of summers as a field archaeologist in Illinois and Labrador. You can imagine my surprise, then, when Bob called me one day about five years later and invited me to come and work with him at "COBWEBS," he called it, a new Outward Bound school he'd started in North Ontario.

I went, and it changed my life. I've never been satisfied in quite the same way with gainful employment again. Bob left before I arrived, however, and was replaced by Australian Alistair McArthur. But Bob and I kept in touch, and I visited him once in Kingston, Ontario. In January 1980, I became the second program director for COBWS when Wendy Pieh moved to Alberta, passing the baton to me.

The last time I saw Bob was when I invited him back to Homeplace to be a guest instructor for one of the first educator courses at the school. A couple

---

1. This essay originally appeared in *Pathways: The Ontario Journal of Outdoor Education* Vol. 9, No. 2 (April 1997).

of weeks before Bob arrived, a forest fire swept to within a mile of Homeplace; the wind miraculously changed direction, which saved the school, but not before we had evacuated all the canoes, food, equipment, and students to Thunder Bay.

We couldn't return to our normal course sites until August; thus, we were forced to run our program in Quetico Provincial Park, near Atikokan, Ontario, and the Boundary Waters Canoe Area in northern Minnesota. For the month of July, we based our operations out of the Lakehead University gymnasium. I didn't realize it then, but I was following in Bob's footsteps of running a program on a shoestring.

When Bob arrived in Thunder Bay, the course had already been in the field for ten days, and the plan was for Bob and me and the course director, Ian Yolles, to paddle into the BWCA and meet the group on a remote lake for a series of workshops. The only vehicle available to us was an old blue pickup truck, which we drove to the end of the Gunflint Trail, where we launched our canoe.

We spent several fun and productive days with the educators, Bob transmitting wisdom without saying a word, it seemed. My story really begins when we left the group about an hour before dark at the end of the third day, when Bob casually informed Ian and me that he needed to catch a plane the next morning for Toronto. (The plan had been to spend the night and paddle out the next day.) We were three hours of brisk paddling from the takeout, and a summer thunderstorm was moving into the area—not a time to be on the water.

However, you couldn't argue with Bob. He would smile quixotically, his eyes would sparkle, and his expression seemed to ask, "*Do you have a problem with this great idea?*"

Of course we did! But we were with the legendary Bob Pieh, who had started two Outward Bound schools and initiated the fabled Outdoor & Experiential Education program at Queen's University. Who were we?

Ian and I quickly took down the tent as Bob dropped our packs into the aluminum Grumman canoe, and we paddled off toward the approaching storm. For a while the wind blew softly in our faces, that fecund, humid summer air that precedes a downpour.

In a couple of hours, it was dark as a cave (before the thunder and lightning created awe all around us). But the two portages were behind us—all that remained was crossing four miles of open water in the pouring rain.

> *How admirable!*
> *To see lightning and not think*
> *Life is fleeting.*
>
> —Basho

Ian and I mentioned to Bob that maybe this was as far as we should go tonight. When we broached our idea to him, he looked crestfallen. His expression seemed to say, "*Why would anyone want to camp here, at the end of the portage trail?*"

"Well, gentlemen, I think we can do it," he said as he looked at us with a wry grin.

Now let's reflect on this for a moment: Bob Pieh is paddling with the program director and course director for COBWS. We've evacuated Homeplace and are running these courses because to cancel them would shut down the school. Alistair McArthur, the new school director, has implored us to run a safe, mobile program.

Two summers before, more than a dozen students had died in another canoeing program when trying to cross Lake Timiskaming. Here stood Bob Pieh, a dean of outdoor education in North America, and he wanted to shove off and paddle across a big lake in a lightning storm.

I do remember it as an exhilarating paddle. A huge cumulus was on fire with the internal electricity of lightning bolts, and the rain pelted us as we dug deep with each stroke to gain the opposite shore. Ian was in the bow, and I was in the stern, following a compass bearing for where I knew we had left the truck. Bob sat on top of a pack in the midsection.

Even now in memory, I can see Ian's bent back, pulling hard, and his arms working as fast as they could. A couple of times, when the lightning was especially bright, or the thunder particularly loud, Bob would look back at me and give me two thumbs-up, his white hair, though wet, standing on end.

Bob appeared to be loving it. I've often wondered about that. Did he believe he lived a charmed life? Or like John Muir, did his spirit need the cataclysmic power of nature in order to feel whole? Or did his genius lie in being bold?

When we hit the other shore and carried our gear to the truck, it wouldn't start. The engine turned over and over without igniting. Finally, we ran down the battery.

"You guys mind sleeping in the truck?" Bob asked. "I know an innkeeper down the road a bit. I can probably stay with him."

It was around midnight when Bob hoisted his pack and disappeared down the Gunflint Trail. Ian and I spent a fitful night. I won the coin toss and got the seat to stretch out on; Ian crawled under the truck to find a dry spot. In my dreams the storm raged around us all night.

At daybreak, around five, Bob woke me up by tapping on the window. He was cleanly shaven and dressed in sport coat and tie. "Just wanted to say thanks," he said.

As we shook hands through the rolled-down window, I asked, "How will you get back to Thunder Bay to catch your plane?"

"I should have no trouble catching a ride in this getup," he said, waving a hand at his polished image. The last time I saw Bob, he wore a tie and sport coat and carried a woods pack as he walked down the Gunflint Trail, a gravel road.

I had fallen back to sleep for maybe an hour or more when I was awakened again by a man at my window.

"Are you with that old man who came in here last night?"

When I said I was, the man replied, "Well, he left early this morning without paying his bill. That will be twenty-eight dollars."

"Twenty-eight dollars for a four-hour nap! Isn't that a bit steep?"

"That old codger ate half the food in my refrigerator!"

For a moment I looked back down the Gunflint Trail, and in my mind's eye, I could still see Bob, smiling, waving goodbye, his white hair freshly combed and spiffy. That was the last time I saw him. Sometimes, though, when I'm fed up with linear-minded supervisors, rules, and regulations, I think of Bob and want to follow again in his footsteps.

Learning to See New Landscapes: The Canadian Outward Bound Wilderness School

Philip Blackford and Stephen Couchman

The real voyage of discovery lies not in seeing new landscapes but in having new eyes.

—Marcel Proust

Originally, the expression *outward bound* referred to a time when sailors headed for open sea, leaving behind the safety of a familiar harbor. Today, at more than thirty Outward Bound schools around the world, it means leaving the comfort and security of family and friends to undertake a challenging voyage of experience, adventure, and self-discovery.[1]

Outward Bound is a nonprofit educational organization, formulated around an interpretation of the educational philosophy of German educator Dr. Kurt Hahn (1886–1974). Hahn's educational philosophy was founded on the utopian vision described in Plato's *Republic*. He was impressed by Plato's notion of nurturing the development of traditional Athenian civic virtues in a "healthy pasture" removed from the corrupting influences of modern society (James 1980).

Hahn's first school was established in 1920. Germany had been ruined by the First World War. The social climate was one of dissolution and despair. Salem School was intended as a force for social and political regeneration. Its purpose was "to train citizens who could, if called upon, make independent decisions, put right action before expediency and the common cause before personal ambition" (Hahn, quoted in James 1980, 19). Hahn's goal was to ensure "the survival of an enterprising curiosity, an undefeatable spirit, and tenacity in pursuit, readiness for sensible self-denial and, above all, compassion."

---

1. This essay, printed with permission, is a chapter from *The Ecology of Health: Identifying Issues and Alternatives*, ed. Jennifer Chesworth (New York: Sage Publications, 1996).

Hahn later went on to establish a number of other innovative and influential organizations, including Gordonstoun School in 1934 and the United World Colleges in 1962. But Outward Bound is his best known and most enduring legacy.

The first Outward Bound school was founded in 1941, in the tiny Welsh seacoast town of Aberdovey. In the early days of World War II, many young recruits to the British merchant marines were succumbing to the hardships they faced when forced into lifeboats in the North Atlantic. Often, their senior colleagues were surviving the ordeal. It was felt that although the younger men might be more physically fit, their older compatriots had at least two advantages: First, they had been through difficult times before and were more psychologically prepared; they knew how to access personal reserves of tenacity and perseverance. Second, they knew the advantages of teamwork and were aware, from experience, that their chances of survival increased dramatically when they worked together.

The initial Outward Bound program was very specific in its purpose. It was a response to an immediate and critical set of circumstances. Even so, Hahn was clear that the Outward Bound training should focus not so much on technical skills as on developing those personal skills of self-reliance, tenacity, and teamwork. Laurence Holt, Hahn's partner in the venture, articulated their shared vision: "The training at Aberdovey must be less a training *for* the sea than *through* the sea, and so benefit all walks of life" (Holt, quoted in Miner and Boldt 1981, 33).

Outward Bound has changed tremendously since those first British sailors arrived in Aberdovey over a half century ago. The more than thirty Outward Bound schools now scattered around the world have all developed their own unique character. Several years ago, a Canadian journalist exploring the origins of Outward Bound remarked:

> There is no blueprint, no set of instructions on how to run an Outward Bound school. I tried to puzzle this out in the schools I visited and came up with a comparison to Common Law. Guided by precedent, successive waves of practitioners have absorbed the basic thinking and adapted it to the special circumstances of each new school (Wilson 1985, 5).

COBWS—or COBWEBS, as it is affectionately known—is by no means the largest or most affluent Outward Bound school in the world. It is, however, unique. The school's main summer site is the most remote Outward Bound base in the world. An hour and a half north of the Trans-Canada Highway near Thunder Bay, Ontario, Homeplace is separated from Hudson Bay by a single railway line, a few logging roads, five or six small Indigenous communities, and several thousand square miles of forest, lakes, and rivers. During the day, you can watch rain squalls sweep across the lake. At night, with no significant sources of artificial light for more than fifty miles in any direction, you can paddle out from shore and watch the stars, meteors, and northern lights reflected in the silent black water.

COBWS has also acquired a reputation within Outward Bound as having a particularly strong orientation to community. Although promoting the skills of working and living together is an important component of all Outward Bound programs, COBWS seems to have singled out this aspect of Hahn's philosophy for special attention. It may have something to do with the school's remoteness. Staff living and working at the school must rely on one another for social as well as professional interaction. And, most certainly, the first staff of the school set a tone early on of community and consensus. This emphasis on community underlies a significant characteristic of the school, which is that COBWS is quite possibly the most diverse Outward Bound school in the world.

In essence, this diversity stems from the belief that no matter who you are—how young or old, rich or poor, whatever the color of your skin or the level of your physical abilities—you have something to gain from participation in an Outward Bound program. As is the case at all Outward Bound schools, COBWS strives to involve a wide cross section of participants. Subsequently, the school recognizes the special needs of individuals. To provide for these needs, the school has developed three program areas.

The largest and most well known of these are the open enrollment programs. As the name suggests, these programs are available for any individual who wishes to experience Outward Bound. Through the Centre for Change, COBWS also provides a wide variety of programs for corporations and organizations. These groups, who are most often experiencing a transition or dealing with difficult issues, or who may simply wish to explore the further potential of their business, find that the communications, group dynamics, and team-building approach of the school can have a significant positive impact on the culture of their organization.

Finally, the school is extremely proud of its Community & Health Services Programs. These programs, which now account for more than a quarter of the school's work, are intended to make the Outward Bound experience available and accessible to a wide range of people who might not normally consider a learning experience of this sort. As part of this program area, COBWS runs courses for troubled youth, women who have experienced violence, older adults, Indigenous participants, and people with differing physical abilities.

It is important to point out that it is not the school's intention to segregate these individuals from the regular stream of courses. Many individuals who might fall into one of these groups choose each year to participate in standard courses. However, the school found that by offering special programs it could sometimes entice participants to join who would not normally take the leap. At the same time, it was felt that richer experiences might be provided for some by creating an environment of heightened emotional safety or by framing a course within a particular context, be it developmental, cultural, or simply shared experience.

> *Often during the day I find myself thinking about the great feelings of camaraderie with other women, and I glow all over again as I remember the wonderful feats I accomplished up there. Each day I remember something positive about my Outward Bound experience, whether it be words of praise or a simple smile of a good friend.*
>
> —Women of Courage program participant

Although the school provides a variety of programs, instructors never stray far from a methodology that has developed along with the school. The focus on this learning process, which consists of experience and adventure within a holistic context, creates a landscape for change. Regardless of the motivation of individual participants, the process through which they explore themselves and their relationship to the world is remarkably similar.

CREATING A LANDSCAPE FOR CHANGE

"The greatest challenge you'll face in Outward Bound was the one you overcame in arriving here today." These are often the first words a student hears on arriving at COBWS. Tired after a long journey to an unfamiliar place, bitten by mosquitoes and blackflies, and asked to pack all their worldly possessions into a small sack, many participants would likely climb right back into the van for a trip home if it were not for a deep-seated spirit of adventure and desire to explore unknown places within themselves and the world around them.

Often, people choose to take an Outward Bound course at an important transition point in their lives, such as finishing school, ending a relationship, or changing jobs. Regardless of the circumstance, more than anything else, the greatest tool for growth is an individual's eagerness to create such an opportunity. Once an individual identifies the will to change within herself or himself, the greatest challenge has been overcome.

The Outward Bound process assumes that learning takes place when people engage in and reflect on experiences in challenging environments. Participants are presented with a series of increasingly difficult physical and mental problems, none designed to be beyond their capability. By confronting difficult tasks, they must call on forgotten or hitherto unrecognized reserves of ingenuity, strength, perseverance, and compassion. By rising to meet these unavoidable challenges, students learn the necessity and the rewards of working well with others. Through direct experience, Outward Bound students are presented with irrefutable evidence that they can succeed far beyond perceived expectations.

EXPERIENCE

The foundation for learning at Outward Bound is experience. There are no textbooks at the schools, nor are there any chalkboards (which is probably for the best because there are no walls). Lessons in geography are learned while participants find their way through the woods, and classes in physics are taught over the din of foaming whitewater. Rather than being passive receptacles of information, participants are encouraged to learn for themselves the skills they will need to accomplish the many challenges placed before them during the course of the program.

Some of these skills, such as how to paddle a canoe in a straight line, pack a wanigan, use a map and compass, and cook lump-free oatmeal, represent technical knowledge. Mastery of these skills is necessary for the group to be able to travel safely and comfortably through the wilderness. At the same time, less tangible but ultimately more important goals such as trust, teamwork, communication, and consensus building are addressed.

The foundation for this model of education is expressed in the work of the educational theorist David Kolb:

> Experiential learning occurs through a four-stage cycle; immediate concrete experience is the basis for observation and reflection. These observations are assimilated into a "theory" from which new implications for action can be deduced. These implications or hypotheses then serve as guides, interacting to create new experiences (Chickering 1977).

Through the course of an Outward Bound program, participants are presented with a series of problem-solving experiences. After each experience, time is given for reflection and group discussion. During these sessions, participants have an opportunity to discuss personal perspectives on the activity and to critique the working relationship of the group in preparation for increasingly difficult tasks to come. In this way, the focus is not on the successful completion of individual tasks, but on the ability of the group to learn to work together effectively. Each of us has strengths in one or more of the stages of the learning cycle Kolb describes. Some of us are better thinkers; others are better doers. Some of us feel most comfortable in learning environments that allow us to watch and reflect; others prefer to tinker with a problem. In a sense, the four stages of the experiential learning cycle also represent four somewhat distinct learning styles. One of the beauties of Kolb's model in a community setting is that it allows for all participants to play a role in the learning process. Most formal educational environments favor a cognitive approach to learning. In experiential learning, the ability to think abstractly is valued equally with an orientation to experiencing things firsthand, the ability to observe and reflect, and a willingness to test out new assumptions through experimentation.

It is important to realize that learning by experience is a much more fundamental and, for most, accessible learning strategy than the more conceptual approach favored throughout the world. In fact, an experiential approach to learning was, until relatively recently, the more common mode of learning.

Think of the time in life when learning is most intense—infancy and early childhood. How do young children accomplish the Herculean tasks of learning to walk, learning a language, learning the principles of cause and effect? They do it through experience. As an adult, there is no reason why this mode of learning cannot and should not remain useful.

Historically, until well into the eighteenth century and certainly prior to Gutenberg's printing press, most of the world's people were information poor but experience rich. People learned what they needed to know through trial and error and by listening to elders, whose life experience was of great value. As society changed, the need to educate people for different tasks through book learning increased. The process has continued to this day. We now live in a society that is information rich but experience poor.

Through presenting challenges in a variety of ways, Outward Bound encourages participants to develop a balanced approach to learning and to recapture the value of experience in understanding the world. At the same time, participants are able to rely on the strengths of other group members.

These various experiences can provide for powerful learning. However, the metaphors of experience elicit even deeper, more lasting lessons. The assumption is that, under stress, individuals behave in roughly the same way, whether they are at Outward Bound or at home. A corporate group that fails to complete an initiative because everyone is talking at once provides insight into an unsuccessful business deal. The young student who found being stuck on a ledge fifty feet off the ground to be the best time to express how peer pressure had so often led him into "impossible" situations is also experiencing the power of metaphor.

Although there are no guarantees that such events will ensure change, highly charged experiences like rock climbing or carrying a canoe across a long, swampy portage are not easily forgotten. The memories and the meaning individuals invest in them remain crystal clear for years to come. It has been suggested that metaphors like these can carry "a depth and complexity of meaning as therapeutically potent as any insight gained from the more conventional psychotherapeutic approaches practiced by mental health professionals" (Couchman 1995).

ADVENTURE

I found the whole experience to be terrific. I began to realize that I had been setting unnecessary limits on my own capabilities. My attitude changed. I'll never put off accepting a challenge again, because I did things on my course there I never dreamed I could do.

When was the last time you had an adventure? When was the last time you did something out of the ordinary, risked uncertain outcomes, or accepted unforeseen or unknown challenges? For many people, the spirit of adventure is something left to the very young, the foolhardy, and *National Geographic* photographers. It is an approach to life abandoned sometime between the ages when you stopped climbing trees and started using credit cards.

For many, the idea of adventure has a macho stigma. Too many Hollywood movies have portrayed the rough-and-tough adventurer, out to win against the wilderness. In this light, an adventure is a test of physical endurance, extreme discomfort, and sheer pigheadedness. However, when speaking to those who have climbed the highest mountains, paddled the longest rivers, sailed oceans, and crossed Arctic waters, what becomes clear is that to be an adventurer is to find peace of mind. Rather than displaying great machismo, adventure requires and promotes more philosophical strengths, such as self-actualization (Hirsch 1992). Boldness and self-confidence are crucial components to achieving great feats, but they are always tempered by a sense of humility that comes from experiencing the power of nature. In the context of Outward Bound, it is adventure that most helps participants overcome old notions of what is and is not possible. In turn, this leads to extraordinary feelings of empowerment and an increased sense of one's own capacities.

The metaphor of a camera serves us well in illustrating the role of adventure at Outward Bound. As children, we begin seeing the world through an almost limitless, wide-angle lens. Over time, however, most of us begin adjusting the focus. Partly out of necessity (there is just too much going on today for most of us to be able to handle life at full throttle) and partly due to the pain and frustration that often accompany maturation, we begin to narrow our attention, interest, and expectations. Although this may not be all bad, it can mislead us into believing that many of our limitations are, in fact, extremely imposed. Through adventure, we allow ourselves to be open to possibilities that are outside the scope of our day-to-day lives.

Tom Price affirms this belief that the most valuable element in the spirit of adventure is the childlike quality of wonder:

> The traveler who, gazing upon the new vista, is not struck by a feeling of wonder and wild surmise will soon settle down and cease his adventuring. Darwin's voyage in the *Beagle* stimulated him to such a sense of wonder that its impetus carried him through thirty years of dedicated toil, a life-long adventure of the mind. It is a childlike quality, but it can be possessed alike by Einstein or by Wordsworth's "Idiot Boy," for it is not a question of intelligence. It is a kind of extreme mental health. The total absence of it, I suppose, is acute depression. One of the great tasks of education is to sustain this childlike sense of wonder into adulthood and, if possible, throughout life (Price n.d., 90).

Adventure can sometimes carry with it a flavor of recklessness and egoism. At Outward Bound, however, the role adventure plays in the learning process is, instead, tied closely to Kurt Hahn's understanding of the central argument of Plato's *Republic*: namely, that human perfection cannot be realized outside of a perfect society. Hahn believed that the purpose of adventure in personal development was to unlock individual capacities, which could then be used to help create a just and harmonious society.

The individual student comes to grips with what must be done to create a just society, within which a human being might aspire to perfection. Here is the true, unadvertised peak climb of an Outward Bound course. An inner transformation precedes outward conquest. This is why Hahn places compassion above all other values of Outward Bound, for it, among all emotions, is capable of reconciling individual strength with collective need (James 1980, 19).

LANDSCAPE

The physical space that COBWS occupies is a vital component to the programs provided. Aesthetic beauty and a sense of space and place, along with powerful lessons taught by wind, rain, lightning, and beaver swamps, are an important part of the school's approach to learning. Matched with this appreciation for the physical world, COBWS attempts to create programs that provide a safe environment for participants to explore their lives.

Most people are familiar with the term *landscape* as it refers to physical settings or their representations. Social commentators, such as Zukin (1991), have expanded the term to include both physical surroundings and an ensemble of material and social practices. In this sense, a theme park such as Disney World is both a physical landscape and social construct loaded with meaning.

The landscape of our daily lives is a testament to ever-increasing alienation. On a physical level, the horizon, consistently obstructed by overpowering buildings, limits our sense of space and place. On a cognitive level, surviving in today's world is largely an exercise in filtering a constant flow of information: television, work, meetings, military coups, the national debt, ozone depletion. In contrast, the "real reality" of a wilderness experience allows individuals to reconnect with vital, sensual information that, according to Bill McKibben (1992, 233–249), is vital to the knowledge of ourselves as human beings. Simply the act of being in a natural environment—of seeing from horizon to horizon without obstruction—places one in a different relation to the world. At the same time, knowing that all you need to survive and live comfortably for three weeks is located in the canoe you are sitting in is extremely reassuring. It is freeing to be rid, even for a brief time, of all the baggage we have accumulated in our lives. Among other things, it allows us the freedom to explore those things that are truly important to us.

Imagine you are 40 miles into the wilderness. A summer storm strikes. You've had the good sense to set up a secure camp beforehand. At that moment, a hot meal in a bowl and a cup of tea overwhelm thoughts of designer clothes, the latest CD equipment, the reupholstering of the sofa in a more contemporary color pattern. In amazes me how simple it is to live life comfortably (Couchman 1995).

The physical landscape of wilderness has a powerful impact on participants in an Outward Bound program. At the same time, the program attempts to engage individuals on all levels: physical, intellectual, emotional, and spiritual. The program is designed to provide for the entire landscape of individual learning. In understanding this landscape, it is important to recognize that the components of personal development are not separated but are simultaneously integrated into every aspect of the program.

The transference of experience back into everyday life is the final crucial step in the learning process. Outward Bound provides its participants with significant learning based on a landscape of adventure and experience in a powerful natural setting. However, ultimately it is up to individuals to use that learning back in the world with which they are most familiar.

For the more than fifteen thousand COBWS participants who have left the security of family and friends to undertake a challenging voyage of experience, adventure, and self-discovery, the effectiveness of experiential learning is quite real. The memories of breakfast in the early-morning mist, aching muscles after a long day's paddle, and peacefulness of solo time are forever etched in their memories. They are reservoirs to be drawn on for strength through life's many experiences. At Outward Bound, the experience of significant personal achievement leads to feelings of empowerment and mastery. To accomplish what a day earlier was thought to be impossible is to see the world anew. It is to begin with the courage to risk and the confidence to try again.

> *Be tough yet gentle*
> *Humble yet bold*
> *Swayed always by beauty and truth.*[2]

---

2. This quotation has long been attributed to Bob Pieh, who died on September 18, 1993. His daughter, Wendy, herself a moving force in Outward Bound, said she believed he had written the short poem.

VIII. PREVIOUSLY PUBLISHED

REFERENCES

Chickering, A. W. 1977. Kolb's Experiential Learning Theory. In *Experience and Learning.* Change Magazine Press.

Couchman, R. 1995. Some Reflection on the Role of Outward Bound in Promoting Change (unpublished manuscript).

Hirsch, J. 1992. The Ecology of an Adventure. *Recreation Canada* 32 (December): 14–15.

James, T. 1980. Sketch of a Moving Spirit: Kurt Hahn. *Journal of Experiential Education* (Spring): 17–22.

McKibben, W. 1992. *The Age of Missing Information.* New York: Random House.

Miner, J., and J. Boldt. 1981. *Outward Bound USA.* New York: William Morrow.

Price, T. n.d. Adventure by Numbers. In *Colorado Outward Bound School Staff Manual.*

Wilson, R. 1985. Kurt Hahn and the Legend of Outward Bound. *Mountain News* (Fall): 5.

Zukin, S. 1991. *Landscapes of Power: From Detroit to Disney World.* Berkeley: University of California Press.

CONTRIBUTORS & ACKNOWLEDGMENTS

We thank the many people who answered our call for submissions back in 2020: those who took the time to remember their connection to COBWS by sending us a short essay, photographs from slides that weren't discarded, and Polaroid prints found in musty journals.

Rob Linscott deserves special mention for returning each year to Homeplace to keep it maintained. Even though Outward Bound Canada closed the site in 2004, to Rob it never really closed. Lorne Tippett and (Victoria) Moon Joyce deserve special recognition for contributing their artwork. Lorne found his hand-drawn illustrations from the 1970s and 1980s in a folder filed away.

We thank author James Raffan for writing the foreword. His words reaffirmed we had a story worth telling. Derek Pritchard, who wrote the historical perspective, at ninety-one years old delighted us with his memories of a career on four continents with Outward Bound.

Raoul Goff, publisher at Insight Editions, gave us early encouragement. His publishing imprint EarthAware speaks volumes about his commitment to the sustainability of life on earth and, more specifically, environmental education. The publishing team at EarthAware—Peter Behravesh, Katie Killebrew, and Amanda Nelson—has been very helpful in preparing this book for publication. We are incredibly grateful for your belief, enthusiasm, guidance, and attention to the many details that went into the publication of this book.

OPPOSITE: *Ropes Course Group Challenge* by Lorne Tippett.

Most of the early contributors dashed off a rough draft and then sent it to us. Soon we had over fifty rough drafts to polish if we wanted to make a book. We did, and over twenty donors seeded us the money necessary to hire a professional copyeditor (Karen Brown) and proofreader (Elizabeth Judkins) to help us prepare the manuscript with over 14,000 edits!

Rachel Seick, then an English major at Western Washington University, helped us in the beginning by contacting many of the authors and offering her astute editorial advice. Rachel kept us moving forward when we were caught in the eddy of "What do we do with this?"

Several artists and photographers contributed their talent to the visual effects. Their documentation of COBWS has enriched the history of a wild community. Mark Zelinski offered us use of seven photographs from his books on Outward Bound. When Wendy Pieh said she had drawings by Wendell Beckwith, we swooned. And thanks as well to Rob Wallis of Outward Bound Canada for his contributions to the timeline in the appendix.

Lastly, we constantly thought of you, our readers. "Who might they be?" we asked. We wondered who would be interested in our story. You, imagined reader, kept us going—we wished to join our spirit with yours. We hope this book inspires you to carry forward the flame that was kindled at COBWS. Onward!

Charles Luckmann

Alistair McArthur

Wendy Pieh

Ian Yolles

The *Carry the Flame* Team

Nearly fifty years ago, the Canadian Outward Bound Wilderness School (COBWS) sprang into existence. Charles Luckmann, Alistair McArthur, Wendy Pieh, and Ian Yolles—all staff during the early years of the school—began meeting in 2020 via Zoom to write the definitive book on the school's place within Outward Bound worldwide. Their efforts have turned into this memoir of over forty contributing authors and artists. As editor and co-founder of Flying Trout Press, Luckmann guided the book to completion, with ongoing input and support from the other three collaborators. Flying Trout Press is a 501(c)(3) literary and charitable nonprofit.

SPECIAL THANKS

The generous contributions from the following donors made possible the publication of this book.

Philip Blackford
Stephen Couchman
Juliet Westgate (Duff)
Susan Fenton Gibson
Patrick Gorry
David Gouthro
Amanda Harris
Sara Harrison
John Huie
Ian Kilborn
Charles Luckmann
Biff Matthews
Alistair McArthur

Peter Morgan
Geoff Murray
Andrew Orr
Charlie Orsak
Wendy Pieh
Will Pooley
Wendy Talbot
David Thomson
Lorne Tippett
Ken Victor
Ian Yolles
Flying Trout Press

OPPOSITE: *Canoe Over Canoe Rescue* by Lorne Tippett.

IN MEMORIAM

On July 19, 1979, sometime after 4:45 p.m., on Boulder Lake near Collins, Ontario, Mark Anthony Bateman drowned. The coroner's jury ruled his death accidental: "Mark was a non-swimmer, who entered the water not wearing a life jacket at a point outside the boundary of his solo site." Mark was a quiet, thoughtful, and introspective person, and we all mourned his death. His mother, Irene Bateman, had worked in the Toronto office of Outward Bound to earn Mark a scholarship. An amazing woman, she continued to be supportive of COBWS and maintained a close friendship with Alistair McArthur, the executive director at the time of the drowning. *We hold Mark and his family forever in our hearts.*

OPPOSITE: *Group Hug* by Lorne Tippett.

AUTHOR & ARTIST BIOGRAPHIES

Philip Blackford

Philip Blackford was born, raised, and to this day remains in Toronto. His whole career has been in education, beginning as a counselor in a rehabilitation hospital for children. For the past twenty-plus years he has worked as a consultant and leadership development coach. During this time he also taught kinesiology in the Outdoor & Experiential Education program at McArthur College of Education. Philip instructed and was a volunteer member of COBWS's program committee from 1982 to 1985, director of program development from 1985 to 1990, and executive director from 1990 to 1998. He shares the distinction with Andrew Orr of temporarily misplacing an entire educators brigade while en route from Whitewater Lake to the Pikitigushi River. His email address is philip.blackford1@gmail.com.

Isabelle Cole

Isabelle Cole has lived in Bellingham, Washington, her whole life. She grew up drawing nature and the landscapes of the Pacific Northwest. She received a transfer degree at Whatcom Community College and is currently continuing to take classes at Skagit Valley College and Whatcom Community College before transferring to a university where she can study fine art as well as biology. She plans on pursuing a career in background art for animated projects. She drew the map illustrations for this book. Her email address is isabellesemail@gmail.com.

Rick Cotter

Rick "Tentfly" Cotter was born in the Royal City of Guelph, Ontario, and currently resides in the Chicopee area of Kitchener, Ontario. He worked at

OPPOSITE: *Climbing at Claghorn Bluffs with Top Belay* by Lorne Tippett.

Homeplace from 1980 to 1985, and again from 1989 to 1992. After Outward Bound, Rick worked as a baker, cook, and chef in bakeries, restaurants, a prison, and a conference center. He recently retired from being a chef at a retirement home. His email address is tentfly@hotmail.com.

Bob Couchman (1937–2008)

Robert "Bob" Couchman grew up in East Toronto. Despite not owning a car, phone, or TV for most of his youth, his parents insisted on two things: a subscription to *National Geographic* and two weeks every summer at a cottage. Bob's first major purchase upon securing a teaching position was a Peterborough cedar-strip canoe, followed closely by a VW Bug with which to carry the canoe to the put-in. Bob brought his passion for the outdoors and for underserved youth to Outward Bound, serving as chair of COBWS from 1984 to 1987, and chair of Outward Bound Canada from 1989 to 1994. Bob's lifelong leadership and advocacy in community and social services and his commitment to taking a risk on good ideas contributed to many of the programs that are still being offered today. He finished his days continuing his work with youth and families in northern British Columbia and the Yukon among the mountains he'd first seen pictured as a boy.

Stephen Couchman

Stephen "Cookie Machine" Couchman grew up in southern Ontario, mostly in Toronto, but spent lots of time with his dad, Bob Couchman, paddling lakes and rivers. He now lives on Georgian Bay in Clarksburg with his wife, Catherine Smart, whom he met when they co-instructed the first Access to Adventure program. Stephen first volunteered at Homeplace in 1984. He then underwent the tutelage of Rick "Tentfly" Cotter and Ginger "Bertha Bumchuckles" Mason before becoming an instructor and finally program director of Contract Programs until February 1999. Stephen has spent much of his career working in private and public philanthropy, most recently in Bhutan. His email address is stephen@smartmove.ca.

Juliet Westgate (Duff)

Juliet Westgate is originally from Vancouver. Nowadays her home is Gaia, while her house is in Ireland; she travels a lot and enjoys Greece. Juliet worked most summers at Homeplace from 1978 to 1985, then moved to Kenya to run a clinic in the Northern Frontier District (where the Samburu tribe lived). She is married and has three sons and two grandchildren. Juliet has played diverse, often seemingly contrasting roles in this life to expand her experience. Connecting threads have been healing arts, conscious evolution, fun, creativity, immersing herself in nature, and adventure. She is currently involved in energetic healing on micro and macro levels to help facilitate our species' evolution and planetary evolution. Her email address is julietduff19@gmail.com.

Susan Fenton Gibson

As a founding director of the Public Affairs Association of Canada, Susan Fenton Gibson has been a lobbyist for women and wilderness for decades from the public, nonprofit, and philanthropic sectors. Born in Toronto in 1942, she has, nomadically since 1988, made her home in Owen Sound, Tobermory, Ottawa, Almonte, and Deep River, Ontario; Metchosin in British Columbia; and Flatrock in Newfoundland and Labrador. She currently lives, partially communally, with other seniors in Picton, Ontario, near where her mother's ancestors, United Empire Loyalists, landed on the northern shore of Lake Ontario. She loves Scottish crime noir and bagpipes from her father's heritage. She cherishes slow, deep-look nature walks and nature travel with her partner, Tom. Her email address is susangibson888@gmail.com.

Ruth Goldman

Ruth spent her formative years hiking and canoeing in New England, and moved to Homeplace after a life-altering experience with two COBWS instructors on a winter course. She spent thirteen years doing the Outward Bound thing at Homeplace, in Toronto, and in British Columbia, paddling, skiing, dogsledding, and mountaineering. Ruth now lives a more sedate life with her husband and dog in Newton, Massachusetts, escaping to the mountains on occasion. Her career passions are still gritty but more urban: environmental justice and youth activism. Her children, Ben and Lucy, have inherited her spirit of adventure and have fled far from Newton, just as she did. Her email address is ruthgoldperson@gmail.com.

Patrick Gorry

In 1980, Patrick was in the first year of a management training program at Scotiabank in Toronto. The program was designed to quickly slot MBAs into branch manager positions. With only two weeks' vacation that first year with the bank, Outward Bound beckoned instead of England to see Grandma. An MBA classmate had been to the Keremeos Outward Bound Mountain School in British Columbia the previous year, so Patrick was primed. Little did he know that snow was typical in late September northwest of Lake Nipigon. His next Outward Bound vacation was on the sunny Colorado River in Utah . . . thankfully with no snow! His email address is patrickgorry@gmail.com.

David Gouthro

David Gouthro invested forty-five years of his early life in Toronto while plotting his escape to the wilds of West Vancouver, British Columbia. In his mid-1980s role as the national training manager for Apple Canada, he coordinated a very successful (and voluntary) Homeplace-based Outward Bound program for employees. Since 1988, he has been helping clients on four continents change and grow through his facilitation, training, and emceeing practice. Current plans are to retire at the tender age of ninety-five, while he still has ample time to engage in new adventures. His email address is david@davidgouthro.com.

Christo Grayling

Christo Grayling grew up in Adelaide and on the coast of South Australia. He now shares his time among a tiny fishing village and surf town in Baja Sur, Mexico; Canmore, Alberta; and the Sunshine and Central Coasts of Australia. He worked summers at Homeplace from 1977 to 1981. Christo cofounded and co-led the Pacific Center for Leadership 1987 to 2012. His email address is yochristo@gmail.com.

Amanda Harris

Amanda Harris left her hometown of Toronto the day after high school graduation. There were places to go, people to meet. She worked at COBWS from 1979 to 1983, with winters spent at Enviros Wilderness School and Project Trust in Calgary. Learning and family have been at the heart of Amanda's life since Outward Bound, raising two awesome daughters, being a joyful registered massage therapist for twenty-five years, and then being able to study fine arts in Vancouver. Becoming a grandma was one of Amanda's COVID-19 blessings. For the past ten years, Amanda and her husband, Jim, have spent winters in Belize having grand adventures. Her email address is achild17@gmail.com.

Sara Harrison

Sara Harrison was born in Minneapolis, Minnesota, and currently lives there. She began working for COBWS in 1980, and spent the next twelve years working as an instructor, course director, and program director for the Canadian Outward Bound Wilderness and Voyageur Outward Bound Schools and Wilderness Inquiry. In 1992, she was invited to join the first all-women's ski traverse of Greenland with Ann Bancroft and two other team members, which was a forty-eight-day expedition. Sara went on to complete a master's in education and was licensed to teach high school social studies. She taught at a Launch Expeditionary Learning Charter School in Saint Paul, Minnesota; the School of Environmental Studies in Apple Valley, Minnesota; and at the Native American Preparatory School in New Mexico. Sara returned to Minneapolis, and in 2005 began working at the University of Minnesota as an academic advisor and transfer admissions counselor, specializing in working with diverse, first-generation, and international student populations. Sara left the University of Minnesota in 2021 and is preparing to move to northern Minnesota to work on local climate change, environmental conservation, and sustainability initiatives.

Ilona Hitchcock

Ilona Hitchcock grew up in Montreal. She is a retired children's librarian and currently resides in Hamilton, Ontario, with her husband, daughter, and grandchildren. The outdoors, books, and travel continue to be her main interests. Her email address is ilonahi@gmail.com.

John Huie

As a boy, John loved to explore the swamps, creeks, springs, and caves around Albany, Georgia. An all-around athlete, he attended Davidson College on a basketball and track scholarship, majoring in history and psychology. While earning his master's at Emory University, he was invited by Bob Pieh in 1965 to work for MOBS, where he found his tribe. Years later, when John served as director of NCOBS, he hired his respected friend and mentor Bob Pieh as a consultant. Over forty thousand students graduated from NCOBS courses on John's watch. He spread the ideals and spirit of Kurt Hahn in many places as a teacher, coach, headmaster, professor, and director of environmental leadership for Warren Wilson College. He lives with his wife, Jaan, in Asheville, North Carolina. His email address is john@johnhuie.com.

(Victoria) Moon Joyce

Absorbed in singing with passengers on the train from Toronto, Moon almost missed her drop-off in Thunder Bay in the spring of 1977. She was eventually picked up and driven up the dusty road to Homeplace, thus beginning her lifetime affection for COBWS, its people, its pedagogy, and the glorious gift of leading people through the wild, spectacular landscape that was the vast classroom surrounding Black Sturgeon Lake. Moon was a high school teacher at the time, and through her experiences at Outward Bound, her understanding of teaching and learning, leadership and service, and culture and community informed every future endeavor she undertook as an educator, activist, musician, and artist. Inspired by the powerful effect that singing had on the Women of Courage (WOC) courses she instructed, Moon went on to complete master's and doctorate degrees, looking at singing as a tool that can help people going through life transitions to find their voice and mobilize a newfound sense of agency. From her WOC experiences of group singing on these intensive courses with women survivors of intimate partner abuse, she witnessed how singing aids in building community and personal support. Her email address is moonjoyce2@gmail.com.

Louise Karch

Louise Karch, EdM, is the best-selling author of *Word Glue* (wordglue.co) and coauthor of *The Carbon Almanac* (thecarbonalmanac.org). Trading snow for sea, the former Canuck now calls Australia home. She was a WOC instructor and course director in the 1990s. Her thinking was shaped by her experience as a student activist fighting to reduce violence against women on campus and as a counselor and advocate at Ontario's London Abused Women's Centre. Her approach was shaped by training from Yvonne Dolan, Sandra Butler, and the writings of Judith

Herman. She recommends leaders become familiar with the Duluth Model's Power and Control Wheel (see www.theduluthmodel.org/training/wheels.html).

Ian Kilborn

Ian Kilborn left his job as an engineer at a nuclear research facility in the mid-1980s to work at COBWS. He spent a summer at Homeplace, instructing mainly adult courses. Over many following years, Ian continued instructing part time, especially courses for organizations and resort-based team-building programs. Ian went on to build challenge courses for Project Adventure and started a climbing gym in Kingston, Ontario. He currently lives on a lake north of Kingston and works part time as a building energy consultant. His email address is iank@kos.net.

Paul Landry

Paul Landry grew up in northeastern Ontario. He started work at COBWS in 1979 and stayed with COBWS until 1989, except for stints at the Hurricane Island Outward Bound School in New England and the Enviros Wilderness School in Alberta. In 1990, Paul moved to Baffin Island, and with Matty McNair, started NorthWinds Arctic Adventures, Ltd. In 2000, Paul shifted to guiding polar expeditions to the North and South Poles and on the Greenland ice cap. Mostly retired from guiding, Paul now spends time in the mountains in Canmore, Alberta, and on his sailboat in Antigua. His email address is paul@polarconsultants.com.

Robert "Rob" Linscott

Rob Linscott was born and raised in Kingston, Ontario. His introduction to Outward Bound was in 1971 as a student at the mountain school in Keremeos, British Columbia. In 1976, he joined COBWS for what was supposed to be one summer. He ended up working there for many years seasonally, and eventually full time for Outward Bound Canada until 2010. Rob had a second seasonal profession in oil-and-gas exploration in Alberta and British Columbia that financially supported his Outward Bound habit. Now retired, Rob lives with his wife, Michelle, in Ottawa, Ontario. His email address is roblinscott@gmail.com.

Charles "Chuck" Luckmann

Chuck Luckmann grew up along the Mississippi River in Illinois, Missouri, and Minnesota. When he was eleven years old he purchased his first canoe for $75, which launched a passion for rivers that has never waned. During a forty-five-year career in education, he taught at nine schools in four countries, including COBWS from 1979 to 1982, where he spent summers at Homeplace and winters in the Toronto office. From 1992 to 1997, he was the executive editor for *The Journal of Experiential Education*. He's written or edited five books, including *X Stories: The Personal Side of Fragile X Syndrome*, *Voices Along the Skagit: Teaching the History of the First People in the Skagit River Watershed*, and *Bellingham Poems*, among others. In

2004 he cofounded Flying Trout Press (a literary and charitable 501(c)3 nonprofit). He lives in Bellingham, Washington, with his wife and son and several honeybee colonies. His email address is charlesluckmann@gmail.com.

Eric MacDonald

Eric MacDonald has been inward and outward bound since his early days in Ontario. He crashed into COBWS in the early 1980s, and it was a chance encounter at Outward Bound Japan that led to a thirty-year career at two international schools in Asia. He and his wife, Naoko, dig living in the hills overlooking the Japanese Alps, where he continues his journey with Outward Bound. As Christo Grayling told the program director who hired Eric, "Eric's from a different planet, but it's a good planet." His email address is ericmjmacdonald@gmail.com.

Ginger Mason

Ginger Mason's Outward Bound nicknames were Bertha Bumchuckles or Chucklebum, as riffed upon by Christo Grayling, or Bertha Bunny, as dubbed by Mary Morgan, after Bunny-Luv carrots. She was born in Belleville, Ontario, and grew up there and in various small towns in British Columbia. She now lives in Victoria, British Columbia. During her eclectic working life, she was a chef, baker, letter carrier, caregiver to adults with special needs, Statistics Canada interviewer, and executive assistant. As Bertha Bumchuckles, she was the seasonal food services coordinator at Homeplace from 1979 to 1989. In 2016, Ginger retired from paid employment, rebranding this new period of her life as inspirement, and she now revels in the pursuit of pleasure and the freedom to do whatever she feels like doing. Her email address is spicyjar8@gmail.com.

Biff Matthews

R. B. "Biff" Matthews has lived most of his life in Toronto. Shortly after he began practicing law in 1974, he became the founding board chair of the Canadian Outward Bound Wilderness School (COBWS). He enjoyed spending time at Homeplace on several occasions, including a ten-day winter camping trip with a sled and huskies in 1988. He now serves as chair of Longview Asset Management, a Toronto-based investment management company. His email address is bmatthews@longviewassets.com.

Alistair McArthur

Australian Alistair McArthur came to COBWS in January 1978 as executive director at age thirty-seven. He started his outdoor education career in 1964 as an instructor at the Ullswater Outward Bound Mountain School in the United Kingdom. He worked as an instructor, senior instructor, chief instructor, and program director at various Outward Bound schools (Ullswater and Devon in the United Kingdom, Australia, Hurricane Island in Maine, and Colorado). Alistair also did community development work for two and a half years with the Department of Native Affairs in Papua New Guinea. As base commander of a British Antarctic Survey expedition for two years, he traveled over fifteen hundred miles by dogsled. Since the early 1990s, he has acted as an advisor and consultant to outdoor education programs based in Australia. Throughout his career he has worked or consulted with over fifty outdoor programs in the United Kingdom, United States, Canada, Asia, and Australia. His email address is a.mcarthur@c031.aone.net.au.

John Mordhorst

John Mordhorst, skilled outdoorsman and outdoor education instructor, was the inaugural musher for the first dogsled team at COBWS. He worked in this role for three winters in the late 1970s and early 1980s. He also worked at Hawaii Bound; MOBS; the Canadian Outward Bound Mountain School in Pemberton, British Columbia; Enviros Wilderness School in Calgary, Alberta; and Nantahala Outdoor Center and Alpine Towers in North Carolina. In 1977, prior to working at COBWS, he organized a significant expedition to the Thelon Wildlife Sanctuary in the Northwest Territories, where he gained valuable experience driving a dogsled team. His email address is actionjohn@frontier.com.

Mary Morgan (1957–2021)

Mary Elizabeth Morgan lived in Toronto and Thornhill, Ontario, before embarking on adventure and social justice work around the globe. In 1974, she left home at the tender age of seventeen to live among the Kunas, an Indigenous people living in the San Blas Islands off the coast of Panama. From there she traveled to South America on a banana boat and lived on $2 a day, returning home in 1976 a changed woman. In 1978, she found her way to COBWS on Black Sturgeon Lake and forever changed the Homeplace community. Mary started a women's bank in the Guatemalan jungle, making $100 loans accessible to women during the country's civil war, then lived and worked in postwar Bosnia. As an economic development consultant, she traveled to Afghanistan, Zambia, Zimbabwe, Morocco, South Africa, Liberia, Sierra Leone, Guinea, and Bangladesh. Mary loved life, was fascinated by culture, and was inspired by humanity even in the harshest of environments. Mary was committed to social justice and attempted to assist the most vulnerable. She died on April 13, 2021, at the age of sixty-four.

Peter Morgan

Peter Morgan grew up in downtown Toronto. He was a student at the Outward Bound Mountain School in Keremeos, British Columbia, in 1981 and worked at COBWS from 1983 to 1985, including the 1985 winter season. After Outward Bound, he taught English in Japan, led Canadian-government-funded development exchange programs in Pakistan and Indonesia, and worked as a consultant in North America. He then headed to China as a project manager of a bilateral education program, and on to the United Kingdom and Singapore to lead health care technology projects. He has recently completed a novel and has had short stories and photographs published. His email address is petermorgan1@gmail.com.

Geoff Murray

Geoff Murray grew up in Winnipeg. He came to COBWS as an intern in 1982, instructing and course directing until 1989. He spent summers and winters at Homeplace, split by a yearlong stint at NCOBS, a spring on Baffin Island, and a summer at the Canadian Outward Bound Mountain School. After Outward Bound, he became a carpenter and now lives in Victoria, British Columbia, where he teaches carpentry at Camosun College. He and Rosemary, married for more than thirty years, have a son, Toby. His email address is geophd@icloud.com.

Andrew Orr

Andrew Orr is originally from Ontario. He worked at COBWS most summers from 1976 to 1986, then full time at Outward Bound Western Canada from 1988 to 1998, the last eight and a half years as director. After traveling to Africa for international development work, he returned to Canada and started a coaching business in Vancouver, retiring in 2015. He maintains an interest in mountains, warm places, wild places, and Africa, not necessarily in that order. His email address is andrew@playforce.ca.

Charlie Orsak

Charlie Orsak is a mostly retired child psychologist living in Duluth, Minnesota, with COBWS staff alumnus and spouse Marian Flammang. In the early 1980s, he was an instructor, course director, and program manager at COBWS. He spends his time doing climate-change advocacy, gravel and mountain biking, and sitting on his deck communing with the birds and other critters that inhabit the woods behind his house. His email address is flamsak@msn.com.

Bob Pieh (1918–1993)

Bob Pieh was born in 1918 in Madison, Wisconsin. From the get-go he was interested in wilderness travel by canoe, physical education, and counseling. He received his BA from the University of Wisconsin and an MA from UCLA. From 1940 to 1958 he taught at Antioch College in Yellow Springs, Ohio, and subsequently accepted a position in physical education at Indian Springs School, a boarding school for boys just south of Birmingham, Alabama. During this time he started a canoe-tripping camp for boys in Ely, Minnesota, at a resort that his family had purchased. In 1963, Bob used this Ely base camp as the location for MOBS, which he founded. In 1967, he joined the inaugural staff at the McArthur College of Education, a new college started at Queen's University in Kingston, Ontario, focusing on group dynamics, outdoor education, and service. Bob founded COBWS in 1976 and served as the executive director for the first two years. He eventually retired from McArthur and lived in his lakefront home outside of Kingston. In 1993, he died of Alzheimer's disease. Bob Pieh had a positive effect on all whom he met.

Wendy Pieh

Wendy Pieh was born in 1948 in Yellow Springs, Ohio. Her first real exposure to social injustice occurred in 1958, when her family moved to Alabama. Wendy decided that working together, compassion, and consensus decision-making would lead to positive change. In the late 1960s, she worked at MOBS as an instructor and course director. In 1976, Wendy joined her father, Bob Pieh, in founding COBWS. She was the program director for the school's first four years.

In 1990, Wendy joined her husband, Peter Goth, the founder of Wilderness Medical Associates, in the small fishing village of Bremen, Maine. She served as a representative in the Maine Legislature for eight years. She was elected to the Board of Selectmen in Bremen in 2004 and has been the chair since 2005. She won reelection by a 75 percent landslide for another three-year term in 2023. Wendy and Peter have been raising Cashmere goats on Springtide Farm since 1997. Her email address is wpieh@tidewater.net.

Will Pooley

Will Pooley took a kayaking course from Matty McNair and Lorne Tippett in June 1980. He lived at Homeplace year-round from 1986 to 1990. His daughters, Jen and Jess, visited several summers; Jen loved helping Bertha Bumchuckles in the kitchen, and Jess loved the dog yard and playing with Eric and Sarah McNair-Landry. Will went to graduate school for a master's in school guidance and counseling, and from 1995 to 2017 was an alternative high school counselor in Eau Claire, Wisconsin, where he now lives and works on his student rental business. He retired and remarried in 2017. You're welcome to get in touch with Will at wpooley@charter.net.

Derek Pritchard

Derek Pritchard took his first Outward Bound course as a trainee at Aberdovey Outward Bound Sea School, Course #97, in July 1950. He went on to accumulate forty-four years of full-time service with Outward Bound on four continents, including serving as an instructor at the Outward Bound Mountain School (OBMS) in Eskdale, UK (1956–1958); a senior instructor at Man O' War Bay, British Cameroons, West Africa (1958–1961); a senior executive officer at the Citizenship and Leadership School Training Centre, Nigeria (1961–1962); a senior instructor at OBMS, Eskdale (1962–1963); a warden at OBMS in Kenya (1963–1968); a warden at OBS at Devon, UK (1968–1973); the school director at the Minnesota Outward Bound School, US (1973–1983); the executive director of HKOBS (1983–1996); and the executive director of Outward Bound International (1996–2000). He lives with his wife Pat on Whidbey Island in Washington State. His email address is ordpritchard@gmail.com.

James Raffan

James Raffan (BSc, BEd, MEd, PhD) was a student of Bob Pieh's in the 1970s, following in his footsteps as professor and coordinator of Outdoor Experiential Education (OEE) at Queen's University. Since leaving Queen's in 1999, James has been a writer and independent scholar, long associated with the Canadian Canoe Museum, in Peterborough, Ontario, serving as its first curator and then executive director (2008–2014). He has written for radio, television, film, and various print media outlets. His best-selling books include *Circling the Midnight Sun*, *Emperor of the North*, *Deep Waters*, and *Ice Walker*, which was recently translated and republished for worldwide distribution in French and Spanish. James has been honored with numerous recognitions and awards, including being named one of Canada's 100 most influential explorers by *Canadian Geographic* and receiving the Queen's Golden and Diamond Jubilee Medals for his community service to the RCGS and the Arctic Institute of North America, and the Meritorious Service Medal from the governor-general of Canada. Years spent as a camper and staff member at Camp Kandalore, from 1959 to 1973, inspired James's lifelong interest in adventure, outdoor education, and canoe culture. His email address is james@jamesraffan.ca.

Pamela Ramage-Morin

Pamela Ramage-Morin was born in Canada, grew up in Australia, and returned to Canada in 1982. Her first exposure to Outward Bound was on a twenty-eight-day course following the Snowy River from Mount Kosciuszko to the Tasman Sea. Once in Canada, Pamela worked with incarcerated youth at the Enviros Wilderness School in Alberta before heading to COBWS, where she worked at Homeplace and Baffin Island from 1985 to 1989. Pamela pursued studies in sociology followed by a master's degree in epidemiology. She recently retired from a twenty-one-year career at Statistics Canada. She is currently living the retired life with her husband, Tim Morin, in Osgoode, Ontario, with frequent trips north to visit their son, Andrew. Her email address is ramage_morin@sympatico.ca.

Bob Ramsay

Bob Ramsay was born in Edmonton, where summers are so short that summer camping isn't a thing. So he had to wait until his thirties, when he was living in Toronto, to discover the joys of the great outdoors in ways only Outward Bound can teach. He never worked for COBWS but has sent dozens of unwitting enthusiasts there. Forty years later, he's still writing and hosting and traveling from Toronto. He's president of Ramsay Inc., a Toronto communications and marketing firm (www.ramsayinc.com), and his email address is bob@ramsayinc.com.

Susie Specter

Susan (Susie) Specter was born and raised in Chicago, Illinois. She graduated from the University of Illinois at Urbana-Champaign in 1981. Following a brief stint in Minneapolis, Minnesota, Susie and her husband relocated to Seattle, Washington. Susie decided to pursue graduate studies in counseling, obtaining her master's from Antioch University Seattle in March 1985, two months after delivering her first child. Full-time parenting of two children became Susie's focus and passion for the next ten years. In 1993, Susie and her family relocated to Bellingham, Washington, where Susie pursued her career providing mental health and social work case management services for twenty-six years. During Susie's time at COBWS, she was able to realize her dream of participating in community building. She has enjoyed staying connected with many of her fellow COBWS workers and dreamers. Her email address is susiespec@gmail.com.

Wendy Talbot

Wendy grew up in London, Ontario. She studied kinesiology at the University of Western Ontario. Later, while attending Queens University, she participated in the Outdoor & Experiential Education program, which led her to COBWS as an intern in 1976. Working both summer and winter courses for ten years proved to be an invaluable foundation for future adventures. After working with several Canadian outdoor education programs, she obtained a master's degree and settled into a career in health care. She spent twenty years as the CEO of NorWest Community Health Centres, which serves the district of Thunder Bay, before retiring. She enjoys golf, appreciates the value of a good physiotherapist (decades of portaging Grumman canoes had taken a toll), and lives happily with her rottweiler in Thunder Bay, Ontario. Her email address is talbotwendy06@gmail.com.

Rod Taylor

Rod Taylor was born in Toronto. He worked for COBWS at Black Sturgeon Lake from 1983 to 1986, at Black Sturgeon Lake and Baffin Island from 1994 to 1995, and in the Yukon from 1993 to 2003. He currently lives with his wife, Martha, and daughter, Hayley, on Vancouver Island and runs a consulting firm that works primarily with First Nation communities across Canada. His email address is rod@legacy-tourism.com.

Bill Templeman

Bill Templeman grew up in Montreal a very long time ago. He now lives in Peterborough, Ontario. He worked at Homeplace from 1979 to 1986, then served on the COBWS board from 1988 to 1991. He was coordinator of the Professional Development Program in the 1990s. After Outward Bound, he worked as a training consultant, college teacher, and career coach; he is now married and has two grown kids. He writes (btwritingportfolio.blogspot.com) and records podcasts (pintsandpolitics.ptbopodcasters.ca). You can find him on Facebook and X (@billtemp) and LinkedIn (www.linkedin.com/in/billtempleman). He is still trying to figure out what he will do when he grows up (suggestions welcome). His email address is bill.templeman@gmail.com.

David Thomson

David Thomson was born and raised in Scarborough, Ontario, and has lived in North Vancouver, British Columbia, since 1997. He worked at COBWS—both at Homeplace and at the Toronto office—from 1982 to 1990, including the summer and winter programs. He also worked in the Everglades for the NCOBS Florida Program one winter. In his later COBWS years, he received a master's of science in organization development from Pepperdine University and then spent the next thirty years working in organizational development consulting, leadership training, and coaching in the corporate and not-for-profit sectors, primarily in the conservation sector. His email address is dgthomson@telus.net.

Lorne Tippett

Lorne Tippett has always had a passion for the outdoors and for creating art. He worked for nearly twenty years in the outdoor field, approximately twelve years with COBWS, and a year and a half with the Hurricane Island Outward Bound School. Along the way, he returned to school, graduated with a degree in social work, and spent fifteen years working as a counselor. He moved to Salt Spring Island off the coast of British Columbia thirteen years ago and has returned to his roots of creating art. Living the dream! He contributed illustrations for this book. His email address is lornetippett@hotmail.com.

Ken Victor

Originally from the Boston area, Ken Victor worked at COBWS seasonally from 1981 to 1989, and then moved to Toronto in 1990 as the director of the Professional Development Program (PDP), where his wife-to-be, Nathalie Belanger, was already working. After COBWS, they moved together to the Gatineau Hills of Quebec, where they still live and where his experience with PDP enabled him to launch his own practice in organizational development. Ken now writes essays and poetry (he's the author of the poetry collection *We Were Like Everyone Else*), takes long walks, and is developing an expertise in afternoon naps. His email address is kvelg@aol.com.

Ian Yolles

Ian Yolles grew up in Toronto. In 1978, he started as an intern at COBWS.

After overcoming his skepticism, he hung around until 1990, working as an assistant instructor, instructor, course director, and program director. In 1985, he became the school's executive director, the youngest person ever appointed to that role in Outward Bound history. Along the way, he received a postgraduate research fellowship from the Thomas J. Watson Foundation, enabling him to work at most of the Outward Bound schools around the world. After Outward Bound he became interested in progressive businesses, leading him to work at the Body Shop, Patagonia, and Nike. Ian then went the entrepreneurial route when he co-founded Nau, an outdoor apparel company. To channel his passion for outdoor education, he served on the board of NatureBridge, including six years as the board chair. Today he lives with his wife, Irene, in Portland, Oregon, works as a venture partner at Closed Loop Partners, and often seeks inspiration in nature. His email address is iyolles@gmail.com.

Mark Zelinski

Mark Zelinski's diverse career as a professional photographer has taken him across eighty countries, with clients ranging from Ford Motor Company to Panasonic. He is also a publisher, writer, painter, filmmaker, fellow of the Royal Canadian. Geographic Society, Explorers Club member, board member of the Niagara Escarpment Biosphere Network, and winner of a Canadian Governor General's Academic Medal. Zelinski is best known for his Books That Heal Initiative—donating 8,000 copies of his photography books to 120 charities around the world. His nine internationally acclaimed photography books include forewords by HRH Prince Philip, the Honorable Lincoln Alexander, and Prime Minister Justin Trudeau. Zelinski photographed Outward Bound schools around the globe to produce the books *Outward Bound: The Inward Odyssey* (volumes one and two) and *One Small Flame: Kurt Hahn's Vision of Education*, his third book in a series about Outward Bound and experiential education. His book *Heart of Turtle Island* and its 2025 sequel *Niagara Escarpment: Land Between Waters* bring exquisite focus to the ecosystems and Indigenous communities of the Niagara Escarpment Biosphere Reserve. Visit Mark's website at www.MarkZelinski.com.

APPENDIX

Establishment of Outward Bound in Canada

Outward Bound is an international network of outdoor education organizations that was founded in the United Kingdom by Laurence Holt and Kurt Hahn in 1941. Today there are Outward Bound schools in over thirty-five countries, with 250 wilderness and urban locations around the world attended by more than 250,000 students each year.

Outward Bound International is a nonprofit membership and licensing organization for the international network of Outward Bound schools. The Outward Bound Trust is an educational charity established in 1946 to operate the schools in the United Kingdom. Separate organizations operate the schools in each of the other countries in which Outward Bound operates.

Outward Bound helped shape the Peace Corps training program and numerous other outdoor adventure programs. Its aim is to foster the personal growth and social skills of participants by using challenging expeditions in the outdoors.

	TIMELINE
1941	The first Outward Bound school is established at Aberdovey, Wales.
1961	The first Outward Bound course in North America is run in Puerto Rico for the Peace Corps.
1962	The Colorado Outward Bound School is established at Marble, Colorado.
1969	The first Outward Bound school in Canada, the Canadian Outward Bound Mountain School (COBMS), is established in the southern interior of British Columbia, at a 184-acre base camp along the Similkameen River, near Keremeos, 250 miles east of Vancouver.
1975	A mobile, summer Outward Bound program is initiated in Quebec.
1976	The second Outward Bound school in Canada, the Canadian Outward Bound Wilderness School (COBWS), is established 100 miles northeast of Thunder Bay, on the western shore of Black Sturgeon Lake, 50 miles south of Armstrong, Ontario. The base camp, an abandoned Ministry of Natural Resources spruce budworm research station, is christened Homeplace.

APPENDIX

1992	Chetwynd, a second Ontario base camp, is established near Burk's Falls, 36 miles west of Algonquin Provincial Park and 160 miles north of Toronto. Staff, equipment, and sled dogs are shared between Chetwynd and Homeplace. Field staff view both Homeplace and Chetwynd as part of COBWS. In the 1990s, the Toronto administrative office begins to refer to Homeplace and Chetwynd as Outward Bound East.
2000	Outward Bound Canada (OBC) is created, uniting COBMS and COBWS.
2004	OBC closes Homeplace on Black Sturgeon Lake.
2010	OBC closes Chetwynd, opting to run mobile Outward Bound courses without a base camp. Most mobile courses in Ontario are run from a private campground ten minutes south of Chetwynd.
2019	OBC celebrates fifty years of Outward Bound in Canada.
2025	OBC operates mobile programs throughout Canada at six centers, including two urban "centers" for accessible short courses catering to younger students, with an administrative office in Toronto, Ontario. In 2024, over 5,000 students participated.

INDEX

A
Aberdovey, Wales, 18, 53, 277, 314
abuse, 160, 164–168. *See also* Women of Courage program
Access to Adventure program, 149*n*1
accidents, 72–74. *See also* Bateman, Mark
adventure, 12, 54, 67, 210
  reflections on, 94–97, 283–284
Ai Weiwei, 169, 172
aloneness, 81. *See also* soloing
Apple Canada custom program, 223–226
Atwood, Margaret, 269

B
Baffin Island expedition, 177, 200–202
Barnett, Hepsi, 132, 149
Bartman, Monica, 89, 170
Bateman, Irene, 35, 114, 295
Bateman, Mark, 12–13, 49, 114, 116, 295
  reflections on, 34, 35, 38, 124, 219
Beckwith, Wendell, 54, 77–79, 85, 145
  canoe expedition visit, 67, 75–77
  reflections on, 98–101, 218, 256
Bertha Bumchuckles. *See* Mason, Ginger
Best Island, 75–77, 98–99
"Be tough yet gentle" maxim (Pieh), 53, 97, 219–220, 249, 258, 286

Blackford, Philip, 13, 143, 149–152, 297
  Homeplace essay, 59–61
  "Learning to See New Landscapes," 267, 276–286
  WOC program, 159–160
blaze marks, 83
Boundary Waters Canoe Area (BWCA), 29, 53, 54

C
Canadian hero archetype, 269–271
Canadian Outward Bound Mountain School, 169, 304, 305, 314
Canadian Outward Bound Wilderness School (COBWS), 19, 25, 47–48, 277
  Bob Pieh on, 38–39
  historical perspective, 17–23
  origins, 29–31, 33, 314
  shaping of, 11–14
Canadian Outward Bound Wilderness School (COBWS) West, 125
canoeing expeditions, 29–30, 88, 113, 224
  reflections on, 54, 62–86
Carry the Flame (Joyce), 266
catholes, 71
Centre for Change, 149, 277–278
Charles III, King, 19

Cole, Isabelle, 21–23, 68, 297
Colorado Outward Bound School, 35, 112, 252, 314
Common, Robert, 179, 181, 201
Community & Health Services Programs, 149, 149*n*1, 279
community meetings, 56–58, 60, 103, 113
  consensus governance and, 89, 142, 143
  reflections on, 129, 190, 219, 237, 243
compassion, 12, 53, 56, 89, 276, 284. *See also* Kurt Hahn philosophy
  reflections on, 35, 54, 60–61, 94–97, 244
consensus governance, 12, 30, 54, 94, 263
  reflections on, 60, 89, 103–104, 144, 158, 219
Cotter, Rick "Tentfly," 103, 109, 126, 128, 156, 297–298
Couchman, Robert, 150–151, 267, 268–271, 298
Couchman, Stephen, 176, 267, 276–286, 298
craftsmanship, 12, 94, 96, 147
creativity, 49, 91, 96, 98
  community and, 89, 143, 145–148
curiosity, 34, 35, 89, 102, 276
  See also Kurt Hahn philosophy

D
Dew Drop Inn (Beckwith), 100
dogsledding program, 113, 135, 175
  Baffin Island expedition, 177, 203–206
  dog-mushing training, 181–185, 201
  reflections on, 179–181
"Dunk 'em and dry 'em" tradition, 54, 232, 246–249

E
education, 53, 89, 102. *See also* five pillars
Elizabeth II, Queen, 18
emergency situations preparedness, 72–74, 81, 83–85
emotional safety protocols (ESP), 150, 150*n*2. *See also* whole person well-being; Women of Courage program
empowerment, 95, 111, 164–168
end-of-course banquets, 91, 142–143
environmental stewardship, 12, 69, 71, 113
  reflections on, 88, 239–242
equality, 56–58, 103, 166–167
experiential learning, 26, 30, 142, 154, 262
  (Victoria) Moon Joyce on, 54, 94–97
  Blackford and Couchman on, 61, 267, 280–286

Bob Pieh commitment to, 13–14, 27, 31

F
Ferguson, Marilyn, 60–61
finances, 112–113, 114, 227–228, 242
fire evacuation, 123–124, 144, 155–157
reflections on, 221–222
first aid, 65, 72, 113
First Nations. *See* Indigenous communities
fitness, 12, 37, 54, 94–97
five pillars, 18, 53, 56, 94, 276
flattened hierarchies. *See* minimal hierarchies
food planning, 67, 69–71, 72, 103. *See also* Mason, Ginger
forest bathing, 166, 241
four pillars, 54, 94–97
fundraising, 113, 227–228

G
gender roles and expression, 12, 59–61, 96–97
geographical isolation, 55–58, 103
reflections on, 60, 267, 268–271
Gibson, Susan Fenton, 231–232, 239–242, 299
Giwaykiwin, 95, 95*n*2, 133, 149*n*1
Goldman, Ruth, 164–165, 299. *See also* Women of Courage program
gorp, 89–90
Gorry, Patrick, 210, 211–215, 299
Gouthro, David, 210, 223–226, 299–300

granola spirit phrase, 265
Grayling, Christo, 102, 216, 217, 300
reflections, 109, 122–125
Greaves, Lorraine, 165
Green, Peter, 113, 114, 115, 116
group dynamics, 113, 277–278
reflections on, 37, 39–41, 255
Gull Bay First Nation, 95, 107, 134

H
Hahn, Kurt, 12, 14, 17, 26, 63, 64, 102, 111. *See also* Kurt Hahn philosophy
Harris, Amanda, 210, 218–220, 300
Harrison, Sara, 177, 203–206, 300
Hawaii Bound, 179, 304
Heraclitus, 53, 231, 258
hero's journey archetype, 103, 209–210, 263
hierarchies. *See* minimal hierarchies
Hitchcock, Ilona, 210, 216–217, 300–301
holographic participation, 13, 104–105
Homeplace, 25, 33, 107–110
1970s to 1980s, 111–114
closing, 11, 12, 315
maintenance, 138–139
maps, 21–23
preparing for use, 42–44
Huie, John, 301
on Bob Pieh, 232, 246–261

I
ice rescue simulation, 194–195, 201, 240
idealism, 232, 262–265
inclusivity, 143, 149–152, 188
indefatigable spirit, 89, 102, 276
Indigenous communities, 75–77, 98–99, 149*n*1
environmental stewardship, 241–242
Gull Bay community, 95, 107, 134
Native Canadian program, 131–133, 132*n*1
pictographs, 73, 91
isolation, 55–58, 103
reflections on, 60, 267, 268–271

J
Joyce, (Victoria) Moon, 12, 35, 132*n*1, 266, 301
on community and creativity, 143, 145–148
emergency situations preparedness, 72–74
on four pillars, 94–97
reflections on, 235, 237–238
WOC program, 163, 167

K
Karch, Louise, 301–302
WOC program, 144, 146, 164–168
Katt, Ray, 132, 133
Kilborn, Ian, 144, 158, 302
Kurt Hahn philosophy, 27, 67, 241, 246, 276–277
five pillars, 18, 53, 56, 94
origins, 262–263

L
Lacelle, Guy, 120, 136, 170, 186, 234

Lachecki, Marge, 129, 136, 186
Landry, Paul, 302
Baffin Island expedition, 177, 200–202
reflections on, 120, 128, 147, 170
winter rescue, 135–136
landscape, 284–286
Lappé, Frances Moore, 69, 89
LaRocque, Olivier, 183
leadership, 33–34, 241. *See also* women leaders
reflections on, 54, 55–58
Lesotho, 34–35, 260
Li, Qing, 166
Lightfoot, Gordon, 171
Linklater, Maria and Walter, 131–132
Linscott, Robert "Rob," 86, 110, 138–139, 146, 302
Luckmann, Charles "Chuck," 11, 25–27, 112, 132*n*1, 291, 302–303
on canoe expedition, 54, 62–86
fire evacuation, 144, 155–157
on idealism, 232, 262–265
relationship with Bob Pieh, 14, 267, 272–275

M
MacDonald, Eric, 109, 127–130, 170, 171, 303
Mason, Ginger, 86, 128, 146, 219, 236, 303
food planning, 69, 87–93, 103
Matthews, R. B. "Biff," 108, 113, 115–116, 303

McArthur, Alistair, 11, 25–27, 59, 291, 303–304
   dogsledding program, 175, 178–180
   executive directorship, 115–116
   fire evacuations, 123–124, 155–156
   on Homeplace from 70s to 80s, 111–114
   reflections on, 35, 108
McNair, Matty, 91, 116, 147, 201–203
mentoring, 12, 109, 127, 209–210
merit badges, 18–19
minimal hierarchies, 31, 62, 94, 103, 120, 143, 145
Ministry of Natural Resources (MNR) research station, 23, 25, 30, 42–43, 107, 314
Minnesota Outward Bound School (MOBS), 19, 27, 53, 156, 260
   origins, 29, 33, 246–249
   reflections on, 37–38, 55–58
Mordhorst, John, 128, 304
   dog-mushing training, 181–185
   dogsledding program, 135, 175, 179–180
Morgan, Mary Elizabeth, 121, 304
   on self-discovery, 231, 235–238
Morgan, Peter, 128, 130, 144, 304–305
   on community, 169–172
Murray, Geoff, 128, 147, 305
   dogsledding expedition, 201–202
   on sled dogs, 177, 197–199
music, 96, 143, 146, 243

N

Native Canadian program, 95, 131–133, 132*n*1
Nawagesic, Patty, 134–135
North Carolina Outward Bound School (NCOBS), 150, 191, 253, 256, 259, 272

O

OBC (Outward Bound Canada), 11, 25, 315
OBI Conference. *See* Outward Bound International Conference
Ojibwe
   Best Island, 75–77, 98–99
   Native Canadian program, 131–133, 132*n*1
   portages, 82, 83
Ontario Native Women's Association, 132
Ontario wilderness school, 25
openness, 41, 141
Orr, Andrew, 31, 42–46, 129, 305
Orsak, Charlie, 51, 109, 117, 136, 231, 233–234, 305
Outward Bound Australia, 25, 122, 151
Outward Bound Canada (OBC), 11, 25, 315
outward bound expression, 26, 276
Outward Bound International (OBI) Conference, 151, 259

Bob Pieh interview, 36–41
Outward Bound Lesotho, 34–35, 260
Outward Bound Mountain Schools, 25, 34, 169, 304, 305, 314
Outward Bound schools, 33, 53, 276–277
   four pillars, 56, 94–97
   worldwide, 25–26
Outward Bound Trust, The, 18
Outward Bound USA, 150, 151

P

Peace Corps, 313, 314
personal growth, 39–40, 54, 95, 165
Philip, Duke of Edinburgh, 17–18
philosophy, 27, 53, 112. *See also* Kurt Hahn philosophy
physical fitness, 12, 37, 54, 94–97
Pieh, Bob, 26–27, 53, 305–306
   Charles Luckmann on, 267, 272–275
   commitment to experiential learning, 13–14, 27, 31
   death, 259–261, 267, 286*n*2
   founding of COBWS, 29–30, 112
   influence on COBWS, 13–14, 19
   John Huie on, 232, 246–261
   OBI Conference interview, 36–41
   on purpose of COBWS, 38–39
   reflections, 36–41
   unobtrusive presence, 43–44
   Wendy Pieh on, 33–35

Pieh, Jerry, 253, 259
Pieh, Wendy, 25–27, 111, 291, 306
   on Bob Pieh, 33–35
   influence on COBWS, 11, 19
   on Wendell Beckwith, 98–101
Plato, 53, 262–263, 276, 284
Pooley, Will, 109, 135, 306
   on Native Canadian program, 131–133
   on Patty Nawagesic, 134–135
   winter rescue, 135–136
Price, Tom, 34–35, 283–284
Pritchard, Derek, 17–23, 306–307

R

racism, 95, 166–167, 255–256
Raffan, James, 11–14, 169, 307
Ramage-Morin, Pamela, 170, 175, 186–187, 307
Ramsay, Bob, 210, 227–228, 307–308
recycling, 71
Republic, The (Plato), 262–263, 276, 284
risk. *See* adventure
ropes course, 61, 66, 224

S

safety, 72–74, 113, 150, 240. *See also* emotional safety protocols; first aid; Women of Courage program
self-denial, 27, 53, 56, 89, 102, 276. *See also* Kurt Hahn philosophy

INDEX

self-discovery, 27, 210
  reflections on, 231, 235–238, 263
self-reliance, 49, 55, 67, 277
  (Victoria) Moon Joyce on, 54, 94–97
  emergency preparations, 72–74
sexism, 95, 235
Shining Trails program, 29, 251
simulations, 72–74, 194–195, 201
singing, 129, 134–135, 161–162, 167, 236–237
skepticism, 54, 101–105
sled dogs, 48, 113, 175
  imagined thoughts, 197–199
  reflections on, 177, 192–194
Snow Goose Lodge (Beckwith), 85
Solit, Barney, 73–74
soloing, 81, 113, 114, 162, 224
  fire evacuation, 221–222
  reflections on, 154, 217, 240, 252
  student participation, 209–210, 211–215
Southern Africa Outward Bound school, 35
Specter, Susan, 210, 221–222, 308
spirituality, 12, 56–58. See also Westgate, Juliet
Strangers to the Land, 95, 95n2, 133
student participation, 209–210, 223–226. See also specific students
summer courses, 113, 314
Survival (Atwood), 269

Swan, Terry, 132, 133, 149

T
Talbot, Wendy, 125, 150, 308
  reflections, 31–32, 47–50
Taylor, Rod, 232, 243–245, 308
  reflections on, 128–129, 170
Templeman, Bill, 129, 170, 171, 308–309
  reflections, 109, 118–121
tenacity, 53, 56, 98, 276, 277. See also Kurt Hahn philosophy
  education and, 89, 102
"Tentfly." See Cotter, Rick
Texas Outward Bound School, 101
Thomsen, Art, 37, 38
Thomson, David, 128, 186, 309
  winter course reflections, 175, 188–196
Thoreau, Henry David, 65, 262
Thunder Bay Indian Friendship Centre, 132
Tippett, Lorne, 128, 129, 147, 309
  Canoe Over Canoe Rescue, 292
  Climbing at Claghorn Bluffs with Top Belay, 296
  Group Hug, 294
  Outward Bound from Homeplace on Canoe Expedition, 106
  Ropes Course Challenge, 140
  Ropes Course Group Challenge, 288
  Sleeping on Solo Under Mosquito Netting, 80
  Solo Paddler, 31
  Supper Cooking on an Open Fire, 84
  Team Challenge at the Ropes Course, 208
  Wall Team Challenge, Ropes Course, The, 52, 53
  Wendell Beckwith's Snail Cabin, 76
  Whitewater Canoeing on Black Sturgeon River, 230

U
Unsoeld, Willi, 104, 105

V
vegetarian diet, 69, 88, 91, 103, 146, 236
Victor, Ken, 12, 36, 109, 128, 149, 309
  poem, 137
  reflections, 55–58
violence against women, 159, 164–165. See also Women of Courage program
Voyageur Outward Bound School, 260

W
waste disposal, 71
Weisinger, Rena, 38
Westgate (Duff), Juliet, 143, 153–154, 236–237, 298
whole person well-being, 94–95, 96, 141, 143, 144
Winds from the Wilderness, 172, 195–196
winter courses, 113, 176, 186–187. See also dogsledding program
  David Thomson on, 175, 188–196
  Paul Landry on, 177, 200–202
winter rescue, 135–136

women, 160, 164–168, 247n1
women leaders, 95, 103, 124
  reflections on, 124, 144, 158, 235, 236
  Susan Gibson on, 231–232, 241–242
Women of Courage (WOC) program, 95, 144, 146, 149n1, 279
  instructor learning, 162–163
  modified program, 159–161
  safety, 164–168
  singing, 161–162
worship, 12, 56–58. See also Westgate, Juliet

Y
Yolles, Ian, 11, 13, 25–27, 59, 61, 291, 309–310
  educational philosophy, 112
  poem, 137
  reflections on, 123, 128, 228
  skepticism, 101–105
Youth Challenge program, 149n1, 150

EARTH AWARE

An Imprint of MandalaEarth
P.O. Box 3088
San Rafael, CA 94912
www.MandalaEarth.com

Publisher Raoul Goff
Associate Publisher Roger Shaw
Publishing Director Katie Killebrew
Editor Peter Adrian Behravesh
Assistant Editor Amanda Nelson
Creative Director Ashley Quackenbush
Senior Designer Stephanie Odeh
Senior Production Manager Joshua Smith
Strategic Production Planner Lina s Palma-Temena

Artwork by Wendell Beckwith, Isabelle Cole, (Victoria) Moon Joyce, and Lorne Tippett

Photography by Sara Harrison, (Victoria) Moon Joyce, Rob Linscott, Charles Luckmann, Peter Morgan, Andrew Orr, David Thomson, and Mark Zelinski

MandalaEarth would also like to thank Bob Cooper, Karen Levy, and Lisa Kingsley. Special thanks to Ian Yolles for connecting Flying Trout Press with MandalaEarth; without him, this book would not exist in its current form.

Copyright © 2025 Flying Trout Press

Flying Trout Press
P.O. Box 1256
Bellingham, WA 98227-1256
www.flyingtroutpress.org

Flying Trout Press is a tax-exempt charitable organization (IRS ID #20-1487477) organized exclusively for charitable, educational, and literary purposes. Its mission is to promote and publish art and literature as regards fragile X syndrome and autism; the natural and cultural landscapes of North America; and by first-time authors.

The publication of this book was supported by individual donations.

All rights reserved. No part of this book may be reproduced in any form without written permission from the publisher.

ISBN: 979-8-88762-125-8

Manufactured in China by Insight Editions
10 9 8 7 6 5 4 3 2 1

Insight Editions, in association with Roots of Peace, will plant two trees for each tree used in the manufacturing of this book. Roots of Peace is an internationally renowned humanitarian organization dedicated to eradicating land mines worldwide and converting war-torn lands into productive farms and wildlife habitats. Roots of Peace will plant two million fruit and nut trees in Afghanistan and provide farmers there with the skills and support necessary for sustainable land use.